Spelling Connections

Teacher Edition **K**

C0-ASI-821

J. Richard Gentry, Ph.D.

Phonemic Awareness

Sound-Symbol Awareness

Letter Awareness

Spelling Awareness

ZB **Zaner-Bloser**

24664

Spelling Connections

The Right Program
Program

Phonemic Awareness

Sound-Symbol Awareness

Letter Awareness

Spelling Awareness

Spelling Success Begins in Kindergarten

Spelling Connections for Kindergarten is a systematic and explicit instructional program that will help your students

- **develop** phonemic awareness
- **practice** and **learn** targeted sounds
- **understand** that spelling is for writing
- **build** foundational spelling and language skills

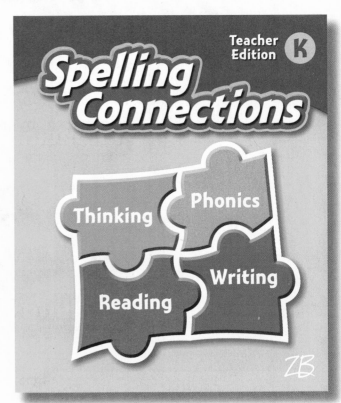

Student Edition helps students develop a solid base for building future spelling and language skills.

Teacher Edition provides complete lesson plans and activities to help teachers plan lessons appropriate for children in various stages of spelling development.

Grade K materials shown

For Spelling Success!

Components

Important Connections
Just Right For Kindergarteners!

◀ **ABC Poem and Picture Charts** are perfect for use with large and small classroom groups. This oversized 20" x 30" flip chart presents one poem and one full-size picture for each letter of the alphabet.

Spelling Connections
Phonemic and Sound-Symbol Awareness

- **Phonemic Awareness**
- **Sound-Symbol Awareness**
- **Letter Awareness**
- **Spelling Awareness**

Student Edition builds foundational skills and makes important connections for spelling success!

Phonemic Awareness ▶ lessons and activities develop this important step in becoming a good reader, writer, and speller.

Children *say*, *hear*, and *identify* the targeted sound.

Sound-Symbol Awareness ▶ lessons develop awareness for each letter of the alphabet and teach children the relationship between spoken sounds and written letters.

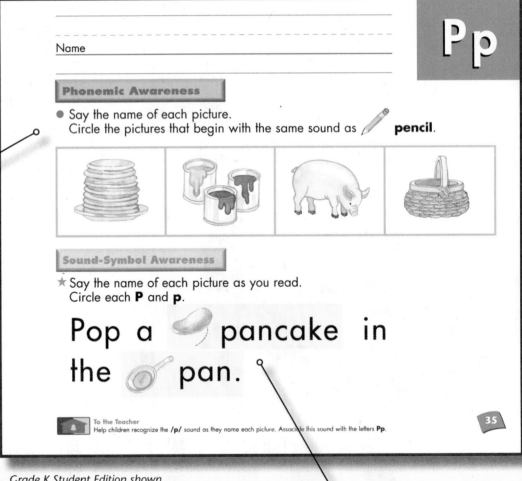

Pp

Name

Phonemic Awareness

● Say the name of each picture. Circle the pictures that begin with the same sound as ✏ **pencil**.

Sound-Symbol Awareness

★ Say the name of each picture as you read. Circle each **P** and **p**.

Pop a 🫘 pancake in the 🍳 pan.

To the Teacher
Help children recognize the **/p/** sound as they name each picture. Associate this sound with the letters **Pp**.

35

Grade K Student Edition shown

Targeted sounds and words are presented in sentence format with picture clues or in picture format with labeled words.

Letter and Spelling Awareness

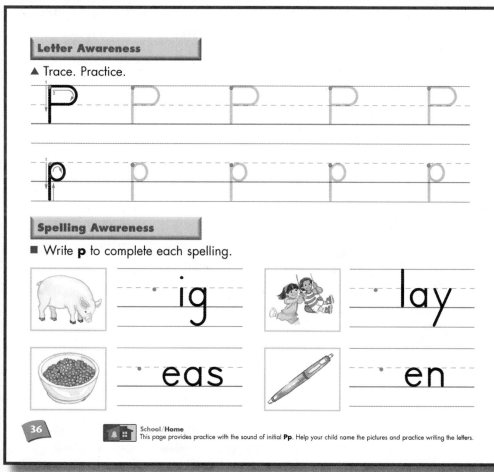

Letter Awareness

▲ Trace. Practice.

P P P P P

p p p p p

Spelling Awareness

■ Write **p** to complete each spelling.

ig

lay

eas

en

36

School/Home
This page provides practice with the sound of initial **Pp**. Help your child name the pictures and practice writing the letters.

> **Letter Awareness**
> provides handwriting practice using correct letter formation for the targeted letter.

> **Spelling Awareness**
> further associates the targeted letter with its sound using word completion activities.

Grade K Student Edition shown

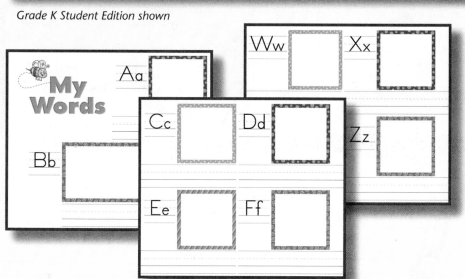

> **My Words**
> serves as a valuable assessment tool for teachers and helps children solidify letter knowledge.

Spelling Connections

Poem and Picture Charts

Phonemic Awareness

Sound-Symbol Awareness

Letter Awareness

Spelling Awareness

Build phonemic awareness and sound-symbol awareness with poetry and nursery rhymes that invite students to see, hear, say, read, and write.

Suggested chart activities are included in the *Spelling Connections for Kindergarten* Teacher Edition.

Use dry erase markers to highlight and emphasize words, pictures, and targeted sounds.

Now with laminated pages!

Umbrellas

Under my
umbrella-top,
Splashing through
the town,
I wonder why
the tulips
Hold umbrellas
Upside down!

—Barbara Juster Esbensen

Phonemic Awareness and Sound-Symbol Awareness

The *Spelling Connections ABC Poem and Picture Charts* help students visually identify letters, make sound-letter relationships through oral language and reading activities, and develop a beginning awareness of spelling patterns. These may be used in any order to complement any language arts program.

Grade K Poem and Picture Charts shown

Use the Picture Charts to
- promote oral language development.
- introduce and review a variety of familiar objects and animals that begin with the targeted letter and sound.
- promote vocabulary development (especially for children acquiring English).

Mix a Pancake

Mix a pancake,
Stir a pancake,
Pop it in the pan.
Fry the pancake,
Toss the pancake—
Catch it if you can.

—Christina Rossetti

Use the Poem Charts to
- introduce familiar nursery rhymes and selections by well-known authors.
- emphasize the targeted consonant or short vowel sound.
- identify high-frequency words and words beginning with targeted sounds.
- present strong patterns of rhythm and rhyme.

Planning Instruction is Easy!

Teacher Edition

Unit Openers include the objectives for both Student Edition and ABC Poem and Picture Chart activities.

Pp

MATERIALS

ABC Poem and Picture Charts
Pp Poem Chart: "Mix a Pancake"
Pp Picture Chart

Student Edition
Pages 35–36

Teacher Edition
Pages T95–T100

Basic Words

pop	pan
pig	pen

★**Note: Basic Words** are starred where they appear in this *Teacher Edition*.

High-Frequency Words

you	if
can	a

Targeted Word Family
-en

OBJECTIVES

ABC Poem and Picture Charts	Student Edition
Phonemic Awareness: Identify the /**p**/ sound	**Phonemic Awareness:** Identify the /**p**/ sound
Letter Recognition: Recognize **P** and **p**	**Letter Recognition:** Recognize **P** and **p**
Sound-Symbol Awareness: Associate the /**p**/ sound with the letters **Pp**	**Sound-Symbol Awareness:** Associate the /**p**/ sound with the letters **Pp**
Early Reading: Engage in repeated readings of the poem "Mix a Pancake"	**Early Reading:** Read a sentence related to the poem "Mix a Pancake"
Early Writing: Write a class story about pretending to be kernels of popcorn	**Early Writing:** Write **Pp**; use developmental spelling to write about things to put in pockets

Language and Cultural Differences

The /**p**/ sound is spelled **p** in English words. It is common in languages around the world, and one of the first sounds that babies produce. The /**b**/ sound is closely related. The Arabic language has /**b**/, but not /**p**/. (Arabic speakers are likely to pronounce **plastic** as /**bi-las-tik**/). Korean /**p**/ is pronounced /**b**/ between vowels.

In English, /**p**/ is pronounced with a puff of air (or aspiration), similar to /**h**/. Speakers of Spanish, French, and other languages may pronounce /**p**/ without the aspiration. To native English speakers, this sounds a bit like /**b**/.

T95

Grade K Teacher Edition shown

Language and Cultural Differences section presents strategies for working with students with different language and cultural backgrounds.

Using the Student Edition: Page 36

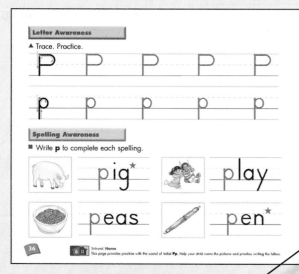

Letter Awareness
and
Spelling Awareness

Share these letter chants. Ask children to write the letters in the air as you chant together.

P

Pull down straight.
Lift and slide.
Curve, slide left.
Write **P** with pride.

p

Pull down straight,
Then push up.
Circle right all the way,
Like a sideways cup.

Point out the red directional arrows and the green dots that show where to begin each letter.

Guide children in tracing and writing **P** and **p** to complete the activities on *Student Edition* page 36.

Use **Meeting Individual Needs** below to extend the practice activities according to the needs of children in your class.

Activities are suggested for each stage of spelling development and used to transition students to the next stage.

Meeting Individual Needs

Stage 0 Spellers

Provide pipe cleaners and show children how to use them to form the letters **P** and **p**. Invite children to trace their pipe cleaner letters with their fingers, following the correct stroke sequence.

Stage 1 Spellers

Use the Stage 0 activity. Then say words from the **Spelling Awareness** activity on *Student Edition* page 36. For prominent sounds, such as /g/ in **pig,** ask children to make a corresponding letter out of pipe cleaners.

Stage 2 Spellers

Use the Stage 0 activity. Then invite children to choose one or more words from the **Spelling Awareness** activity and model it with pipe cleaners.

Stage 3 Spellers

A few children may be ready to produce conventional (correct) spellings. Call out words from the **Spelling Awareness** activity. Ask children to write the words (or model them with pipe cleaners) and check their spelling.

Building Words With Word Families

den, hen, men, pen, ten, then, when

Point out the word part **-en** in the **Spelling Awareness** activity on *Student Edition* page 36. Write **en** on the chalkboard and say /en/. Then say these sounds: /d/, /h/, /m/, /p/, /t/, /th/, and /wh/. For each sound, invite a volunteer to provide the corresponding letter, write it beside **en,** and say the new word. Add the **-en** words to your word wall or to a list of words for writing.

Unit Assessment

See page Z16 for more information.

You may wish to check progress by having children write **P, p,** and one or more **Basic Words (pop, pan, pig, pen).** Note spellings to determine each child's stage of spelling development.

Have children record one **p** word in their **My Words** book (following *Student Edition* page 56).

T99

Assessment activities are included at the end of every unit and help teachers monitor children's spelling and literacy growth.

Grade K Teacher Edition shown

Home Involvement

Keeps families involved and up-to-date. Reproducible versions of each unit's rhyming poem are included in the Teacher Edition.

Introduction to Spelling Development

by J. Richard Gentry, Ph.D.

About the Author

"I myself am a struggling speller. I have a personal record of 252 scores of 100 on the Friday spelling test, but I've always struggled with spelling in my own writing. I know what it's like for a child who scores 100 on the Friday test, but the following week misspells those very same words in his own writing. Spelling is complex. There are many better ways to learn spelling than memorizing a list of words."

Dr. Gentry began his career as a classroom teacher. Later, he earned his Ph.D. in Reading Education from the University of Virginia and served as professor of elementary education and reading at Western Carolina University, where he directed the reading center. As a result of his spelling research and educational experience, he has become a well-known authority on how spelling ability develops and how it contributes to a child's writing and overall literacy development.

In addition to writing the popular books The Science of Spelling, Spel...Is a Four-Letter Word, Teaching Kids to Spell, My Kid Can't Spell!, *and* The Literacy Map, *Dr. Gentry continues to conduct workshops that have helped thousands of school districts throughout the United States adopt better practices for spelling instruction. A popular speaker at educational conferences nationwide, Dr. Gentry has spent much of his successful career finding better ways to teach spelling.*

Spelling Connections embraces a research base calling for children in emergent literacy to create developmentally appropriate spellings that will enable them to write for their own purposes, even as they learn correct spellings. A compelling body of research now supports children's use of what the researchers term "invented spellings" at emergent levels. Generating these non-adult spellings is a developmentally appropriate activity (IRA, 1998). This research reports how the act of generating spellings actually enhances children's letter knowledge and phonemic awareness skills, solidifies knowledge of sound-symbol relationships, and leads to success with reading in first grade (Juel, 1994; Snow, Burns, & Griffin, 1998).

Spelling Connections also resonates with research-based Vygotskian concepts such as teaching in the zone of proximal development (Vygotsky, 1978), as well as scaffolding techniques (Wood, Bruner, & Ross, 1976), including scaffolded writing (Bodrova & Leong, 1998). The program also helps teachers use research-based techniques such as Elkonin Boxes, or "letter boxes," which employ tangible objects or physical actions to teach children challenging mental concepts, such as segmenting sounds in words or making sound-symbol matches (Elkonin, 1963; Galperin, 1969; Clay, 1993; Bodrova & Leong, 1998).

In particular, the research base for *Spelling Connections for Kindergarten* includes a deep and broad perspective of developmental aspects of learning to spell that grew out of Piagetian theory underpinning the notion that aspects of cognitive development proceed by way of qualitative stage-like change. This theory aligned with

- Charles Read's classic studies of children's classification of speech sounds (1971, 1975);
- research conducted by Carol Chomsky (1970);
- a body of developmental spelling research conducted by Ed Henderson and a group of researchers at the University of Virginia (Beers, 1974; Gentry, 1977, 1978; Henderson, 1981; Henderson & Beers, 1980; Templeton, 1979; Zutell, 1975, 1979; reported in Gentry, 2000).

These seminal works began to identify developmental guideposts for when certain accomplishments with spelling might be expected. Spelling, we learned, was not merely memorization of correct spellings, but a more complex acquisition of many aspects of word knowledge gained over time. Over the years, these findings have received widespread acceptance by researchers (Snow, Burns, & Griffin, 1998; Read & Hodges, 1982) and practitioners

(IRA, 1998) and has been extended to incorporate aspects of development in reading (Ehri, 1997) and writing (Bodrova & Leong, 1998; Gentry, 2005).

A synthesis of this research base led to the Gentry Writing Scale (Bodrova & Leong, 1998; Gentry, 2004). (The Gentry Writing Scale appears on pages Z11–Z15 of this Teacher Edition.) This scale, which goes far beyond assessing stages of developmental spelling, will help you lead your students to make important connections between spelling and reading and writing. Originally described as a "writing scale" in a kindergarten research project by Bodrova and Leong (1998), the Gentry Writing Scale not only measures developmental stages of spelling (Gentry, 1977, 1982, 2000), but also tracks reading and writing development by helping you see evidence of the child's changing concept of the alphabetic principle. The scale demonstrates how emergent readers and writers use the underlying knowledge sources you teach for spelling when they read and write. These include concept of word, segmenting sounds in words, recognizing letters, and learning how letters relate to sounds. In addition to phases of word learning and reading, the scale is backed by research showing how spelling stages are, in fact, writing stages in kindergarten (Bodrova & Leong, 1998; Gentry, 2004).

Following Linnea Ehri's research, the scale shows how spelling stages dovetail with phases of word learning and reading. (Ehri demonstrated how the Gentry scale corresponds almost perfectly with her own pre-alphabetic, partial alphabetic, full alphabetic, and consolidated alphabetic phases of word learning. [Research reported in "Learning to read and learning to spell are one and the same, almost," (Ehri, 1997).] This scale is also compatible with other independent but similar studies, such as the work of Darrell Morris (1981).

The Gentry Writing Scale will help you identify levels of emergent reading, writing, and spelling as you follow each child's progress from one level to the next. The scale makes it easy for you to consider each child's development based on his or her use of letter approximations versus real letters, complete-ness of phonemic representation, qualitative differences in invented spelling, sophistication of sound-symbol correspondence, and representation of the alphabetic principle (Gentry, 2004). The scale will help you follow five stages in the child's knowledge and application of how print works in writing. (Keep in mind that the child's writing stage likely impacts his or her strategies for reading.)

Note: A child is considered to be in a particular stage when **more than half** of his or her developmental spellings fit the criteria for that stage.

Stage 0 Spellers

Stage 0 is the minimal competency expected at the beginning of kindergarten. It describes non-alphabetic writing.

Indicators in Child's Writing

- scribbled or approximated letter forms; "wavy" or "loopy" writing
- no true distinguishable alphabetic letters
- no developmental or created spelling
- little awareness of how print "works"
- does not write his/her name

Instructional Recommendations for Transitioning to Stage 1

- Use poetry and rhymes to help the child notice prominent sounds, phonograms, and rhyming words.
- Use oral activities to promote phonemic awareness.
- Read aloud and discuss stories.
- Model reading, engage in shared reading, and do repeated readings of easy-to-read material.
- Begin teaching letters and sounds.
- Teach the child to write his/her name.
- Encourage the child to use letters in his/her name (and newly learned letters) to represent messages and in place of scribbles and "wavy" or "loopy" writing.
- Accept what he or she can do to build confidence.
- Allow the child to write for his/her own purposes.
- Look at the child's independent writing to assess growth and foster the child's expanding literacy knowledge.

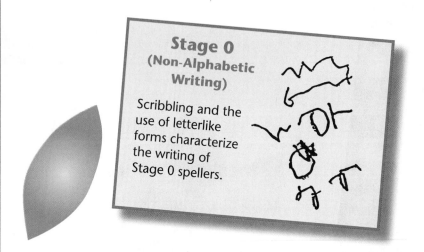

Stage 0
(Non-Alphabetic Writing)

Scribbling and the use of letterlike forms characterize the writing of Stage 0 spellers.

Gentry Writing Scale

Stage 1 Spellers

Stage 1 is the minimal competency expected by mid-kindergarten. It describes writing that is pre-alphabetic. Pre-communicative spelling is typical of this stage.

Indicators in Child's Writing

- writes in letters that appear to be random with no matches to sounds
- uses known letters, such as those in the child's name

Instructional Recommendations for Transitioning to Stage 2

- Sort picture cards based on sounds.
- Have the child match pictures by beginning sounds, then letters.
- Teach letters of the alphabet.
- Read aloud and do book talks.
- Do shared and interactive reading with beginner-oriented text.
- Encourage the child to do independent reading of wordless books, picture books, easy alphabet or letter books, caption books, and easily decodable books.
- Help writers attend to initial sounds in spoken words by modeling the sound as you elongate and accentuate it.
- Model how to stretch out sounds in words.
- Use Elkonin Boxes (see Teacher Edition page T173) to help the child segment the sounds in words.

- Encourage the child to match prominent sounds in words with a letter that "says" the sound.
- Model the process of connecting a prominent sound within a word to a letter.
- Do sound-matching activities first and move to the more difficult tasks such as isolating sounds and segmenting sounds in words (Yopp & Yopp, 2000).
- Use poetry and rhymes to help the child notice sounds, phonograms, and rhyming words. Focus especially on learning letters and sounds in prominent positions in words (e.g., initial and ending letter/sound positions).
- Build confidence by using the writer's attempts to convey messages he/she wishes to write as a vehicle for individualized teaching. Continue supportive literacy activities in reading and phonological awareness.
- Encourage the child to write for his/her own purposes.
- Look at the child's independent writing to assess growth and foster the child's expanding literacy knowledge.

Stage 1
(Pre-Alphabetic Writing)

Dan's grocery list reads "milk, bran flakes, doughnuts." Note that at Stage 1, Dan did not know that letters represent sounds.

Stage 2 Spellers

Stage 2 is the minimal competency expected by the end of kindergarten. It describes writing that is partial alphabetic. Semi-phonetic spelling is typical of this stage.

Indicators in Child's Writing

- begins to use letters to represent sounds
- uses partial letter-matches to sounds (i.e., not all sounds are represented by letters)
- focuses on prominent sounds, especially consonants (e.g., *boat* is spelled **BT**)
- long vowels and other letter name spellings are employed (e.g., *eighty* is spelled **AT**)
- uses a few memorized spellings that make messages readable (e.g., *my motor boat* is spelled **MY MR BT**)
- limited knowledge of letter-sound matching and how letters work in words
- growing, but incomplete, knowledge of the alphabetic system

Instructional Recommendations for Transitioning to Stage 3

- Read aloud and do book talks.
- Introduce and model more advanced beginner-oriented text.
- Encourage independent reading of wordless books, picture books, easy alphabet or letter books, caption books, and easily decodable books. Move to higher levels than in Stage 1.
- Do shared and interactive reading with beginner-oriented text.
- Model how to stretch out sounds in words.

- Sort picture cards based on sounds.
- Use letter tiles for making words.
- Work with onsets (e.g., *c* in *cat*) and rimes (e.g., *at* in *cat*).
- Continue the use of Elkonin Boxes (See Teacher Edition page T173).
- Have students match pictures by beginning sounds, then letters.
- Continue to teach letters of the alphabet that have not yet been mastered.
- Encourage the child to connect each sound in a word to a letter.
- Use poetry and rhymes to help the child notice sounds, phonograms, and rhyming words. Focus especially on medial sounds. This focus on medial sounds will help the child move from **BT** to **BOT** to spell *boat*.
- Accept partial alphabetic spelling but model full alphabetic spelling by helping the writer connect all sounds in a word to a letter.
- Begin to help the child focus on four basic high-frequency phonics patterns: consonant-vowel-consonant (as in *cat*), consonant-vowel (as in *he*), consonant-vowel-consonant-silent e (as in *bike*), and consonant-vowel-vowel-consonant, (as in *beat*).
- Do word sorts to help the child read and recognize the phonics patterns described above. Continue through stages 2, 3, and 4 until the patterns are mastered.
- Encourage children to write for their own purposes.
- Look at the child's independent writing to assess growth and foster the child's expanding literacy knowledge.

Stage 2
(Partial Alphabetic Writing)

Leslie used Stage 2 spelling to label Humpty Dumpty. Stage 2 spellings are often abbreviated.

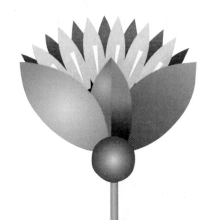

Gentry Writing Scale

Stage 3 Spellers

Stage 3 is the minimal competency expected by the middle of first grade. It describes full alphabetic writing. Phonetic spelling is typical of this stage.

Indicators in Child's Writing

- writes a letter for virtually every sound in a word to create spellings that are very readable phonetically but not necessarily close to the correct spelling (e.g., *eighty* spelled **ATE**, *motor boat* spelled **MOTR BOT**)
- intersperses correct spellings of first-grade words and words important to the child (e.g., names of family members) in writing
- phonetically able to write anything he/she can say

Instructional Recommendations for Transitioning to Stage 4

- Read aloud and conduct book talks.
- Introduce and model more advanced beginning to middle level first-grade texts.
- Encourage independent reading of books at levels 3–8 or C–H. (Match books to child for easy reading.)
- Continue to teach phonics explicitly.
- Model how to stretch out sounds in words to get all the sounds in the word and full alphabetic spellings.
- Use letter tiles for making words.

- Help children move from Stage 3 spellings, such as **BOT** for boat, to spelling in chunks of phonics patterns, such as **BOTE**. Introduce word sorts with patterns such as -oat and -ote. Continue this type of word analysis through Stages 3 and 4.
- Continue working with basic patterns such as consonant-vowel-consonant (as in *hop*) for short vowels and consonant-vowel-consonant-silent e (as in *hope*) for long vowels. (Once Stage 3 writers internalize basic patterns such as these, they move into Stage 4.)
- Focus on high-frequency word families and other chunking activities.
- Work with onsets (e.g., c in *cat*) and rimes (e.g., -at in *cat*).
- Focus attention on medial vowels.
- Do word sorts.
- Use word walls to teach sight words.
- Model conventions for basic capitalization and punctuation.
- Encourage the child to write for his/her own purposes.
- Look at the child's independent writing to assess growth and foster the child's expanding literacy knowledge.

Stage 3
(Full Alphabetic Writing)

This sample shows that Stage 3 spellers represent all the surface sound features in words. This *Tooth Fairy* story reads, "One night I was in my bed and the tooth fairy came."

tuth Fare wm hit I wsh mi Bed and the tuth Fare cam.

Stage 4
(Consolidated Alphabetic Writing)

Writing stories using developmental spelling helps set the foundations for later spelling competency. This story includes Stage 4 spelling.

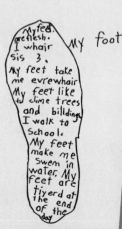

My feet are flesh. I whair sis 3. My feet take me evrewhair My feet like to clime trees and bildings I walk to school. My feet make me Swem in water. My feet are tiyerd at the end of the day

Stage 4 Spellers

Stage 4 is the minimal competency expected by the end of first grade. It describes consolidated alphabetic writing. Transitional spelling is typical of this stage.

Indicators in Child's Writing

- writes with spelling patterns in chunks of letters that mark vowels and show evidence of phonics knowledge
- spells syllables and one-syllable words in chunks of letter patterns such as consonant-vowel-consonant-silent e (as in *cave*) and consonant-vowel-vowel-consonant (as in *beat*), though word knowledge may be incomplete (e.g., the child may write **BOTE** for *boat*)
- uses developmental spellings that look more like English spelling (e.g., *fried* is spelled **FRIDE**)
- writes a majority of developmental spellings in chunks

Instructional Recommendations for Continued Growth

- Integrate spelling instruction in reading and writing anchored in studies of developmentally appropriate word lists and patterns.
- Provide comprehensive, research-based spelling instruction. Teach spelling and word-specific knowledge to enable the writer to determine if it's *mene* or *mean*, or *seperate* or *separate*.

Selected Bibliography

Complete bibliography can be found at www.zaner-bloser.com

Beers, J. (1974). *First and second grade children's developing orthographic concepts of tense and lax vowels.* Unpublished doctoral dissertation, University of Virginia, Charlottesville.

Bodrova, E., & D.J. Leong, (1998). Scaffolding emergent writing in the zone of proximal development. *Literacy Teaching and Learning*, 3(2), 1–18.

Clay, M.M. (1993). *Reading Recovery: A Guidebook for Teachers in Training.* Portsmouth, NH: Heinemann.

Ehri, L.C. (1997). Learning to read and learning to spell are one and the same, almost. In C.A. Perfetti, L. Rieben, & M. Fayol (Eds.), *Learning to Spell* (pp. 237–269). London: Lawrence Erlbaum Associates.

Ehri, L.C. & S. McCormick (1998). Phases of word learning: Implications for instruction with delayed and disabled readers. *Reading & Writing Quarterly*, 14, 135–163.

Gentry, J.R. (1977). *A study of the orthographic strategies of beginning readers.* Unpublished doctoral dissertation, University of Virginia, Charlottesville.

Gentry, J.R. (1978). Early spelling strategies. *The Elementary School Journal*, 79, 88–92.

Gentry, J.R. (1982). An analysis of developmental spelling in GNYS at WRK. *The Reading Teacher*, 36, 192–200.

Gentry, J.R. (2000). A retrospective on invented spelling and a look forward. *The Reading Teacher*, 54(3), 318–332.

Gentry, J.R. (2002). *The Literacy Map: Guiding Children to Where They Need to Be* (4–6). New York: Mondo.

Gentry, J.R. (2004). *The Science of Spelling: The Explicit Specifics That Makes Great Readers and Writers (and Spellers!).* Portsmouth, NH: Heinemann.

Gentry, J.R. (2005). Instructional techniques for emerging writers and special needs students at kindergarten and grade 1 levels. *Reading and Writing Quarterly 21*, 113–34.

Henderson, E. & J. Beers, (Eds.), (1980). *Developmental and Cognitive Aspects of Learning to Spell: A Reflection of Word Knowledge.* Newark, DE: International Reading Association.

Henderson, E. (1981). *Learning to Read and Spell: The Child's Knowledge of Words.* DeKalb, IL: Northern Illinois University Press.

International Reading Association, (1998). Learning to read and write: Developmentally appropriate practices for young children. *The Reading Teacher*, 52, 193–214.

Juel, C. (1994). *Learning to Read and Write in One Elementary School.* New York: Springer-Verlag.

Paulesu, E., J.F. Demonet, F. Fazio, E. McCrory, V. Chanoine, N. Brunswick, S.F. Cappa, G. Cossu, M. Habib, C.D. Frith, & U. Frith, (2001). Dyslexia: Cultural diversity and biological unity. *Science*, Volume 291, Number 5511, March 16, 2001.

Read, C. & R. Hodges, (1982). Spelling. *Encyclopedia of Educational Research*, 5th ed., edited by Mitzel, H. New York: Macmillan.

Silva, C. & M. Alvew-Martins, (2002). Phonological skills and writing of presyllabic children. *Reading Research Quarterly*, 37, 466–483.

Snow, C., M.W. Burns, & P. Griffin, (1998). *Preventing Reading Difficulties in Young Children.* Washington, DC: National Academy Press.

Templeton, S. (1979). Spelling first, sound later: The relationship between orthography and higher order phonological knowledge in older students. *Research in the Teaching of English*, 13, 255–264.

Vygotsky, L.S. (1978). *Mind and Society: The Development of Higher Mental Processes.* Cambridge, MA: Harvard University Press. (Original work published in 1930, 1933, 1935.)

Wood, D., J.C. Bruner, & G. Ross, (1976). The role of tutoring in problem solving. *Journal of Child Psychology and Psychiatry*, 17, 89–100.

Yopp, H.K. & R.H. Yopp, (2000). Supporting phonemic awareness development in the classroom. *The Reading Teacher*, 54(2), 130–143.

Assessing Growth

By observing children working with words—identifying them, analyzing their spellings, and using them in writing—teachers can learn a great deal about each child's knowledge of letters, sounds, and spelling patterns. Units in *Spelling Connections for Kindergarten* do not present weekly "spelling words." Instead, teachers are encouraged to accept and value children's developmental spellings while modeling correct spelling. Children are encouraged to use developmental spelling as they grow in four key areas—phonemic awareness, sound-symbol awareness, letter awareness, and spelling awareness.

Assessing Growth by Conducting a Developmental Spelling Check

The **Basic Words** listed in each unit of this *Teacher Edition* provide an appropriate means to take a "snapshot" of a child's spelling development. **Basic Words** are short, familiar words chosen to represent each unit's letter and sound. Children encounter these words several times in each unit as they work with the **Poem Chart, Picture Chart**, and *Student Edition*.

You may wish to use the **Basic Words** to administer a weekly or bi-weekly **Developmental Spelling Check**. Pronounce each **Basic Word** and use it in a sentence. If possible, point to a picture that represents the word. Ask children to write the word, giving one letter for each sound. Encourage children to do their best, but remind them that you realize they will use developmental (or "sound") spelling.

Observe each child's spellings to determine his or her stage of spelling development. (See pages Z10–Z15.) Use the following chart as a guide.

*Each spelling of **boat** reveals a stage of spelling development.*

Word	Developmental Spelling	Stage of Spelling Development
boat		**Stage 0:** The child has no knowledge of the alphabetic principle.
boat	EMJXR	**Stage 1:** The writer uses letters, but does not show an awareness that letters represent sounds.
boat	BT	**Stage 2:** The writer uses some letters to represent prominent sounds, but has limited knowledge of the way that letters represent sounds to make words.
boat	BOT	**Stage 3:** The writer gives a letter for each phoneme heard in the word.
boat	BOTE	**Stage 4:** The writer consolidates phonemic awareness and phonics knowledge to spell words in syllables or "chunks." Many familiar words and short vowel words are spelled conventionally (correctly).

Assessing Growth Through Children's Writing

Observing spellings in children's independent writing can be an effective way to monitor spelling growth. As children write, they exercise their skills in phonemic awareness, letter recognition, and sound-symbol correspondence. Three important types of writing promote children's spelling development.

Writing to Learn

The teaching suggestions found in **Meeting Individual Needs** in each unit recommend quick, informal writing as a fundamental way for children to learn about letters, sounds, and spelling patterns. As children work with the **Poem Chart, Picture Chart**, and *Student Edition*, they are asked to write developmental spellings in response to the teacher's questions. They may write with magnetic letters, on scrap paper, or on the *ABC Poem and Picture Charts'* **Dry Erase Overlay**. The children's responses will help you gauge their spelling growth.

Group Writing

Teachers can encourage children to think about spelling as they lead group writing activities, such as writing a class big book or poem. For example, as children think of words to contribute to a big book page, teachers may ask volunteers to suggest letters for prominent sounds they hear. The teacher demonstrates how to stretch out sounds in words and how to match letters to the sounds. Group writing suggestions are found throughout the *Teacher Edition*. The children's responses will help you gauge their spelling growth.

Personal Writing

Children grow as spellers when they use words to express their own ideas. In response to a writing prompt, some children may write only a word or two, while others will give several sentences. Encourage children to use appropriate developmental spelling and to illustrate their work. Word banks or word walls of target words and high-frequency words will support young writers. Suggestions for personal writing are found throughout the *Teacher Edition*.

You may wish to collect a weekly or bi-weekly writing sample from each child. Analyze writing based on the child's own knowledge of sounds and letters and not on spellings copied from word walls, word lists, or other supports. Analyze several words in each sample to determine the child's stage of spelling development. Use the chart shown on Page Z16 and the information on pages Z10–Z15 as a guide.

My Words

The **My Words** book (following *Student Edition* page 56) is a personal word journal where children write and illustrate one word for each letter of the alphabet. The completed booklet can provide evidence of spelling growth. Corresponding *Teacher Edition* pages (T161–T166) list all target words encountered in *Spelling Connections for Kindergarten*.

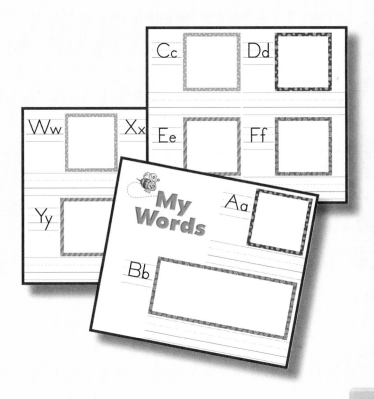

Picture Book Resources

Alphabet Books for Everyone

- Ada, Alma Flor. *Gathering the Sun: An Alphabet in Spanish and English*. Lothrop, Lee & Shepard Books.
- Bunting, Eve. *Girls A to Z*. Boyds Mills Press.
- Capucilli, Alyssa Satin. *Mrs. McTats and Her Houseful of Cats*. Margaret K. McElderry Books.
- Carlson, Nancy. *ABC: I Like Me!* Viking.
- Demarest, Chris L. *Firefighters A to Z*. Margaret K. McElderry Books.
- Fain, Kathleen. *Handsigns: A Sign Language Alphabet*. Chronicle Books.
- Fleming, Denise. *Alphabet Under Construction*. Henry Holt & Co.
- Hoban, Tana. *A, B, See!* Greenwillow Books.
- Magee, Doug and Robert Newman. *All Aboard ABC*. Cobblehill Books.
- Pratt, Kristin Joy. *A Swim Through the Sea*. Dawn Publishing.
- Rogers, Jacqueline. *Kindergarten ABC*. Scholastic Inc.
- Shahan, Sherry. *The Jazzy Alphabet*. Philomel Books.
- Wildsmith, Brian. *ABC (Español)*. Star Bright Books.

Fun With Letters and Words

- Cahoon, Heather. *Word Play ABC*. Walker and Co.
- Dunn, Opal. *Acka Backa Boo: Playground Games From Around the World*. Henry Holt and Co.
- Elting, Mary. *Q Is for Duck: An Alphabet Guessing Game*. Clarion Books.
- Falwell, Cathryn. *Word Wizard*. Clarion Books.
- Faulkenberry, Lauren. *What Do Animals Do on the Weekend? Adventures From A to Z*. Novello Festival Press.
- Frampton, David. *My Beastie Book of ABC: Rhymes and Woodcuts*. HarperCollins.
- Garten, Jan. *The Alphabet Tale*. Greenwillow Books.
- Jackson, Alison. *I Know an Old Lady Who Swallowed a Pie*. Dutton Children's Books.
- Rockwell, Anne. *Albert B. Cub & Zebra: An Alphabet Storybook*. Thomas Y. Crowell.
- Wood, Audrey. *Alphabet Adventure*. Blue Sky Press.
- Yolen, Jane. *Elfabet: An ABC of Elves*. Little, Brown and Co.

Poems, Rhymes, and Fingerplays

- Cole, Joanna. *Six Sick Sheep: 101 Tongue Twisters*. Morrow Junior Books.
- Floella, Benjamin, ed. *Skip Across the Ocean: Nursery Rhymes From Around the World*. Orchard Books.
- Foster, John, ed. *First Verses: Finger Rhymes, Action Rhymes, Counting Rhymes, Chanting Rhymes*. Oxford University Press.
- Jaramillo, Nelly Palacio. *Grandmother's Nursery Rhymes/Las Nanas de Abuelita*. Henry Holt and Co.
- Merriam, Eve. *Higgle Wiggle: Happy Rhymes*. Morrow Junior Books.
- Orozco, José-Luis. *Diez deditos: Ten Little Fingers & Other Play Rhymes and Action Songs From Latin America*. Dutton Children's Books.
- Pomerantz, Charlotte. *The Piggy in the Puddle*. Macmillan.
- Prelutsky, Jack. *It's Raining Pigs & Noodles*. Greenwillow Books.
- Rosen, Michael, ed. *Walking the Bridge of Your Nose: Wordplay, Poems, Rhymes*. Kingfisher.
- Schiller, Pamela Byrne, ed. *The Complete Book of Rhymes, Songs, Poems, Finger-plays, and Chants: Over 700 Selections*. Gryphon House.
- Trapani, Iza. *Baa Baa Black Sheep*. Whispering Coyote.

TABLE OF CONTENTS

Aa T5
Using the ABC Poem and Picture Charts T6
Using the Student Edition T8
Take-Home Poem: "Ants" T10

Bb T11
Using the ABC Poem and Picture Charts T12
Using the Student Edition T14
Take-Home Poem: "Baa! Baa! Black Sheep" T16

Cc T17
Using the ABC Poem and Picture Charts T18
Using the Student Edition T20
Take-Home Poem: "Cows Play Tag" T22

Dd T23
Using the ABC Poem and Picture Charts T24
Using the Student Edition T26
Take-Home Poem: "Hey, Diddle, Diddle" T28

Ee T29
Using the ABC Poem and Picture Charts T30
Using the Student Edition T32
Take-Home Poem: "Meg's Egg" T34

Ff T35
Using the ABC Poem and Picture Charts T36
Using the Student Edition T38
Take-Home Poem: "Fee, Fi, Fo, Fum" T40

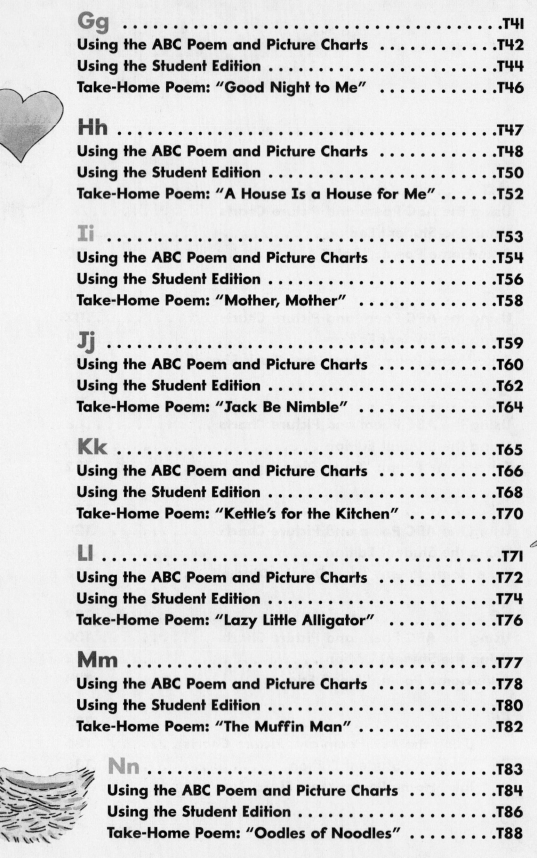

Gg **T41**
Using the ABC Poem and Picture Charts **T42**
Using the Student Edition **T44**
Take-Home Poem: "Good Night to Me" **T46**

Hh **T47**
Using the ABC Poem and Picture Charts **T48**
Using the Student Edition **T50**
Take-Home Poem: "A House Is a House for Me" **T52**

Ii **T53**
Using the ABC Poem and Picture Charts **T54**
Using the Student Edition **T56**
Take-Home Poem: "Mother, Mother" **T58**

Jj **T59**
Using the ABC Poem and Picture Charts **T60**
Using the Student Edition **T62**
Take-Home Poem: "Jack Be Nimble" **T64**

Kk **T65**
Using the ABC Poem and Picture Charts **T66**
Using the Student Edition **T68**
Take-Home Poem: "Kettle's for the Kitchen" **T70**

Ll **T71**
Using the ABC Poem and Picture Charts **T72**
Using the Student Edition **T74**
Take-Home Poem: "Lazy Little Alligator" **T76**

Mm **T77**
Using the ABC Poem and Picture Charts **T78**
Using the Student Edition **T80**
Take-Home Poem: "The Muffin Man" **T82**

Nn **T83**
Using the ABC Poem and Picture Charts **T84**
Using the Student Edition **T86**
Take-Home Poem: "Oodles of Noodles" **T88**

Oo T89
Using the ABC Poem and Picture Charts T90
Using the Student Edition T92
Take-Home Poem: "O Is Very Useful" T94

Pp T95
Using the ABC Poem and Picture Charts T96
Using the Student Edition T98
Take-Home Poem: "Mix a Pancake" T100

Qq T101
Using the ABC Poem and Picture Charts T102
Using the Student Edition T104
Take-Home Poem: "Big Q, Little q" T106

Rr T107
Using the ABC Poem and Picture Charts T108
Using the Student Edition T110
Take-Home Poem: "R Is for Ribbon" T112

Ss T113
Using the ABC Poem and Picture Charts T114
Using the Student Edition T116
Take-Home Poem: "Way Down Deep" T118

Tt T119
Using the ABC Poem and Picture Charts T120
Using the Student Edition T122
Take-Home Poem: "Teddy Bear, Teddy Bear" T124

Uu T125
Using the ABC Poem and Picture Charts T126
Using the Student Edition T128
Take-Home Poem: "Umbrellas" T130

Vv T131
Using the ABC Poem and Picture Charts T132
Using the Student Edition T134
Take-Home Poem: "Roses Are Red" T136

Ww .T137
Using the ABC Poem and Picture Charts T138
Using the Student Edition T140
Take-Home Poem: "Fingers Like to Wiggle, Waggle" . . .T142

Xx T143
Using the ABC Poem and Picture Charts T144
Using the Student Edition .T146
Take-Home Poem: "Fox in a Box" T148

Yy T149
Using the ABC Poem and Picture Charts T150
Using the Student Edition .T152
Take-Home Poem: "When I Get Up in the Morning" . . .T154

Zz T155
Using the ABC Poem and Picture Charts T156
Using the Student Edition .T158
Take-Home Poem: "In Winter When It's Zero" T160

My Words

Using the My Words pages in the
   Student Edition T161
Spelling Connections for Kindergarten
   Word List T161

Elkonin Boxes Practice Page T167
How to Use the Elkonin Boxes Practice
   Page T168

MATERIALS

ABC Poem and Picture Charts
Aa Poem Chart: "Ants"
Aa Picture Chart

Student Edition
Pages 5–6

Teacher Edition
Pages T5–T10

Basic Words

ants	apple
and	alligator

★**Note: Basic Words** are starred where they appear in this *Teacher Edition*.

High-Frequency Words

at	and
I	to

Targeted Word Family

-an

OBJECTIVES

ABC Poem and Picture Charts	Student Edition
Phonemic Awareness: Identify the **short a** sound	**Phonemic Awareness:** Identify the **short a** sound
Letter Recognition: Recognize **A** and **a**	**Letter Recognition:** Recognize **A** and **a**
Sound-Symbol Awareness: Associate the **short a** sound with the letters **Aa**	**Sound-Symbol Awareness:** Associate the **short a** sound with the letters **Aa**
Early Reading: Engage in repeated readings of the poem "Ants"	**Early Reading:** Read picture labels that begin with **a**
Early Writing: Write a class story with **short a** words	**Early Writing:** Write **Aa**; use developmental spelling to write about being an astronaut

Language and Cultural Differences

All languages have consonant sounds and vowel sounds. In pronouncing consonant sounds, air is blocked in some way before it exits the mouth. For example, **/p/** is produced by blocking the air at the lips and then releasing it suddenly. Vowel sounds are produced by vibrating the vocal cords and changing the shape of the tongue and mouth to vary the sound without actually blocking it.

The letter **a** stands for a number of different sounds in English words. This unit focuses on the **short a** sound heard at the beginning of **alligator**. In parts of the southern United States, **short a** may become a diphthong—two vowel sounds—so that **grass** sounds like **/gray-us/**.

Using the **ABC** Poem and Picture Charts: Aa Poem Chart

Read "Ants" aloud, pointing to each word. Ask children to repeat the poem once in a whisper, once at regular volume, and once in a shouting voice.

Say **apple**. Isolate the initial sound and explain that this is the **short a** sound. (This unit focuses on **short a**.) Have children repeat /ă/, noticing how the mouth looks and feels. Associate this sound with **Aa** at the top of the chart.

Use **Meeting Individual Needs** below to develop phonemic awareness and sound-symbol awareness according to the needs of the children in your class.

School/Home
You may wish to duplicate the page that follows *Teacher Edition* page T9 so that children have their own copy of the poem.

Ants
I like to watch
   the ants＊at work
When I am out
   at play.
I like to see them
   run about
And＊carry
   crumbs away.

—Mary Ann Hoberman

＊**Note: Basic Words** are starred.

Meeting Individual Needs

Stage 0 Spellers

Have fun with **short a**. Ask if children can say /ă/ with their mouths closed. (no) With their tongues out? (sort of) While whispering? (yes) Shouting? (yes) Read the poem together, emphasizing /ă/ in **ants**.

Stage 1 Spellers

Give these letter cards to volunteers: **a, n, t, s**. Have the volunteers stand in a line to form **ants**. Name each letter and say its sound: /ă/, /n/, /t/, /s/. Read the word. Ask, *"How many sounds?"* (four) *"How many letters?"* (four)

Stage 2 Spellers

Repeat **a** words from the poem: **ants, at,** and **and**. Invite volunteers to write the words, giving one letter for each sound. Accept developmental spellings (e.g., **ATS** for **ants**).

Stage 3 Spellers

A few children may be ready for more spelling patterns. Invite children to use letter tiles or cards to make new words with **at**. (bat, cat, fat, sat)

For more information on the Stages of Spelling Development, see pages Z10–Z15.

High-Frequency Words
at, and, I, to

Point out **at, and, I,** and **to** in the poem. Ask volunteers to name the letters in each word. Clap and chant the spellings by clapping together as each letter is said. Add the words to your word wall or to a list of words for writing.

ＡＢＣ Using Manipulatives

Ask each child to glue three black circles together to make an ant. Have them use a white crayon to write **a** on the second circle and **t** on the third. Ask them to write **b, c, f, h, m, r,** or **s** on the first circle to make a word such as **hat** or **rat**. Display the ants and read the words together.

Using the **ABC** Poem and Picture Charts:
Aa Picture Chart

Invite children to describe the scene on the chart. Children may wish to tell about a time they used sidewalk chalk.

Point to **Aa**. Ask what sound **a** makes in the word **apple**. (/ă/) Use **Meeting Individual Needs** below to develop phonemic awareness and sound-symbol awareness according to the needs of the children in your class.

Note: If you wish to contrast **short a** with **long a,** also include the pictures identified for **long a**.

Pictured Words · · · · · · · · · · · · · · · · · ·

short a: ★ants, ★alligator, astronaut, ★apple, alphabet, anchor, arrow, acrobat, anthill

long a: acorn, ape, apron

Meeting Individual Needs

Stage 0 Spellers
Prompt children to find pictures of items whose names begin with /ă/. Ask, *"Do you see an alligator? Alligator begins with /ă/."* Write each word on chart paper. Ask a volunteer to underline **a** in each word.

Stage 1 Spellers
As children find pictures with **/ă/,** stretch and count the sounds in each word (e.g., **apple** = /ă/ + /p/ + /l/). Write the words, asking children to provide letters for prominent sounds.

Stage 2 Spellers
Challenge children to find all nine pictures with **short a**. Pronounce the words and ask children to write a letter (or choose a magnetic letter) for each sound. Accept developmental spellings (e.g., **ALGTR** for **alligator**).

Stage 3 Spellers
A few children may be ready for more spelling patterns. Have children find **short a** and **long a** pictures. Write the words in a list.

For more information on the Stages of Spelling Development, see pages Z10–Z15.

ABC Poem and Picture Charts
Use dry erase markers on the laminated pages to highlight and emphasize words, pictures, and targeted sounds.

- Highlight letters on the **Poem Chart**.
- Underline high-frequency words on the **Poem Chart**.
- Circle pictures on the **Picture Chart**.
- Label objects on the **Picture Chart**.

Spelling and Writing
See page Z17 for more information.

Write **short a** words on cards and distribute them to children. Give a story starter such as "An ant got lost." Have each child add something to the story that includes the word on his or her card. Write the story on chart paper. Ask children to provide letters for prominent sounds.

Help children follow the directions on *Student Edition* page 5.

Use **Meeting Individual Needs** below to extend the practice activities according to the needs of the children in your class.

One-Minute Handwriting Hint

Remind children that the vertical stroke in lowercase **a** must touch the circle stroke.

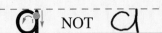

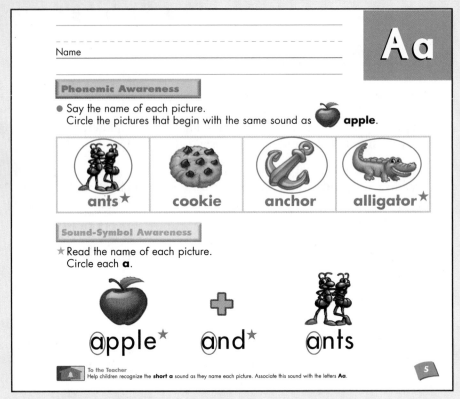

★**Note: Basic Words** are starred.

Meeting Individual Needs

Stage 0 Spellers

Write each of these words on a card: **ant, am, at, and**. Say each word in "slow motion," stretching out the sounds (e.g., **and** = /ă/ + /n/ + /d/). Ask a volunteer to blend the sounds and say the complete word. If the child responds correctly, present the word card and ask him or her to say the word and the names of the letters it contains.

Stage 1 Spellers

Use the Stage 0 activity. After children say each word correctly, ask questions about prominent sounds. For example, ask, *"What letter spells the /ă/ sound in at?"* (a) *"What letter spells the /t/ sound in at?"* (t)

Stage 2 Spellers

Say each word from the Stage 0 activity slowly, stretching its sounds. Then invite a volunteer to write the word on chart paper, giving one sound for each word. Accept developmental spellings.

Stage 3 Spellers

A few children may be ready for more spelling patterns. Start with **an**. Make new words using the **-an** pattern. (man, fan, can, van, Dan)

For more information on the Stages of Spelling Development, see pages Z10–Z15.

Spelling and Writing

See page Z17 for more information.

Have children write words or sentences about what they might do as an astronaut taking a trip to space. Ask them to include a description of what the earth looks like from space. Encourage the use of developmental spelling.

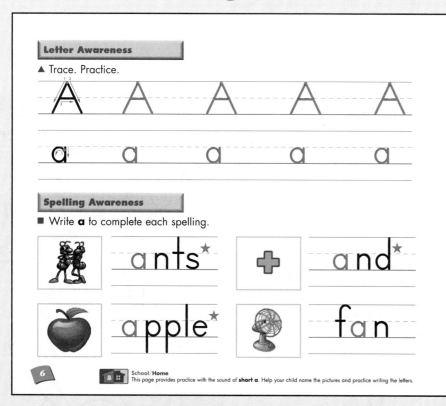

Letter Awareness

▲ Trace. Practice.

A A A A A A

a a a a a a

Spelling Awareness

■ Write **a** to complete each spelling.

ants★   ＋ and★

apple★   fan

6

School/Home
This page provides practice with the sound of **short a**. Help your child name the pictures and practice writing the letters.

Letter Awareness and Spelling Awareness

Share these letter chants. Ask children to write the letters in the air as you chant together.

A

Slant left. Slant right.
You've come partway.
Now lift and slide
To write uppercase **A**.

a

Circle back.
Go around all the way.
Push up, pull down
To write lowercase **a**.

Point out the red directional arrows and the green dots that show where to begin each letter.

Guide children in tracing and writing **A** and **a** to complete the activities on *Student Edition* page 6.

Use **Meeting Individual Needs** below to extend the practice activities according to the needs of the children in your class.

Meeting Individual Needs

Stage 0 Spellers

Allow children to write **A** and **a** in a large size on the chalkboard. Alternately, allow them to paint with a wide brush on an easel. Make sure children are following the correct stroke sequence.

Stage 1 Spellers

Use the Stage 0 activity. Slowly say words from the **Spelling Awareness** activity on *Student Edition* page 6. Ask children to write or paint letters for prominent sounds they hear in the words.

Stage 2 Spellers

Use the Stage 0 activity. Slowly say words from the **Spelling Awareness** activity. Ask children to write a letter for each sound they hear. Accept developmental spellings (e.g., **APL** for **apple**).

Stage 3 Spellers

A few children may be ready to produce conventional (correct) spellings. Call out words from the **Spelling Awareness** activity. Ask children to write or paint them and then check their spelling.

Building Words With Word Families

can, fan, man, pan, ran, tan, van

Point out the word part **-an** in the **Spelling Awareness** activity on *Student Edition* page 6. Write **an** on the chalkboard. Say /an/. Then say these sounds: /k/, /f/, /m/, /p/, /r/, /t/, /v/. Ask a volunteer to give a corresponding letter for each sound, write it beside **an,** and say the new word. Add the **-an** words to your word wall or to a list of words for writing.

Unit Assessment

See page Z16 for more information.

You may wish to check progress by having children write **A, a,** and one or more **Basic Words** (**ants, apple, and, alligator**). Note spellings to determine each child's stage of spelling development.

Have children record one **a** word in their **My Words** book (following *Student Edition* page 56).

Ants

I like to watch
   the ants at work
When I am out
   at play.
I like to see them
   run about
And carry
   crumbs away.

—Mary Ann Hoberman

School/Home

Read the poem several times with your child. Chant the poem together while clapping. Then look for words in the poem that contain **A** or **a**. Read and write the **a** words together, emphasizing the **short a** sound heard at the beginning of **alligator**.

MATERIALS

ABC Poem and Picture Charts

Bb Poem Chart: "Baa! Baa! Black Sheep"

Bb Picture Chart

Student Edition

Pages 7–8

Teacher Edition

Pages T11–T16

Bb

Basic Words

bag	boy
bus	bat

★ **Note: Basic Words** are starred where they appear in this *Teacher Edition.*

High-Frequency Words

have	the
for	you

Targeted Word Family

-at

OBJECTIVES

ABC Poem and Picture Charts

Phonemic Awareness:
Identify the /b/ sound

Letter Recognition:
Recognize **B** and **b**

Sound-Symbol Awareness:
Associate the /b/ sound with the letters **Bb**

Early Reading:
Engage in repeated readings of the poem "Baa! Baa! Black Sheep"

Early Writing:
Use developmental spelling to write a big book about colors

Student Edition

Phonemic Awareness:
Identify the /b/ sound

Letter Recognition:
Recognize **B** and **b**

Sound-Symbol Awareness:
Associate the /b/ sound with the letters **Bb**

Early Reading:
Read a sentence related to the poem "Baa! Baa! Black Sheep"

Early Writing:
Write **Bb;** use developmental spelling to write a bus safety rules sign

Language and Cultural Differences

The letter **b** represents only one sound, /b/, in English, though it is sometimes silent, as in **lamb**. The sound /b/ is closely related to /p/. Arabic has /b/, but not /p/, making Arabic speakers likely to pronounce English **plastic** as /bi-las-tik/. Korean /p/ is pronounced /b/ between vowels, but otherwise there is no /b/ in Korean. Spanish **b** has a sound between /b/ and /v/: **cabo** (**end**) is /cah-voh/. Ask Spanish-speaking children to share Spanish words that have /b/, such as **balón** (**ball**), **bicicleta** (**bicycle**), **banana** (**banana**), **barco** (**boat**), **libro** (**book**), and **abeja** (**bee**).

Using the ABC Poem and Picture Charts: Bb Poem Chart

Read "Baa! Baa! Black Sheep" aloud, pointing to each word. Ask children to sing the poem, tapping their feet to the rhythm.

Say **bus**. Explain that **bus** begins with the **/b/** sound. (**Note:** Be sure to say **/b/,** not **/buh/,** to isolate the consonant sound.) Have children repeat **/b/,** noticing how the mouth looks and feels. Associate this sound with **Bb** at the top of the chart.

Use **Meeting Individual Needs** below to develop phonemic awareness and sound-symbol awareness according to the needs of children in your class.

School/Home
You may wish to duplicate the page that follows *Teacher Edition* page T15 so that children have their own copy of the poem.

Bb

Baa! Baa! Black Sheep
Baa! Baa! Black sheep,
Have you any wool?
Yes, sir, yes, sir,
Three bags full.

One for the mister,
And one for the dame,
And one for the little boy★
Who lives down the lane.

★**Note: Basic Words** are starred.

Meeting Individual Needs

Stage 0 Spellers
Ask if any children have **B** or **b** in their names. Read the poem, asking children to say "Baa!" when they hear a word that begins with **/b/**. For each **b** word, ask a volunteer to point to the letter **b**.

Stage 1 Spellers
Read the poem, asking children to say "Baa!" when they hear a word that begins with **/b/**. For each **b** word, ask questions such as *"What letter spells the /b/ sound in bag?"* (b) *"Can you write the letter b?"*

Stage 2 Spellers
Read the poem, asking children to say "Baa!" when they hear a word that begins with **/b/**. Say each **b** word slowly, stretching its sounds (e.g., **bag** = /b/ + /ă/ + /g/). Ask volunteers to write a letter (or choose a magnetic letter) for each sound.

Stage 3 Spellers
A few children may be ready for more spelling patterns. Use the Stage 2 activity. Point out the **bl** digraph and the **ck** spelling of **/k/** in **black**. Make new words with the **-ack** pattern. (back, pack, stack)

For more information on the Stages of Spelling Development, see pages Z10–Z15.

High-Frequency Words
have, the, for, you

Point out **have, the, for,** and **you** in the poem. Ask volunteers to name the letters in each word. Clap and chant the spellings by clapping together as each letter is said. Ask volunteers to find the words in the poem.

Using Manipulatives

Write each letter of the alphabet on a blank card. Provide drawing materials and old magazines. Ask children to draw a picture or paste a picture on the back of each card. The picture should begin with the corresponding sound (e.g., a boy for **b**). Put the cards in a center for ongoing spelling practice.

Using the ABC Poem and Picture Charts: Bb Picture Chart

Invite children to describe the scene on the chart. Children may wish to tell about an outdoor picnic or festival they attended.

Point to **Bb** and ask children what sound it makes. (/b/) Use **Meeting Individual Needs** below to develop phonemic awareness and sound-symbol awareness according to the needs of the children in your class.

Pictured Words......................
barn, ★bag, ★boy, balloon, baseball, ★bat, bingo, bicycle, ★bus, bee, bird, bow

---

Meeting Individual Needs

Stage 0 Spellers
Prompt children to find pictures of items whose names begin with /b/. Ask, *"Do you see a bee? Bee begins with /b/."* Write each word on chart paper. Ask a volunteer to underline **b** in each word.

Stage 1 Spellers
Ask children to find pictures whose names begin with /b/. Stretch and count the sounds in each word (e.g., **bus** = /b/ + /ŭ/ + /s/). Write the words, asking children to provide letters for prominent sounds.

Stage 2 Spellers
Challenge children to find all 12 pictures that begin with /b/. Pronounce the words and ask children to write a letter (or choose a magnetic letter) for each sound. Accept developmental spellings (e.g., **BASBL** for **baseball**).

Stage 3 Spellers
A few children may be ready for more spelling patterns. Write a list of /b/ words children identify. Point out that **bag, bat,** and **bus** each have three letters with the vowel letter in the middle.

For more information on the Stages of Spelling Development, see pages Z10–Z15.

ABC Poem and Picture Charts

Use dry erase markers on the laminated pages to highlight and emphasize words, pictures, and targeted sounds.

- Highlight letters on the **Poem Chart**.
- Underline high-frequency words on the **Poem Chart**.
- Circle pictures on the **Picture Chart**.
- Label objects on the **Picture Chart**.

Spelling and Writing

See page Z17 for more information.

Write a big book about colors. On each page, write the sentence pattern "___ are (color name)." Ask children to complete each sentence with a **B** word and a color. For example, "Basketballs are orange." Accept developmental spellings. Have children illustrate the book.

Help children follow the directions on *Student Edition* page 7.

Use **Meeting Individual Needs** below to extend the practice activities according to the needs of children in your class.

One-Minute Handwriting Hint

Use flashcards to provide practice in recognizing **b** and **d**. Help children avoid reversals of these letters by reminding them that **b** begins at the headline while **d** begins at the midline.

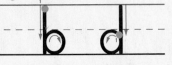

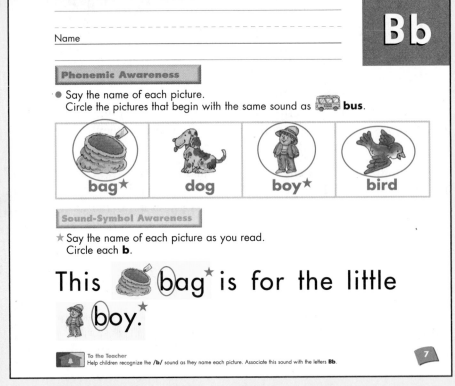

★**Note: Basic Words** are starred.

Meeting Individual Needs

Stage 0 Spellers

Draw an outline of a bag on the chalkboard. Provide cotton balls and tape. Tell children they can help fill the boy's bag with wool. Pronounce pairs of words that begin with different sounds, such as **apple/banana, bus/car, boy/toy, look/book, fox/box, bear/dog, rag/bag,** and **bird/nest**. Ask children to repeat the word in each pair that begins with **/b/**. For each correct response, ask a child to tape a piece of "wool" inside the bag.

For more information on the Stages of Spelling Development, see pages Z10–Z15.

Stage 1 Spellers

Use the Stage 0 activity. Choose several **b** words to write beside the bag. Say them slowly and ask children to provide letters for prominent sounds. Accept developmental spellings (e.g., **BRD** for **bird**).

Stage 2 Spellers

Use the Stage 0 activity. Repeat several of the **b** words, stretching out the sounds (e.g., **bus** = /b/ + /ŭ/ + /s/). Ask volunteers to write the words on the chalkboard, giving one letter for each sound.

Stage 3 Spellers

A few children may be ready for more spelling patterns. Start with **boy**. Ask children to write new words that have the **-oy** pattern. (toy, joy)

Spelling and Writing

See page Z17 for more information.

Talk about children's experiences with riding on a school bus. Then ask them to write a sign giving several bus safety rules. Accept developmental spellings. Have children illustrate and display their signs.

Using the Student Edition: Page 8

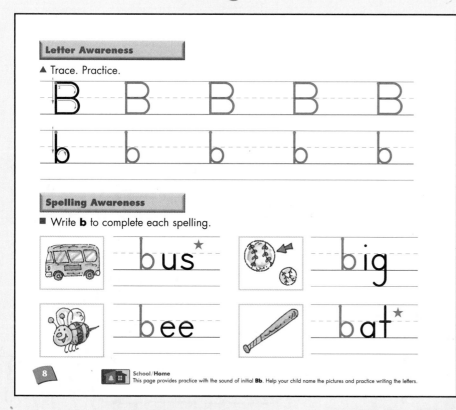

Letter Awareness and Spelling Awareness

Share these letter chants. Ask children to write the letters in the air as you chant together.

B

Pull down straight. Lift. Slide right.
Curve forward right, then slide left.
Don't stop now, there's more to do yet.
Slide right. Curve right. Now slide left.
When you look back, **B** seems easy, I'll bet.

b

Pull down straight. Push up without a sound.
Now circle right. Go all the way around.
Keep that bottom very close to the ground.

Point out the red directional arrows and the green dots that show where to begin each letter.

Guide children in tracing and writing **B** and **b** to complete the activities on *Student Edition* page 8.

Use **Meeting Individual Needs** below to extend the practice activities according to the needs of children in your class.

Meeting Individual Needs

Stage 0 Spellers
Provide a zip-top bag for each child. Spread a small amount of washable paint in each bag and seal it. Ask children to lay the bags flat and use them as "magic slates" for finger-tracing **B** and **b**. Check to make sure they are following the correct stroke sequence.

Stage 1 Spellers
Use the Stage 0 activity. Slowly say words from the **Spelling Awareness** activity on *Student Edition* page 8. Ask children to trace letters for prominent sounds they hear in the words.

Stage 2 Spellers
Use the Stage 0 activity. Slowly say words from the **Spelling Awareness** activity. Ask children to trace a letter for each sound they hear. Accept developmental spellings (e.g., **BE** for **bee**).

Stage 3 Spellers
A few children may be ready to produce conventional (correct) spellings. Call out words from the **Spelling Awareness** activity. Ask children to trace them on the "magic slates" and then check their spelling.

Building Words With Word Families
bat, cat, fat, hat, mat, pat, rat, sat

Point out the word part **-at** in the **Spelling Awareness** activity on *Student Edition* page 8. Write **at** on a large card and ask a child to hold it. Say /at/. Write the letters **b, c, f, h, m, p, r,** and **s** on smaller cards and give them to volunteers. Ask each volunteer to hold his or her letter card beside **at**. Say the new words together. Add the **-at** words to your word wall or to a list of words for writing.

Unit Assessment

See page Z16 for more information.

You may wish to check progress by having children write **B, b,** and one or more **Basic Words** (**bag, boy, bus, bat**). Note spellings to determine each child's stage of spelling development.

Have children record one **b** word in their **My Words** book (following *Student Edition* page 56).

Bb

Baa! Baa! Black Sheep

Baa! Baa! Black sheep,
Have you any wool?
Yes, sir, yes, sir,
Three bags full.

One for the mister,
And one for the dame,
And one for the little boy
Who lives down the lane.

School/Home
Read the poem several times with your child. Sing the poem together. Then look for words in the poem that begin with **B** and **b**. Read and write the **b** words together, emphasizing the /b/ sound heard in **boy**.

MATERIALS

ABC Poem and Picture Charts

Cc Poem Chart: "Cows Play Tag"
Cc Picture Chart

Student Edition

Pages 9–10

Teacher Edition

Pages T17–T22

Basic Words

cows	cat
cup	can

★**Note: Basic Words** are starred where they appear in this *Teacher Edition*.

High-Frequency Words

can	if
you	play

Targeted Word Family

-ap

OBJECTIVES

ABC Poem and Picture Charts

Phonemic Awareness:
Identify the **/k/** sound

Letter Recognition:
Recognize **C** and **c**

Sound-Symbol Awareness:
Associate the **/k/** sound with the letters **Cc**

Early Reading:
Engage in repeated readings of the poem "Cows Play Tag"

Early Writing:
Use developmental spelling to write a class poem about a game children like to play

Student Edition

Phonemic Awareness:
Identify the **/k/** sound

Letter Recognition:
Recognize **C** and **c**

Sound-Symbol Awareness:
Associate the **/k/** sound with the letters **Cc**

Early Reading:
Read picture labels that begin with **c**

Early Writing:
Write **Cc**; use developmental spelling to write about a visit to a farm

Language and Cultural Differences

This unit focuses on the **c** spelling of the **/k/** sound. One difference between the **/k/** sound in English and the corresponding sound in Spanish, French, and many other languages is that the English **/k/** is accompanied by a puff of air (or aspiration). Some non-native English speakers pronounce **/k/** without aspiration, making it sound a bit like **/g/**. Help children recognize **/k/** by saying words with and without the **hard c** or **/k/** sound (e.g., **cat** and **hat**). Ask children to pat their heads when they hear a word with **/k/**.

Using the ABC Poem and Picture Charts:
Cc Poem Chart

Phonemic Awareness and **Sound-Symbol Awareness**

Read "Cows Play Tag" aloud, pointing to each word. Read it again, asking children to shout the last word (i.e., the rhyming words) in every other line. For example, you say, *"When cows play tag in fields of"* and children shout, *"hay."*

Say **cow**. Explain that **cow** begins with **/k/**. (**Note:** Be sure to say **/k/**, not **/kuh/**, to isolate the consonant sound.) Have children repeat **/k/**, noticing how the mouth looks and feels. Associate this sound with **Cc** at the top of the chart.

Use **Meeting Individual Needs** below to develop phonemic awareness and sound-symbol awareness.

School/Home
You may wish to duplicate the page that follows *Teacher Edition* page T21 so that children have their own copy of the poem.

Cows Play Tag
Cows* play tag
In fields of hay.
"Catch me if
You can!" they say.

You ought to see
Them dash away,
When cows play tag
In fields of hay.
—David L. Harrison

★**Note: Basic Words** are starred.

Meeting Individual Needs

Stage 0 Spellers
Show children how to cup their left hands to make a **C** shape. Read the poem aloud. Ask children to hold up their **C** hands when they hear a word that begins with **/k/**. Have them repeat each **c** word and say **/k/**.

Stage 1 Spellers
As for Stage 0, have children hold up their **C** hands when you come to a **/k/** word in the poem. Stretch out and count the sounds in each **c** word (e.g., **cows** = **/k/** + **/ow/** + **/z/**). Ask questions such as *"What letter spells /n/ in can?"* (n)

Stage 2 Spellers
As for Stages 0 and 1, have children hold up **C** hands for **/k/** words in the poem. Cover the poem and ask children to provide letters for each sound as you write the **c** words. Accept developmental spellings (e.g., **CATC** for **catch**).

Stage 3 Spellers
A few children may be ready for more spelling patterns. Point out the **ow** spelling of the **/ow/** sound in **cows** and ask children for rhyming words. (how, now, wow) Discuss the **silent t** and the **ch** digraph in **catch**.

For more information on the Stages of Spelling Development, see pages Z10–Z15.

High-Frequency Words
can, if, you, play
Point out **can, if, you,** and **play** in the poem. Ask volunteers to name the letters in each word. Clap and chant the spellings by clapping together as each letter is said. Ask volunteers to find the words in the poem.

ABC Using Manipulatives
Give each child a handful of candy corn. Invite children to use the candy pieces to form **c, C,** and other letters and words. Continue by pronouncing prominent consonant sounds (e.g., **/b/, /g/, /f/, /l/**) and asking children to form the corresponding letters.

Using the ABC Poem and Picture Charts: Cc Picture Chart

Invite children to describe the scene on the chart. Children may wish to share their own experiences of being on a farm.

Point to **Cc** and ask children to identify the letter and its sound. (/k/) Use **Meeting Individual Needs** below to develop phonemic awareness and sound-symbol awareness according to the needs of the children in your class.

Pictured Words. . . . .
corn, ★can, cow, camera, ★cat, caterpillar, computer, candy, ★cup, cap, cloud

Meeting Individual Needs

Stage 0 Spellers

Prompt children to find pictures of items that begin with **/k/**. Ask, *"Do you see a camera? Camera begins with /k/."* Write each word on chart paper. Ask a volunteer to underline **c** in each word.

Stage 1 Spellers

As children find **/k/** pictures, stretch the sounds in each word (e.g., **cap** = /k/ + /ă/ + /p/). Write the words, asking children to provide letters for prominent sounds to yield developmental spellings such as **CRN** for **corn**.

Stage 2 Spellers

Challenge children to find all 11 pictures that begin with **/k/**. Pronounce the words and ask children to write a letter (or choose a magnetic letter) for each sound. Accept developmental spellings (e.g., **CANDE** for **candy**).

Stage 3 Spellers

A few children may be ready for more spelling patterns. Write **/k/** words children identify as volunteers provide spellings. Point out the **cl** blend that begins **cloud**.

For more information on the Stages of Spelling Development, see pages Z10–Z15.

ABC Poem and Picture Charts

Use dry erase markers on the laminated pages to highlight and emphasize words, pictures, and targeted sounds.

- Highlight letters on the **Poem Chart**.
- Underline high-frequency words on the **Poem Chart**.
- Circle pictures on the **Picture Chart**.
- Label objects on the **Picture Chart**.

Spelling and Writing

See page Z17 for more information.

Write a class poem like "Cows Play Tag." Have children vote for a game such as soccer, freeze tag, or checkers. Ask them to provide developmental spellings to finish the poem: We play __ in __. "__," we say. You ought to see us __ when we play __ in __.

Using the Student Edition: Page 9

Phonemic Awareness and Sound-Symbol Awareness

Help children follow the directions on *Student Edition* page 9.

Use **Meeting Individual Needs** below to extend the practice activities according to the needs of children in your class.

One-Minute Handwriting Hint

C and **c** are like cookies with a bite taken out. Begin them just below the headline (**C**) or midline (**c**) to keep the letters open.

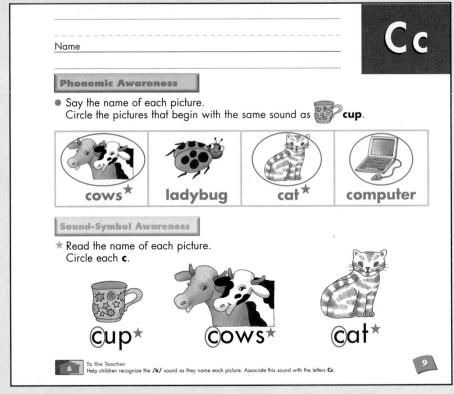

★**Note: Basic Words** are starred.

Meeting Individual Needs

Stage 0 Spellers

Model how to make new words by adding **/k/** to the beginning of words you say. Use these words: **at** (cat), **up** (cup), **an** (can), **are** (car), **air** (care), **ape** (cape), **old** (cold), **at** (cat), **ow** (cow), **oats** (coats). Although some word pairs have different spelling patterns, help children hear the matching **/k/** sound at the beginning of the new words. Write the new words. Underline **c** in each word.

For more information on the Stages of Spelling Development, see pages Z10–Z15.

Stage 1 Spellers

Use the Stage 0 activity. For each new **/k/** word, write a developmental spelling by asking volunteers to provide letters for prominent sounds. Help children by asking questions such as *"What letter spells /p/ in cup?"* (p)

Stage 2 Spellers

Use the Stage 0 activity. Ask children to count the sounds in each new **/k/** word (e.g., **coats** has four sounds: **/k/ + /ō/ + /t/ + /s/**). Have volunteers provide a letter for each sound as you write developmental spellings.

Stage 3 Spellers

A few children may be ready for more spelling patterns. Use the Stage 0 activity. Have children write each pair of **/k/** words on paper and underline the matching spelling patterns (e.g., **at, c̲a̲t**).

Spelling and Writing

See page Z17 for more information.

Ask children to write and illustrate words, a sentence, or a story about visiting a farm. Writing may include the words **corn, cows, cat,** and **can**. Encourage the use of developmental spelling.

Using the Student Edition: Page 10

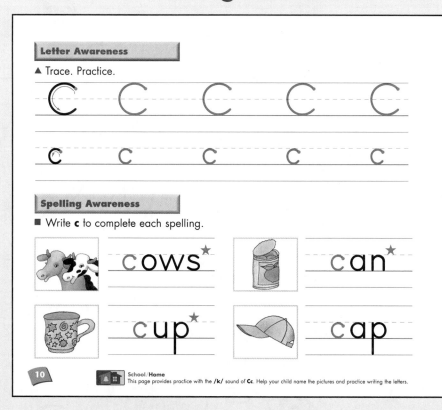

Letter Awareness

and

Spelling Awareness

Share this letter chant. Ask children to write the letters in the air as you chant together.

Cc
Circle back left,
That's all you do
To write uppercase **C**
And lowercase **c,** too.

Point out the red directional arrows and the green dots that show where to begin each letter.

Guide children in tracing and writing **C** and **c** to complete the activities on *Student Edition* page 10.

Use **Meeting Individual Needs** below to extend the practice activities according to the needs of children in your class.

Meeting Individual Needs

Stage 0 Spellers

Provide cups of water and clean paintbrushes. Allow groups of children to go to the chalkboard and paint **C** and **c** with water. Make sure they are using the correct starting point for each letter.

Stage 1 Spellers

Use the Stage 0 activity. Slowly say words from the **Spelling Awareness** activity on *Student Edition* page 10. Ask children to paint letters for prominent sounds they hear in the words.

Stage 2 Spellers

Use the Stage 0 activity. Write words from the **Spelling Awareness** activity in a large size on the chalkboard. Invite children to either paint over your words or paint the words directly below your model.

Stage 3 Spellers

A few children may be ready to produce conventional (correct) spellings. Call out words from the **Spelling Awareness** activity. Ask children to paint them with water and then check their spelling.

Building Words With Word Families

cap, gap, lap, map, nap, tap, zap

Point out the word part **-ap** in the **Spelling Awareness** activity on *Student Edition* page 10. Write **ap** on chart paper. Say /ap/. Make a card for each of these letters: **c, g, l, m, n, t, z**. Give the cards to volunteers and ask each child to hold his or her letter next to **ap** and say its sound. Then say the new words together. Add the **-ap** words to your word wall or to a list of words for writing.

Unit Assessment

See page Z16 for more information.

You may wish to check progress by having children write **C, c,** and one or more **Basic Words** (**cows, cat, cup, can**). Note spellings to determine each child's stage of spelling development.

Have children record one **c** word in their **My Words** book (following *Student Edition* page 56).

Cc

Cows Play Tag

Cows play tag
In fields of hay.
"Catch me if
You can!" they say.

You ought to see
Them dash away,
When cows play tag
In fields of hay.

—David L. Harrison

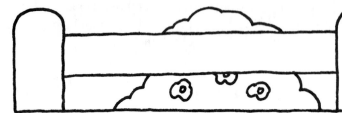

School/Home
Read the poem several times with your child. You may wish to make up a tune for the poem and sing it together.
Then look for words in the poem that begin with **C** and **c**. Read and write the **c** words together, emphasizing the
/k/ sound heard at the beginning of **cow**.

MATERIALS

ABC Poem and Picture Charts

Dd Poem Chart: "Hey, Diddle, Diddle"
Dd Picture Chart

Student Edition

Pages 11–12

Teacher Edition

Pages T23–T28

OBJECTIVES

ABC Poem and Picture Charts	Student Edition
Phonemic Awareness: Identify the /d/ sound	**Phonemic Awareness:** Identify the /d/ sound
Letter Recognition: Recognize **D** and **d**	**Letter Recognition:** Recognize **D** and **d**
Sound-Symbol Awareness: Associate the /d/ sound with the letters **Dd**	**Sound-Symbol Awareness:** Associate the /d/ sound with the letters **Dd**
Early Reading: Engage in repeated readings of the poem "Hey, Diddle, Diddle"	**Early Reading:** Read a sentence related to the poem "Hey, Diddle, Diddle"
Early Writing: Use developmental spelling to write in the voice of a character from the poem "Hey, Diddle, Diddle"	**Early Writing:** Write **Dd**; use developmental spelling to write about a dog

Language and Cultural Differences

The letter **d** always represents the /**d**/ sound in English. This sound is common in languages around the world. Children begin saying /**d**/ very early (as in **dada**), and it seldom causes pronunciation problems.

Make use of the illustrations in this unit when working with children who are acquiring English. Point to and identify objects that begin with **d** and have children repeat the words.

Using the **ABC** Poem and Picture Charts:
Dd Poem Chart

Phonemic Awareness and **Sound-Symbol Awareness**

Read "Hey, Diddle, Diddle" aloud, pointing to each word. Divide into two groups. Have one group shout the first line of the poem and the other group reply by shouting the next line. Continue for the rest of the poem.

Say **dance**. Explain that **dance** begins with /**d**/. (**Note:** Be sure to say /**d**/, not /**duh**/, to isolate the consonant sound.) Have children repeat /**d**/, noticing how the mouth looks and feels. Associate this sound with the letters **Dd** at the top of the chart.

Use **Meeting Individual Needs** below to develop phonemic awareness and sound-symbol awareness.

School/Home
You may wish to duplicate the page that follows *Teacher Edition* page T27 so that children have their own copy of the poem.

Hey, Diddle, Diddle
Hey, diddle, diddle!
The cat and the fiddle,
The cow jumped over
 the moon.

The little dog* laughed
To see such sport,
And the dish* ran away
 with the spoon.

★**Note: Basic Words** are starred.

Meeting Individual Needs

Stage 0 Spellers

Ask if anyone has **D** or **d** in his or her name. If so, say the names slowly, emphasizing /**d**/. Read the poem. Ask children to shout *"Diddle!"* when you read a word that has /**d**/. Have volunteers point to each **d** in the poem.

For more information on the Stages of Spelling Development, see pages Z10–Z15.

Stage 1 Spellers

Use the Stage 0 activity. Stretch and count the sounds in **d** words children identify (e.g., **dog** = /**d**/ + /ŏ/ + /**g**/). Ask questions such as *"What letter spells /**g**/ in **dog**?"* (g) Focus on prominent (beginning and ending) sounds.

Stage 2 Spellers

Use the Stage 0 activity. Cover the poem. Say the **d** words slowly. Ask a volunteer to choose a magnetic letter to spell each sound. Accept developmental spellings (e.g., **DIDL** for **diddle**).

Stage 3 Spellers

A few children may be ready for more spelling patterns. Ask them to write new words with the **-ish** pattern seen in **dish**. (fish, wish, swish)

High-Frequency Words
and, little, see, with

Point out **and, little, see,** and **with** in the poem. Ask volunteers to name the letters in each word. Clap and chant the spellings. Ask volunteers to find each word in the poem. Add the words to your word wall or to a list of words for writing.

ABC Using Manipulatives

Make a transparency of the page that follows *Teacher Edition* page T27. Put it on an overhead projector. Have children place bingo chips or colored acetate squares over each **D** or **d** in the poem. Continue by asking children to mark other letters you name.

Using the **ABC** Poem and Picture Charts: Dd Picture Chart

Invite children to describe the scene on the chart. Children may wish to tell about a time they attended a football game or watched one on television.

Point to **Dd** and ask children to identify the letter and its sound. (/d/) Use **Meeting Individual Needs** below to develop phonemic awareness and sound-symbol awareness according to the needs of the children in your class.

Pictured Words.....................
deer, dinosaur, ★dog, doll, dolphin, ★duck, doughnuts, dress, drum, ★dish

GO, DOG, GO!

Dd

Meeting Individual Needs

Stage 0 Spellers

Prompt children to find pictures that begin with **/d/**. Ask, *"Do you see the little pig's doll? **Doll** begins with /d/."* Write the **/d/** words on chart paper and invite a volunteer to underline **d** in each word.

Stage 1 Spellers

Ask volunteers to find pictures that begin with **/d/**. Write each **d** word on chart paper, pausing to ask children to provide letters for prominent sounds, such as **/g/** in **dog**.

Stage 2 Spellers

Challenge children to find all ten items that begin with **/d/**. Count the sounds in each word (e.g., **duck** = **/d/ + /ŭ/ + /k/**). Ask volunteers to write the words on chart paper. Accept developmental spellings (e.g., **DUK** for **duck**).

Stage 3 Spellers

A few children may be ready for more spelling patterns. Write **dr** and ask children to blend the **/d/** and **/r/** sounds. Then ask them to find two objects in the picture that begin with this blend. (dress, drum)

For more information on the Stages of Spelling Development, see pages Z10–Z15.

ABC Poem and Picture Charts

Use dry erase markers on the laminated pages to highlight and emphasize words, pictures, and targeted sounds.

• Highlight letters on the **Poem Chart**.
• Underline high-frequency words on the **Poem Chart**.
• Circle pictures on the **Picture Chart**.
• Label objects on the **Picture Chart**.

Spelling and Writing

See page Z17 for more information.

Discuss characters in "Hey, Diddle, Diddle": cat, cow, dog, dish, and spoon. Have children choose a character, then write and illustrate a sentence from that point of view. The cow might write "I jump over the moon." Accept developmental spelling.

Phonemic Awareness and Sound-Symbol Awareness

Help children follow the directions on *Student Edition* page 11.

Use **Meeting Individual Needs** below to extend the practice activities according to the needs of children in your class.

One-Minute Handwriting Hint

Have children begin at the midline and form the *circle first* when writing **d**. This helps children distinguish it from **b**, which begins at the headline.

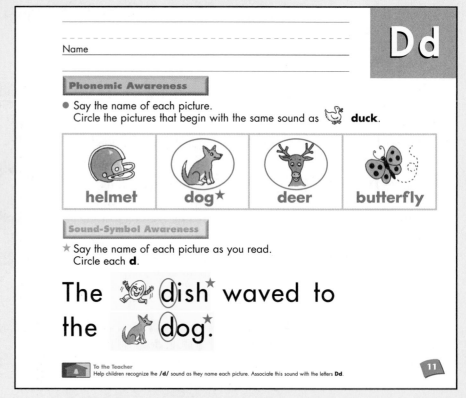

★**Note: Basic Words** are starred.

Meeting Individual Needs

Stage 0 Spellers

Model adding /d/ to the beginning of **add** to make **dad**. Then ask children to shout out words they make by adding /d/ to the beginning of these words: **ark** (dark), **or** (door), **ear** (deer), **inner** (dinner), **air** (dare), **ash** (dash), **I'm** (dime), **Andy** (dandy), **ate** (date), **ugh** (dug). Help children hear the /d/ sound at the beginning of each new word. Write several words and ask volunteers to underline **d** in each one.

For more information on the Stages of Spelling Development, see pages Z10–Z15.

Stage 1 Spellers

Use the Stage 0 activity. Repeat **d** words from the activity as well as words pictured on *Student Edition* page 11. Write the words, asking questions about prominent sounds. For example, ask, *"What letter spells /g/ in dog?"* (g)

Stage 2 Spellers

Use the Stage 0 activity. Repeat several **d** words from the activity as well as words pictured on *Student Edition* page 11. Stretch and count the sounds in each word. Ask volunteers to provide developmental spellings (e.g., **DER** for **deer**).

Stage 3 Spellers

A few children may be ready for more spelling patterns. Ask them to make new words with the **-ate** pattern seen in **date**. (ate, rate, late, skate) Have them continue by making words with the **-ug** pattern seen in **dug**. (bug, tug, mug, rug)

Spelling and Writing

See page Z17 for more information.

Invite children to draw a picture of a dog they know or a dog they would like to own. Ask them to write a description that tells how the dog looks and acts. Encourage the use of developmental spelling.

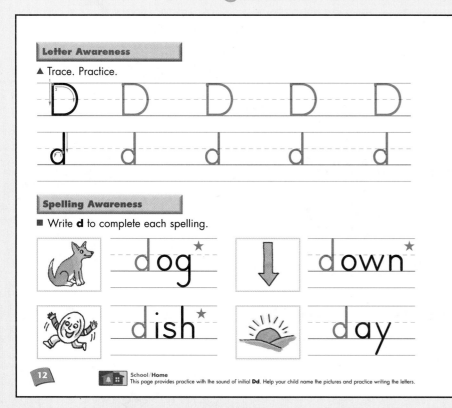

Letter Awareness

▲ Trace. Practice.

D D D D D

d d d d d

Spelling Awareness

■ Write **d** to complete each spelling.

d og ★   ↓ d own ★

d ish ★   d ay

12 School/Home
This page provides practice with the sound of initial **Dd**. Help your child name the pictures and practice writing the letters.

Letter Awareness

and

Spelling Awareness

Share these letter chants. Ask children to write the letters in the air as you chant together.

D

Pull down straight.
Then lift, and off we go.
Slide right. Curve right. Slide left.
For uppercase **D**
That's all you need to know!

d

Circle back left, all the way around.
Keep that bottom close to the ground.
Push up straight. Pull down straight, too.
No one writes lowercase **d**
Better than you!

Point out the red directional arrows and the green dots that show where to begin each letter.

Guide children in tracing and writing **D** and **d** to complete activities on *Student Edition* page 12.

Use **Meeting Individual Needs** below to extend the practice activities according to the needs of children in your class.

Meeting Individual Needs

Stage 0 Spellers

Provide pipe cleaners and show children how to use them to form the letters **D** and **d**. Invite children to trace their pipe cleaner letters with their fingers, following the correct stroke sequence.

Stage 1 Spellers

Use the Stage 0 activity. Then say words from the **Spelling Awareness** activity on *Student Edition* page 12. For prominent sounds, such as /n/ in **down,** ask children to make a corresponding letter out of pipe cleaners.

Stage 2 Spellers

Use the Stage 0 activity. Then invite children to choose one or more words from the **Spelling Awareness** activity to model with pipe cleaners.

Stage 3 Spellers

A few children may be ready to produce conventional (correct) spellings. Call out words from the **Spelling Awareness** activity. Ask children to write the words (or model them with pipe cleaners) and check their spelling.

Building Words With Word Families

day, hay, may, pay, ray, say, way

Point out the word part **-ay** in the **Spelling Awareness** activity on *Student Edition* page 12. Write **ay** on the chalkboard and say /ay/. Then say **day, hay, may, pay, ray, say,** and **way**. For each word, invite a volunteer to come to the chalkboard and write a consonant letter in front of **ay**. Correct spellings as needed. Say the new words together. Add the **-ay** words to your word wall or to a list of words for writing.

Unit Assessment

See page Z16 for more information.

You may wish to check progress by having children write **D, d,** and one or more **Basic Words (dog, dish, duck, down)**. Note spellings to determine each child's stage of spelling development.

Have children record one **d** word in their **My Words** book (following *Student Edition* page 56).

T27

Dd

Hey, Diddle, Diddle

Hey, diddle, diddle!
The cat and the fiddle,
The cow jumped over
the moon.

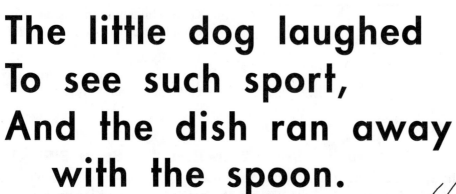

The little dog laughed
To see such sport,
And the dish ran away
with the spoon.

School/Home
Read the poem several times with your child. Encourage him or her to recite the poem while clapping. Then look for words in the poem that begin with **D** or **d**. Read and write the **d** words together, emphasizing the /d/ sound heard at the beginning of **dance**.

MATERIALS

ABC Poem and Picture Charts

Ee Poem Chart: "Meg's Egg"
Ee Picture Chart

Student Edition

Pages 13–14

Teacher Edition

Pages T29–T34

Ee

Basic Words

egg   elf
Meg   net

★Note: **Basic Words** are starred where they appear in this *Teacher Edition*.

High-Frequency Words

likes   not
or   but

Targeted Word Family

-et

OBJECTIVES

ABC Poem and Picture Charts

Phonemic Awareness:
Identify the **short e** sound

Letter Recognition:
Recognize **E** and **e**

Sound-Symbol Awareness:
Associate the **short e** sound with the letters **Ee**

Early Reading:
Engage in repeated readings of the poem "Meg's Egg"

Early Writing:
Cook a snack of scrambled eggs and write about the experience

Student Edition

Phonemic Awareness:
Identify the **short e** sound

Letter Recognition:
Recognize **E** and **e**

Sound-Symbol Awareness:
Associate the **short e** sound with the letters **Ee**

Early Reading:
Read a sentence related to the poem "Meg's Egg"

Early Writing:
Write **Ee;** use developmental spelling to write about a creature that will hatch from an unusual egg

Language and Cultural Differences

The letter **e** represents several vowel sounds in English. It is often silent as well. This makes it difficult for children to associate the sounds and the symbol. In languages around the world, /ĕ/ and /ē/ are common, though English is unusual in using **e** to represent both sounds.

In Spanish, **long e** (as in **meet**) is written with the letter **i** or **y**. Ask Spanish-speaking children to suggest Spanish words that have the sound of **long e**. If possible, write these on the chalkboard and contrast the ways the sound is written in Spanish and English. Then ask children to find pictures in this unit whose names have the **short e** sound in Spanish. These include **elefante** (**elephant**), **huevo** (**egg**), and **elfo** (**elf**).

T29

Using the ABC Poem and Picture Charts: Ee Poem Chart

Phonemic Awareness
and
Sound-Symbol Awareness

Read "Meg's Egg" aloud, pointing to each word. Chant the poem together. Ask children to pat their knees for each syllable in the poem and to clap each time they say **egg**.

Say **egg**. Isolate the initial sound and explain that this is the **short e** sound. (This unit focuses on **short e**.) Have children repeat /ĕ/, noticing how the mouth looks and feels. Associate this sound with **Ee** at the top of the chart.

Use **Meeting Individual Needs** below to develop phonemic awareness and sound-symbol awareness according to the needs of the children in your class.

School/Home
You may wish to duplicate the page that follows *Teacher Edition* page T33 so that children have their own copy of the poem.

Meg's Egg
Meg★ likes
A *regular egg*★

Not a poached
Or a fried
But a *regular egg*

An *eggular*
Megular
Regular
Egg!

—Mary Ann Hoberman

★**Note: Basic Words** are starred.

Meeting Individual Needs

Stage 0 Spellers

Sing "The ABC's," stopping at **e**. Read the poem together. Ask children to join you in repeating the words **Meg, egg, regular, eggular,** and **Megular,** stretching out and holding the /ĕ/ sound in each word.

Stage 1 Spellers

Have children say /ĕ/. Have them add /g/ to the end and say the word. (egg) Ask them to add /m/ to **egg**. (Meg) Have them change /m/ to /r/ to make a nonsense rhyming word. (reg, as in regular)

Stage 2 Spellers

Tape blank cards over **egg, Meg,** and **regular**. Read the poem and invite volunteers to write the missing words on the cards. Accept developmental spellings (e.g., **RAGULR** for **regular**).

Stage 3 Spellers

A few children may be ready for more spelling patterns. Use the Stage 2 activity. Lift the cards and compare the developmental spellings to correct spellings. Point out double **g** in **egg** and **silent e** in **likes**.

For more information on the Stages of Spelling Development, see pages Z10–Z15.

High-Frequency Words
likes, not, or, but

Point out **likes, not, or,** and **but** in the poem. Ask volunteers to name the letters in each word. Clap and chant the spellings. Ask volunteers to find the words in the poem. Add the words to your word wall or to a list of words for writing.

ABC Using Manipulatives

Use a permanent marker to write word parts on plastic colored eggs. For example, write **n** on one-half of the egg and **et** on the other half. The two parts snap together to form **net**. Place the egg parts in a center. Ask children to copy the words they make.

Using the ABC Poem and Picture Charts: Ee Picture Chart

Invite children to describe the scene on the chart. Children may wish to tell how their artwork is displayed at home.

Point to **Ee**. Ask what sound **e** makes in the word **egg**. (/ĕ/) Use **Meeting Individual Needs** below to develop phonemic awareness and sound-symbol awareness according to the needs of the children in your class.

Note: If you wish to contrast **short e** with **long e,** also include the pictures identified for **long e**.

Pictured Words • • • • • • • • • • • • • • • • • •

short e: ★egg, ★Meg, ★elf, envelope, ★net, elephant, engine, ear, elbow, eggplant

long e: eraser, eagle, eleven

Meeting Individual Needs

Stage 0 Spellers
Prompt children to find pictures of items whose names contain /ĕ/. Ask, *"Do you see an elephant? **Elephant** begins with /ĕ/."* Write each word on chart paper. Ask a volunteer to underline **e** in each word.

Stage 1 Spellers
As children find pictures with /ĕ/, stretch and count the sounds in each word (e.g., **net** = /n/ + /ĕ/ + /t/). Write the words, asking children to provide letters for prominent sounds.

Stage 2 Spellers
Challenge children to find all ten pictures with /ĕ/. Pronounce the words and ask children to write a letter (or choose a magnetic letter) for each sound. Accept developmental spellings (e.g., **EG** for **egg**).

Stage 3 Spellers
A few children may be ready for more spelling patterns. Ask children to find pictures whose names contain **short e** or **long e**. Write each word, pointing out patterns such as **consonant-vowel-consonant** in **Meg** and **net**.

For more information on the Stages of Spelling Development, see pages Z10–Z15.

ABC Poem and Picture Charts
Use dry erase markers on the laminated pages to highlight and emphasize words, pictures, and targeted sounds.

- Highlight letters on the **Poem Chart**.
- Underline high-frequency words on the **Poem Chart**.
- Circle pictures on the **Picture Chart**.
- Label objects on the **Picture Chart**.

Spelling and Writing
See page Z17 for more information.

Make scrambled eggs in an electric skillet. Let children help by cracking the eggs and stirring in milk and grated cheese. After children have eaten, invite them to write about the cooking experience and tell what they did and did not like about the eggs.

Phonemic Awareness and **Sound-Symbol Awareness**

Help children follow the directions on *Student Edition* page 13.

Use **Meeting Individual Needs** below to extend the practice activities according to the needs of the children in your class.

One-Minute Handwriting Hint

Remind children that the circle back line must touch the first, horizontal line in **e**.

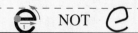 NOT

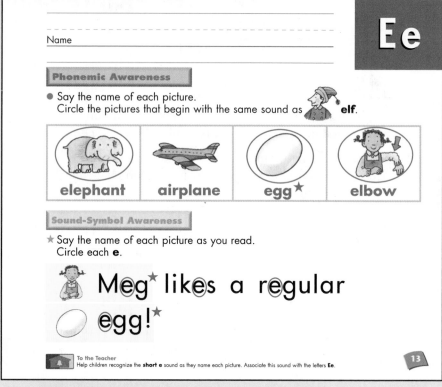

★**Note: Basic Words** are starred.

Meeting Individual Needs

Stage 0 Spellers

Tell children you will say a word in slow motion and ask them to say the word in a normal way. For example, if you say **pet** as /p/ + /ĕ/ + /t/, the children should respond, "*pet.*" Use words that have a **short e** sound and no more than three phonemes, such as **let, men, egg, Meg, red, set, met, tell, wet, hen, yes, bell, leg, neck, ten, sell, yet, beg, jet,** and **den**.

For more information on the Stages of Spelling Development, see pages Z10–Z15.

Stage 1 Spellers

Use the Stage 0 activity. After children say each word correctly, ask questions about prominent sounds. For example, ask, "*What letter spells the /ĕ/ sound in egg?*" (e) "*What letter spells the /g/ sound in Meg?*" (g)

Stage 2 Spellers

Use the Stage 0 activity. Draw a number of egg outlines on the chalkboard. After children say each word correctly, invite a volunteer to write it inside one of the eggs. Accept developmental spellings (e.g., **LAG** for **leg**).

Stage 3 Spellers

A few children may be ready for more spelling patterns. Ask them to write new words with the **-eg** pattern seen in **Meg**. (beg, peg, leg)

Spelling and Writing

See page Z17 for more information.

Provide a cardboard egg stencil. Invite children to trace around the stencil and decorate their egg with spots, stripes, or other unusual patterns. Ask them to write a description of the type of imaginary creature that will hatch from the egg. Encourage the use of developmental spelling.

Using the Student Edition: Page 14

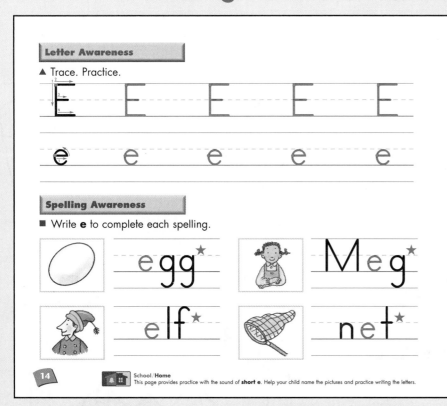

Letter Awareness and Spelling Awareness

Share these letter chants. Ask children to write the letters in the air as you chant together.

E

Pull down straight. Lift and slide right.
Lift again and then slide right in the middle.
One more lift and another slide right—
There's an uppercase **E** that's fit as a fiddle.

e

Slide right, straight across;
To the left circle back.
Your pencil should glide
Like a train on its track.

Point out the red directional arrows and the green dots that show where to begin each letter.

Guide children in tracing and writing **E** and **e** to complete the activities on *Student Edition* page 14.

Use **Meeting Individual Needs** below to extend the practice activities according to the needs of the children in your class.

Meeting Individual Needs

Stage 0 Spellers

Have children use their fingers to trace **E** and **e** in the air, on their tabletops, and on a partner's back. Check to make sure children are using the correct stroke sequence.

Stage 1 Spellers

Say a word from the **Spelling Awareness** activity on *Student Edition* page 14. Ask, *"What is one sound you hear? What letter spells the sound?"* After children respond with a letter, have them trace it on a partner's back.

Stage 2 Spellers

Have children work in pairs. The first child should choose a word from the **Spelling Awareness** activity and trace some or all of the letters on the second child's back. The second child should try to guess the word. Partners should then trade roles.

Stage 3 Spellers

A few children may be ready to produce conventional (correct) spellings. Use the Stage 2 activity. After the word is guessed, ask both partners to write it correctly on lined paper.

Building Words With Word Families

bet, get, jet, let, met, net, pet, set, vet, wet, yet

Point out the word part **-et** in the **Spelling Awareness** activity on *Student Edition* page 14. Write **et** on the chalkboard and say /et/. Hide cards with these letters around the room: **b, g, j, l, m, n, p, s, v, w, y.** Invite volunteers to spot a card, retrieve it, and place it in front of **et**. Say the new words together. Add the **-et** words to your word wall or to a list of words for writing.

Unit Assessment

See page Z16 for more information.

You may wish to check progress by having children write **E, e,** and one or more **Basic Words** (**egg, elf, Meg, net**). Note spellings to determine each child's stage of spelling development.

Have children record one **e** word in their **My Words** book (following *Student Edition* page 56).

Ee

Meg's Egg

Meg likes
A *regular* egg

Not a poached
Or a fried
But a *regular* egg

An *eggular*
Megular
Regular
Egg!

—Mary Ann Hoberman

School/Home
Read the poem several times with your child. Chant the poem together, asking your child to omit the word **egg** and clap in its place. Then look for words in the poem that contain **E** or **e**. Read and write the **e** words together, emphasizing the **short e** sound heard at the beginning of **egg**.

MATERIALS

ABC Poem and Picture Charts
Ff Poem Chart: "Fee, Fi, Fo, Fum"
Ff Picture Chart

Student Edition
Pages 15–16

Teacher Edition
Pages T35–T40

Basic Words
finger   fish
fox   fence

★**Note: Basic Words** are starred where they appear in this *Teacher Edition*.

High-Frequency Words
see   my
so   is

Targeted Word Family
-og

OBJECTIVES

ABC Poem and Picture Charts

Phonemic Awareness:
Identify the **/f/** sound

Letter Recognition:
Recognize **F** and **f**

Sound-Symbol Awareness:
Associate the **/f/** sound with the letters **Ff**

Early Reading:
Engage in repeated readings of the poem "Fee, Fi, Fo, Fum"

Early Writing:
Write a class fingerplay that includes **f** words

Student Edition

Phonemic Awareness:
Identify the **/f/** sound

Letter Recognition:
Recognize **F** and **f**

Sound-Symbol Awareness:
Associate the **/f/** sound with the letters **Ff**

Early Reading:
Read a sentence from the poem "Fee, Fi, Fo, Fum"

Early Writing:
Write **Ff**; use developmental spelling to write a story about a frog and a fish

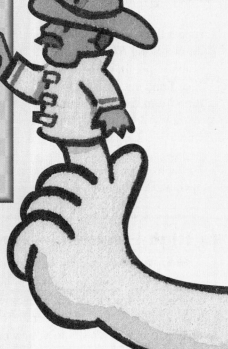

Language and Cultural Differences

In English, the letter **f** almost always stands for the **/f/** sound (in **of,** it stands for **/v/**). The **/f/** sound is called a fricative because air is forced through a narrow space, causing friction. Children who are missing front teeth won't be able to make **/f/** accurately.

Some languages lack **/f/**. To produce the closest sound in Japanese, the lips are brought close together and air is blown through the opening. For children acquiring English, point to pictures in this unit and ask children to repeat their names after you.

Using the ABC Poem and Picture Charts: Ff Poem Chart

Phonemic Awareness and **Sound-Symbol Awareness**

Read "Fee, Fi, Fo, Fum" aloud, pointing to each word. Have pairs of children make up hand motions to use while reciting the poem together.

Say **fun**. Explain that **fun** begins with the **/f/** sound. (**Note:** Be sure to say **/f/,** not **/fuh/,** to isolate the consonant sound.) Have children repeat **/f/,** noticing how the mouth looks and feels. Associate this sound with **Ff** at the top of the chart.

Use **Meeting Individual Needs** below to develop phonemic awareness and sound-symbol awareness according to the needs of children in your class.

School/Home
You may wish to duplicate the page that follows *Teacher Edition* page T39 so that children have their own copy of the poem.

Fee, Fi, Fo, Fum
Fee, fi, fo, fum,
See my finger,★
 see my thumb.

Fee, fi, fo, fum,
Finger's gone,
 so is thumb.

★**Note: Basic Words** are starred.

Meeting Individual Needs

Stage 0 Spellers
Ask if any children have **F** or **f** in their names. If so, repeat the names together, emphasizing **/f/**. As you read the poem, point to each **F** or **f** and encourage children to make the **/f/** sound as they hold up their pointer fingers.

For more information on the Stages of Spelling Development, see pages Z10–Z15.

Stage 1 Spellers
Read the poem, asking children to count the sounds they hear in each **f** word (e.g., **fum** = **/f/** + **/ŭ/** + **/m/**). Ask questions such as *"What letter spells the /g/ sound in **finger**?"* (g)

Stage 2 Spellers
Read the poem, pausing to spell **fee, fi, fo,** and **fum** aloud. Clap and chant the spellings. Point out that in **fee, fi,** and **fo,** the vowels say their names. **Fum** has the **short u** sound heard in **umbrella**.

Stage 3 Spellers
A few children may be ready for more spelling patterns. Point out the **ee** spelling of **long e** in **fee**. Make a list of words that end in **ee**. (bee, tree, see, knee, wee)

High-Frequency Words
see, my, so, is

Point out **see, my, so,** and **is** in the poem. Ask volunteers to name the letters in each word. Clap and chant the spellings. Ask volunteers to find each word in the poem. Add the words to your word wall or to a list of words for writing.

Using Manipulatives

Write the **Basic Words** (**finger, fish, fox, fence**) and other **f** words from the unit on blank cards. If you wish, illustrate each word on the back of the card. Then cut **f** from each card in a curved or zigzag pattern to make a simple jigsaw puzzle. Allow children to work the puzzles in a learning center.

Using the **ABC** Poem and Picture Charts:
Ff Picture Chart

Phonemic Awareness and **Sound-Symbol Awareness**

Invite children to describe the scene on the chart. Children may wish to compare the classroom shown on the chart with your classroom.

Point to **Ff** and ask children what sound it makes. (/f/) Use **Meeting Individual Needs** below to develop phonemic awareness and sound-symbol awareness according to the needs of the children in your class.

Pictured Words..................
fan, ★fence, ★fish, farmer, firefighter, fire engine, forest, flag, ★finger, flamingo, flashlight, ★fox, frog

Meeting Individual Needs

Stage 0 Spellers

Prompt children to find pictures of items whose names begin with /f/. Ask, *"Do you see a fence? Fence begins with /f/."* Write each word on chart paper. Ask a volunteer to underline **f** in each word.

For more information on the Stages of Spelling Development, see pages Z10–Z15.

Stage 1 Spellers

Ask children to find pictures whose names begin with /f/. Stretch and count the sounds in each word (e.g., **fish** = /f/ + /ĭ/ + /sh/). Write the words, asking children to provide letters for prominent sounds.

Stage 2 Spellers

Challenge children to find all 13 pictures that begin with /f/. Pronounce the words and ask children to write a letter (or choose a magnetic letter) for each sound. Accept developmental spellings (e.g., **FRMR** for **farmer**).

Stage 3 Spellers

A few children may be ready for more spelling patterns. Write /f/ words children identify. Ask which picture names begin with **fl**. (flag, flamingo, flashlight)

ABC Poem and Picture Charts

Use dry erase markers on the laminated pages to highlight and emphasize words, pictures, and targeted sounds.

- Highlight letters on the **Poem Chart**.
- Underline high-frequency words on the **Poem Chart**.
- Circle pictures on the **Picture Chart**.
- Label objects on the **Picture Chart**.

Spelling and Writing

See page Z17 for more information.

Work as a class to write a new fingerplay using **fee, fi, fo, fum, finger,** and other words. Ask children to suggest words and accompanying hand motions. Write the fingerplay on chart paper and perform it together.

Phonemic Awareness *and* **Sound-Symbol Awareness**

Help children follow the directions on *Student Edition* page 15.

Use **Meeting Individual Needs** below to extend the practice activities according to the needs of children in your class.

One-Minute Handwriting Hint

Remind children to begin **F** by pulling down straight from the top. Have them practice making the first stroke of **f** in one, fluid motion.

★**Note: Basic Words** are starred.

Meeting Individual Needs

Stage 0 Spellers

Have children practice making the **/f/** sound. Then pronounce pairs of words. Ask children to hold up their thumbs if the word does not begin with **/f/**. Ask them to hold up their pointer fingers if the word does begin with **/f/**. Use these word pairs: fence/sense, can/fan, fat/bat, fog/dog, fox/box, car/far, beat/feet, fear/dear, bin/fin, fell/bell, bed/fed, fine/dine, finger/linger, dish/fish, fuzz/buzz, bit/fit, dare/fair.

For more information on the Stages of Spelling Development, see pages Z10–Z15.

Stage 1 Spellers

Use the Stage 0 activity. Choose several of the **f** words to pronounce slowly. Help children count the sounds in each word (e.g., **fox** = /f/ + /ŏ/ + /ks/). Then ask questions such as *"What letter spells the /ŏ/ sound in fox?"* (o)

Stage 2 Spellers

Use the Stage 0 activity. Choose several of the **f** words to pronounce slowly. Ask a volunteer to write each word on the chalkboard, giving one letter for each sound. Accept developmental spellings (e.g., **FINS** for **fence**).

Stage 3 Spellers

A few children may be ready for more spelling patterns. Use the Stage 0 activity. Write several of the word pairs. Point out spelling patterns such as **an** in **can** and **fan**.

Spelling and Writing

See page Z17 for more information.

Invite children to imagine and write about the adventures of a frog and a fish who are friends. Challenge them to include one page (with a few words or a sentence) for the beginning, one page for the middle, and one page for the end. Encourage the use of developmental spelling.

Using the Student Edition: Page 16

Letter Awareness
and
Spelling Awareness

Share these letter chants. Ask children to write the letters in the air as you chant together.

F

Pull down straight—that's how to begin.
Lift. Slide right. Lift and slide right again.
Write uppercase **F** in green, blue, or red.
Now write friendly letters to Franny and to Fred.

f

Curve back left;
Pull down straight.
Lift and slide right;
Your **f** should be great.

Point out the red directional arrows and the green dots that show where to begin each letter.

Guide children in tracing and writing **F** and **f** to complete the activities.

Use **Meeting Individual Needs** below to extend the practice activities.

Meeting Individual Needs

Stage 0 Spellers

Dispense a small amount of shaving cream on each child's tabletop. Show how to spread it out to make a "magic cloud" for finger-writing. Ask children to write **F** and **f**, following the correct stroke sequence.

Stage 1 Spellers

Use the Stage 0 activity. Slowly say words from the **Spelling Awareness** activity on *Student Edition* page 16. Ask children to finger-write letters for prominent sounds they hear.

Stage 2 Spellers

Use the Stage 0 activity. Pronounce the words from the **Spelling Awareness** activity and ask children to finger-write them, giving one letter for each sound they hear. Accept developmental spellings.

Stage 3 Spellers

A few children may be ready to produce conventional (correct) spellings. Call out words from the **Spelling Awareness** activity. Ask children to finger-write them in shaving cream and then check their spelling.

Building Words With Word Families
dog, fog, hog, jog, log, frog

Point out the word part **-og** in the **Spelling Awareness** activity on *Student Edition* page 16. Display the magnetic letters **og** and say /og/. Then show a consonant magnetic letter (**d, f, h, j, l, fr**). Ask a volunteer to say its sound and add it to **og** to make a new word. Say the new words together. Add the **-og** words to your word wall or to a list of words for writing.

Unit Assessment

See page Z16 for more information.

You may wish to check progress by having children write **F, f,** and one or more **Basic Words** (**finger, fish, fox, fence**). Note spellings to determine each child's stage of spelling development.

Have children record one **f** word in their **My Words** book (following *Student Edition* page 56).

Ff

Fee, Fi, Fo, Fum

Fee, fi, fo, fum,
See my finger,
  see my thumb.

Fee, fi, fo, fum,
Finger's gone,
  so is thumb.

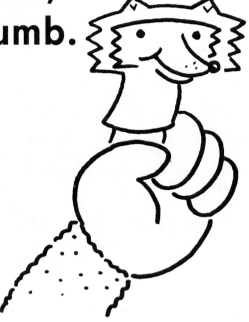

School/Home

Read the poem several times with your child. Make up hand motions to perform together as you recite the poem. Then look for words in the poem that begin with **F** or **f**. Read and write the **f** words together, emphasizing the **/f/** sound heard at the beginning of **fun**.

Gg

MATERIALS

ABC Poem and Picture Charts

Gg Poem Chart: "Good Night to Me"
Gg Picture Chart

Student Edition

Pages 17–18

Teacher Edition

Pages T41–T46

Basic Words

girls	goats
game	gate

★ Note: **Basic Words** are starred where they appear in this *Teacher Edition*.

High-Frequency Words

big	and
good	me

Targeted Word Family

-ot

OBJECTIVES

ABC Poem and Picture Charts

Phonemic Awareness:
Identify the **/g/** sound

Letter Recognition:
Recognize **G** and **g**

Sound-Symbol Awareness:
Associate the **/g/** sound with the letters **Gg**

Early Reading:
Engage in repeated readings of the poem "Good Night to Me"

Early Writing:
Use developmental spelling to write a *Good Night* book

Student Edition

Phonemic Awareness:
Identify the **/g/** sound

Letter Recognition:
Recognize **G** and **g**

Sound-Symbol Awareness:
Associate the **/g/** sound with the letters **Gg**

Early Reading:
Read picture labels that begin with **g**

Early Writing:
Write **Gg**; use developmental spelling to write about a favorite game

---

Language and Cultural Differences

The letter **g** stands for two sounds in English: **hard g** (as in **gold**) and **soft g** (as in **gem**). This unit focuses on **/g/,** the **hard g** sound. The /g/ sound appears in most languages and is produced early by babies (as in **gaga**). Some languages, however, including Arabic and Thai, don't have /g/. For children acquiring English, use instruction words that begin with **/g/,** such as *"Give…,"* *"Go…,"* *"Get…,"* etc. Have children repeat and follow the commands.

Using the ABC Poem and Picture Charts: Gg Poem Chart

Read "Good Night to Me" aloud, pointing to each word. Read it again, pointing to pictures on the chart to cue children to shout out the **g** words (e.g., **girls, geese, garbage trucks**).

Say **goat**. Explain that **goat** begins with the **/g/** sound. (**Note:** Be sure to say **/g/,** not **/guh/,** to isolate the consonant sound.) Have children repeat **/g/,** noticing how the mouth looks and feels. Associate this sound with **Gg** at the top of the chart.

Use **Meeting Individual Needs** below to develop phonemic awareness and sound-symbol awareness according to the needs of children in your class.

School/Home
You may wish to duplicate the page that follows *Teacher Edition* page T45 so that children have their own copy of the poem.

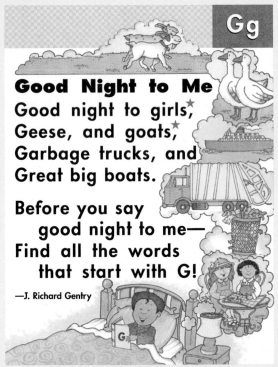

Good Night to Me

Good night to girls,⋆
Geese, and goats,⋆
Garbage trucks, and
Great big boats.

Before you say
    good night to me—
Find all the words
    that start with G!

—J. Richard Gentry

⋆**Note: Basic Words** are starred.

Meeting Individual Needs

Stage 0 Spellers

Have children practice saying **/g/**. Ask if any children have this sound in their name. Read the poem again, asking children to clap when they hear a word that begins with **/g/**. Have volunteers point to each **G** and **g** on the chart.

Stage 1 Spellers

Read the poem, asking children to clap when they hear a word that begins with **/g/**. For each **g** word, ask questions such as *"What letter spells the /g/ sound in geese?"* (g) *"What spells /s/ in geese?"* (s)

Stage 2 Spellers

Ask children to clap when they hear a word in the poem that begins with **/g/**. Cover the chart. Slowly say each **g** word, stretching the sounds (e.g., **goats** = **/g/** + **/ō/** + **/t/** + **/s/**). Ask a volunteer to write a letter for each sound.

Stage 3 Spellers

A few children may be ready for more spelling patterns. Use the Stage 2 activity. As volunteers write the words, point out the **oat** pattern in **goat**. With children's help, write a list of **-oat** words. (oat, boat, float)

For more information on the Stages of Spelling Development, see pages Z10–Z15.

High-Frequency Words
big, and, good, me

Point out **big, and, good,** and **me** in the poem. Ask volunteers to name the letters in each word. Clap and chant the spellings. Ask volunteers to find the words in the poem. Add the words to your word wall or to a list of words for writing.

Using Manipulatives

Have each child cut a **g** shape from black construction paper and decorate it with gold stars, gold markers or paint, or gold glitter. In a learning center, allow children to use their gold letters, along with magnetic letters, to spell **g** words.

Using the ABC Poem and Picture Charts: Gg Picture Chart

Phonemic Awareness and **Sound-Symbol Awareness**

Invite children to describe the scene on the chart. Children may wish to tell about a dream they had.

Point to **Gg** and ask children what sound it makes. (/g/) Use **Meeting Individual Needs** below to develop phonemic awareness and sound-symbol awareness according to the needs of the children in your class.

Pictured Words. . . . .
★girls, ★game, geese, goat, garden, ★gate, grass, guitar, gift, grapes

Meeting Individual Needs

Stage 0 Spellers

Prompt children to find pictures of items whose names begin with /g/. Ask, *"Do you see a game? Game begins with /g/."* Write each word on chart paper. Ask a volunteer to underline **g** in each word.

Stage 1 Spellers

As children find pictures whose names begin with /g/, stretch and count the sounds in each word (e.g., **gate** = /g/ + /ā/ + /t/). Write the words, asking children to provide letters for prominent sounds.

Stage 2 Spellers

Challenge children to find all ten pictures that begin with /g/. Pronounce the words and ask children to write a letter (or choose a magnetic letter) for each sound. Accept developmental spellings (e.g., **GRILS** for **girls**).

Stage 3 Spellers

A few children may be ready for more spelling patterns. Write a list of /g/ words children identify. Point out that **grapes** and **grass** begin with **gr**.

For more information on the Stages of Spelling Development, see pages Z10–Z15.

ABC Poem and Picture Charts

Use dry erase markers on the laminated pages to highlight and emphasize words, pictures, and targeted sounds.

- Highlight letters on the **Poem Chart**.
- Underline high-frequency words on the **Poem Chart**.
- Circle pictures on the **Picture Chart**.
- Label objects on the **Picture Chart**.

Spelling and Writing

See page Z17 for more information.

Talk about bedtime routines. On the chalkboard, write "Good night to ___." Have children write and complete the sentence on several blank pages. Encourage the use of developmental spelling. Have children illustrate the books and staple them together.

Phonemic Awareness
and
Sound-Symbol Awareness

Help children follow the directions on *Student Edition* page 17.

Use **Meeting Individual Needs** below to extend the practice activities according to the needs of children in your class.

One-Minute Handwriting Hint

The "tail" of **g** should curve left and fill the descender space. Children should practice writing **G** with one continuous stroke.

★**Note: Basic Words** are starred.

Meeting Individual Needs

Stage 0 Spellers

Draw a goose on chart paper. Also cut 10–15 egg shapes from yellow paper and write **g** on each egg. Explain that this is Gilda the Goose and she lays golden eggs. Ask children to practice saying the /**g**/ sound. Then challenge them to think of words they know that begin with /**g**/. For each correct response, tape a golden egg beside the goose.

Stage 1 Spellers

Use the Stage 0 activity. Choose several **g** words children suggest. Say the words slowly, then write them beside the goose. Ask children to provide letters for prominent sounds they hear (e.g., **m** for /**m**/ in **game**).

Stage 2 Spellers

Use the Stage 0 activity. Choose several **g** words children suggest. Stretch the sounds in each word (e.g., **geese** = /**g**/ + /ē/ + /s/). Ask volunteers to write the words beside the goose. Accept developmental spellings (e.g., **GES** for **geese**).

Stage 3 Spellers

A few children may be ready for more spelling patterns. Use the Stage 0 activity. Ask volunteers to write several **g** words beside the goose. Give a golden egg for each correct spelling.

Spelling and Writing

See page Z17 for more information.

Ask children to draw a picture of themselves playing a favorite game. It may be a board game or an outdoor game. Ask them to write a few words or a sentence about the game. Accept developmental spelling.

For more information on the Stages of Spelling Development, see pages Z10–Z15.

Using the Student Edition: Page 18

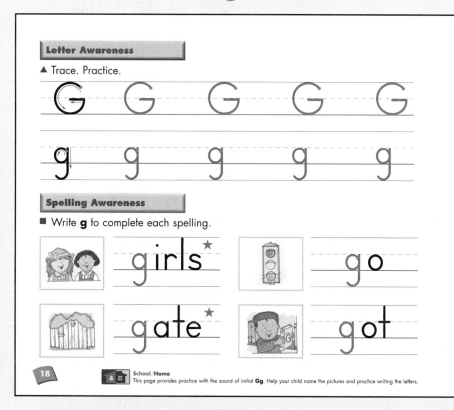

Share these letter chants. Ask children to write the letters in the air as you chant together.

G

Circle back left.
Slide left. Say "Whee!"
Now you can make
Uppercase **G**.

g

Circle back left, all the way around.
Keep that bottom down to the ground.
Push up straight. Pull down the same.
Writing small **g** feels like a game.
Curve back left. Keep your strokes loose.
With this little **g** you can write **goose**.

Point out the red directional arrows and the green dots that show where to begin each letter.

Guide children in tracing and writing **G** and **g** to complete the activities on *Student Edition* page 18.

Use **Meeting Individual Needs** below to extend the practice activities.

Meeting Individual Needs

Stage 0 Spellers

Allow children to write **G** and **g** in a large size on the chalkboard. Alternately, allow them to paint with a wide brush on an easel. Make sure children are following the correct stroke sequence.

Stage 1 Spellers

Use the Stage 0 activity. Slowly say words from the **Spelling Awareness** activity on *Student Edition* page 18. Ask children to write or paint letters for prominent sounds they hear in the words.

Stage 2 Spellers

Use the Stage 0 activity. Slowly say words from the **Spelling Awareness** activity. Ask children to write a letter for each sound they hear. Accept developmental spellings (e.g., **GRILS** for **girls**).

Stage 3 Spellers

A few children may be ready to produce conventional (correct) spellings. Call out words from the **Spelling Awareness** activity. Ask children to write or paint them and then check their spelling.

Building Words With Word Families
cot, dot, got, hot, not, pot

Point out the word part **-ot** in the **Spelling Awareness** activity on *Student Edition* page 18. Write **ot** on a large card and ask a child to hold it. Say **/ot/**. Write letters **c, d, g, h, n,** and **p** on smaller cards and give them to volunteers. Ask each volunteer to hold his or her letter card beside **ot**. Say the new words together. Add the **-ot** words to your word wall or to a list of words for writing.

Unit Assessment

See page Z16 for more information.

You may wish to check progress by having children write **G, g,** and one or more **Basic Words** (**girls, goats, game, gate**). Note spellings to determine each child's stage of spelling development.

Have children record one **g** word in their **My Words** book (following *Student Edition* page 56).

Gg

Good Night to Me

Good night to girls,
Geese, and goats,
Garbage trucks, and
Great big boats.

Before you say
 good night to me—
Find all the words
 that start with G!

—J. Richard Gentry

School/Home
Read the poem several times with your child. Sit and recite the poem together, patting your knees to the rhythm. Then look for words in the poem that begin with **G** or **g**. Read and write the **g** words together, emphasizing the /g/ sound heard in **game**.

MATERIALS

ABC Poem and Picture Charts

Hh Poem Chart: "A House Is a House for Me"

Hh Picture Chart

Student Edition

Pages 19–20

Teacher Edition

Pages T47–T52

Basic Words

hill	house
hole	hat

★**Note: Basic Words** are starred where they appear in this *Teacher Edition*.

High-Frequency Words

for	house
is	me

Targeted Word Family

-and

OBJECTIVES

ABC Poem and Picture Charts

Phonemic Awareness:
Identify the **/h/** sound

Letter Recognition:
Recognize **H** and **h**

Sound-Symbol Awareness:
Associate the **/h/** sound with the letters **Hh**

Early Reading:
Engage in repeated readings of the poem "A House Is a House for Me"

Early Writing:
Write a class big book about places where animals and objects make their homes

Student Edition

Phonemic Awareness:
Identify the **/h/** sound

Letter Recognition:
Recognize **H** and **h**

Sound-Symbol Awareness:
Associate the **/h/** sound with the letters **Hh**

Early Reading:
Read a sentence related to the poem "A House Is a House for Me"

Early Writing:
Write **Hh**; use developmental spelling to write about home

Language and Cultural Differences

The letter **h** is silent in Spanish and French. French **homme** and Spanish **hombre,** both of which mean "man," are pronounced **/uhm/** and **/ohmbray/**. Portuguese, Italian, and Russian also lack **/h/**. Children who are acquiring English may tend to omit **/h/** or substitute another sound.

Tell children that **h** is the "laughing letter." On the chalkboard, write "Ho! Ha! He!" Pronounce **/h/** as you say each word several times while laughing: *"Ho, ho, ho,"* etc. Ask children to repeat after you.

Using the ABC Poem and Picture Charts: Hh Poem Chart

Read "A House Is a House for Me" aloud, pointing to each word. Read the poem again, asking children to shout **house** each time it appears.

Say **house**. Explain that **house** begins with the **/h/** sound. (**Note:** Be sure to say **/h/,** not **/huh/,** to isolate the consonant sound.) Have children repeat **/h/,** noticing how the mouth looks and feels. Associate this sound with **Hh** at the top of the chart.

Use **Meeting Individual Needs** below to develop phonemic awareness and sound-symbol awareness.

School/Home
You may wish to duplicate the page that follows *Teacher Edition* page T51 so that children have their own copy of the poem.

A House Is a House for Me

A hill★ is a house★
    for an ant, an ant.
A hive is a house
    for a bee.
A hole★ is a house
    for a mole
    or a mouse
**And a house is a house
    for me!**

—Mary Ann Hoberman

★**Note: Basic Words** are starred.

Meeting Individual Needs

Stage 0 Spellers

Sing "The ABC's," stopping at **h**. Ask if anyone has this letter in his or her name. If so, repeat the names, emphasizing **/h/**. Ask volunteers to find each **h** in the poem.

Stage 1 Spellers

Read the poem. Ask children to clap when they hear a word that begins with **/h/**. Ask questions about sounds and letters in the **h** words. For example, ask, *"What letter spells /l/ in hill?"* (l)

Stage 2 Spellers

After reading the poem, ask, *"What is a house for (a bee, an ant, a mouse, me)?"* Have children write their responses on scrap paper and hold them up. Accept developmental spellings (e.g., **HOL** for **hole, HOWS** for **house**).

Stage 3 Spellers

A few children may be ready for more spelling patterns. Use the Stage 2 activity. Compare children's developmental spellings with correct spellings. Point out double **l** in **hill** and **silent e** in **hive, hole,** and **house**.

For more information on the Stages of Spelling Development, see pages Z10–Z15.

High-Frequency Words

for, house, is, me

Point out **for, house, is,** and **me** in the poem. Ask volunteers to name the letters in each word. Clap and chant the spellings. Ask volunteers to find the words in the poem. Add the words to your word wall or to a list of words for writing.

ABC Using Manipulatives

For each child, provide a small handful of bingo chips or colored acetate squares. Allow time for children to find **H** and **h** in books and on the walls of your classroom. They may cover each **H** or **h** with a chip.

Using the ABC Poem and Picture Charts:
Hh Picture Chart

Phonemic Awareness
and
Sound-Symbol Awareness

Invite children to describe the scene on the chart. Children may wish to talk about animal homes they have seen.

Point to **Hh** and ask children what sound it makes. (/h/) Use **Meeting Individual Needs** below to develop phonemic awareness and sound-symbol awareness according to the needs of the children in your class.

Pictured Words . . . .
★hole, ★hat, heart, hippo, hedgehog, hose, horn, ★house, hive, ★hill, hook, hammock, happy face, hay, hot dog

Meeting Individual Needs

Stage 0 Spellers
Prompt children to find pictures of items whose names begin with /h/. Ask, *"Do you see a hot dog? **Hot dog** begins with /h/."* Write each word on chart paper. Ask a volunteer to underline **h** in each word.

Stage 1 Spellers
As children find pictures whose names begin with /h/, stretch and count the sounds in each word (e.g., **hat** = /h/ + /ă/ + /t/). Write the words, asking children to provide letters for prominent sounds.

Stage 2 Spellers
Challenge children to find all 15 pictures that begin with /h/. Pronounce the words and ask children to write a letter (or choose a magnetic letter) for each sound. Accept developmental spellings (e.g., **HOL** for **hole**).

Stage 3 Spellers
A few children may be ready for more spelling patterns. Write /h/ words children identify. Point out the double consonants in **hippo, happy,** and **hammock**.

For more information on the Stages of Spelling Development, see pages Z10–Z15.

ABC Poem and Picture Charts

Use dry erase markers on the laminated pages to highlight and emphasize words, pictures, and targeted sounds.

• Highlight letters on the **Poem Chart**.
• Underline high-frequency words on the **Poem Chart**.
• Circle pictures on the **Picture Chart**.
• Label objects on the **Picture Chart**.

Spelling and Writing

See page Z17 for more information.

Talk about where different animals and objects make their homes. Then work together to write a class big book that completes this sentence on each page: "A ___ is a house for ___." (Possible responses: A sock is a house for my toes. A cave is a house for a bear.)

Using the Student Edition: Page 19

Phonemic Awareness and Sound-Symbol Awareness

Help children follow the directions on *Student Edition* page 19.

Use **Meeting Individual Needs** below to extend the practice activities according to the needs of the children in your class.

One-Minute Handwriting Hint

The letters **h** and **n** are easily confused. Explain that **h** "reaches up **high**" to touch the top line.

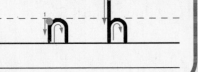

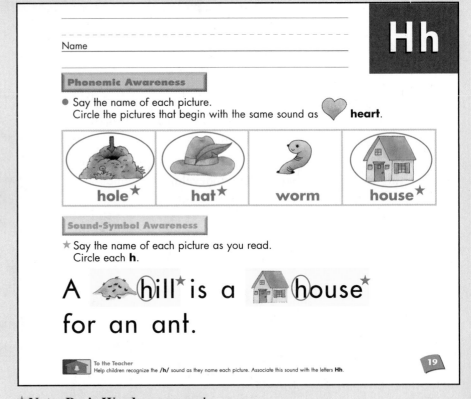

Name

Phonemic Awareness
● Say the name of each picture.
Circle the pictures that begin with the same sound as ♥ **heart**.

| hole★ | hat★ | worm | house★ |

Sound-Symbol Awareness
★ Say the name of each picture as you read.
Circle each **h**.

A hill★ is a house★
for an ant.

To the Teacher
Help children recognize the /h/ sound as they name each picture. Associate this sound with the letters **Hh**.

19

★**Note: Basic Words** are starred.

Meeting Individual Needs

Stage 0 Spellers

Ask children to answer these riddles with /h/ words:
- What has five fingers? (hand)
- What can you climb? (hill)
- What is the opposite of sad? (happy)
- What is a house for your brain? (head)
- What can you wear on your head? (hat)

Write the answers on chart paper. Point out that all the words begin with **h**.

For more information on the Stages of Spelling Development, see pages Z10–Z15.

Stage 1 Spellers

Use the Stage 0 activity. As children respond to the riddles, ask questions about prominent sounds in each /h/ word. For example, ask, *"What letter spells the /h/ sound in **hill**?"* (h) *"What letter spells the /p/ sound in **happy**?"* (p)

Stage 2 Spellers

Use the Stage 0 activity. Say each /h/ word slowly, stretching the sounds (e.g., **hat** = /h/ + /ă/ + /t/). Invite volunteers to write the words on chart paper. Accept developmental spellings (e.g., **HOWS** for **house**).

Stage 3 Spellers

Use the Stage 0 activity. After children write each riddle answer, challenge them to write a new word with the same spelling pattern as each riddle answer (e.g., **band, fill, snappy,** etc.). Have them give themselves a **hug** for each correct answer!

Spelling and Writing

See page Z17 for more information.

Ask children to draw a picture of their home and write a label, description, or story about it. They may use the **h** words **house** and **home**. Encourage the use of developmental spelling.

T50

Using the Student Edition: Page 20

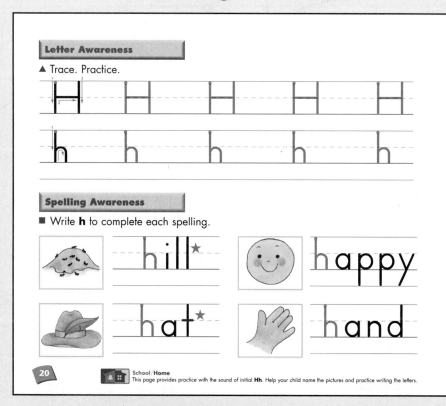

Letter Awareness and Spelling Awareness

Share these letter chants. Ask children to write the letters in the air as you chant together.

H

Pull down straight
Not once but twice.
Slide in the middle
And **H** will look nice.

h

Pull down straight.
Push up, and hold steady.
Curve right. Pull down straight,
And your **h** will be ready.

Point out the red directional arrows and the green dots that show where to begin each letter.

Guide children in tracing and writing **H** and **h** to complete the activities on *Student Edition* page 20.

Use **Meeting Individual Needs** below to extend the practice activities according to the needs of the children in your class.

Meeting Individual Needs

Stage 0 Spellers

Provide cups of water and clean paintbrushes. Allow groups of children to go to the chalkboard and paint **H** and **h** with water. Check to make sure children are using the correct starting point and stroke sequence.

Stage 1 Spellers

Use the Stage 0 activity. Slowly say words from the **Spelling Awareness** activity on *Student Edition* page 20. Ask children to paint letters for prominent sounds they hear in the words.

Stage 2 Spellers

Use the Stage 0 activity. Write words from the **Spelling Awareness** activity in a large size on the chalkboard. Invite children to either paint over your words or paint the words directly below your model.

Stage 3 Spellers

A few children may be ready to produce conventional (correct) spellings. Call out words from the **Spelling Awareness** activity. Ask children to paint them with water and then check their spelling.

Building Words With Word Families
and, band, hand, land, sand, grand, stand

Point out the word part **-and** in the **Spelling Awareness** activity on *Student Edition* page 20. Display the magnetic letters **and**. Say /and/. Then distribute these magnetic letters to volunteers: **b, h, l, s, gr,** and **st**. Ask volunteers to stand and hold their letter(s) in front of **and**. Say the new words together. Add the **-and** words to your word wall or to a list of words for writing.

Unit Assessment

See page Z16 for more information.

You may wish to check progress by having children write **H, h,** and one or more **Basic Words** (**hill, house, hole, hat**). Note spellings to determine each child's stage of spelling development.

Have children record one **h** word in their **My Words** book (following *Student Edition* page 56).

Hh

A House Is a House for Me

A hill is a house
for an ant, an ant.
A hive is a house
for a bee.
A hole is a house
for a mole
or a mouse
*And a house is a house
for me!*

—Mary Ann Hoberman

School/Home
Read the poem several times with your child. Encourage your child to use his or her hands to make a triangular rooftop shape whenever you read the word **house** in the poem. Then look for words in the poem that begin with **H** or **h**. Read and write the **h** words together, emphasizing the **/h/** sound heard at the beginning of **happy**.

MATERIALS

ABC Poem and Picture Charts

Ii Poem Chart: "Mother, Mother"
Ii Picture Chart

Student Edition

Pages 21–22

Teacher Edition

Pages T53–T58

Basic Words

in	pin
ink	inch

★**Note: Basic Words** are starred where they appear in this *Teacher Edition*.

High-Frequency Words

I	in
the	came

Targeted Word Family

-ig

OBJECTIVES

ABC Poem and Picture Charts

Phonemic Awareness:
Identify the **short i** sound

Letter Recognition:
Recognize **I** and **i**

Sound-Symbol Awareness:
Associate the **short i** sound with the letters **Ii**

Early Reading:
Engage in repeated readings of the poem "Mother, Mother"

Early Writing:
Write a class big book about going to the doctor

Student Edition

Phonemic Awareness:
Identify the **short i** sound

Letter Recognition:
Recognize **I** and **i**

Sound-Symbol Awareness:
Associate the **short i** sound with the letters **Ii**

Early Reading:
Read picture labels that begin with **i**

Early Writing:
Write **Ii;** use developmental spelling to write about something that is six inches tall

Language and Cultural Differences

This unit focuses on **short i**. Spanish does not have separate sounds for the **short i** heard in **hit** and the **long e** heard in **heat**. For this reason, Spanish speakers often confuse such English words. (Some might pronounce **it** as **eat,** for example.) Have children pronounce the /ĭ/ sound several times, then add consonants (e.g., **pip, zip, lip**), repeating each word until they have mastered the pronunciation.

The **long i** sound in **ivy** glides into a second vowel sound within the same syllable. Many languages lack this type of sound, and learners may need special practice in pronouncing words with **long i**.

Using the ABC Poem and Picture Charts: Ii Poem Chart

Phonemic Awareness and Sound-Symbol Awareness

Read "Mother, Mother" aloud, pointing to each word. Assign the roles of mother, sick child, doctor, nurse, and lion. Chant the poem together as the characters act it out.

Say **in**. Isolate the initial sound and explain that this is the **short i** sound. (This unit focuses on **short i**.) Have children repeat /ĭ/ several times, noticing how the mouth looks and feels. Associate this sound with the letters **Ii** at the top of the chart.

Use **Meeting Individual Needs** below to develop phonemic awareness and sound-symbol awareness.

School/Home
You may wish to duplicate the page that follows *Teacher Edition* page T57 so that children have their own copy of the poem.

Mother, Mother
Mother, mother,
  I am ill.
Call the doctor
  over the hill.

In★ came the doctor,
In came the nurse,
In came the lion
With the itty-bitty
  purse.

★**Note: Basic Words** are starred.

Meeting Individual Needs

Stage 0 Spellers

Use masking tape to make a "box" on the floor. Read the poem slowly. Ask children to step *in* the box when they hear a word that contains **short i**. (ill, hill, in, itty-bitty) Invite volunteers to point to **i** in each word.

For more information on the Stages of Spelling Development, see pages Z10–Z15.

Stage 1 Spellers

Tell children that on a cue (such as touching your *chin*), they should make the /ĭ/ sound. Read the poem, stopping to say each sound in the **short i** words (e.g., /h/ + cue + /l/ = **hill**). Ask children to say the complete words.

Stage 2 Spellers

Read the poem, asking children to stand when they hear a word with **short i**. Ask a volunteer to point to each word and name its letters. Then ask questions such as *"What letter spells the /n/ sound in the word in?"* (n)

Stage 3 Spellers

A few children may be ready for more spelling patterns. Point out the **-ill** spelling pattern in **ill** and **hill**. Ask children to write more words with the **-ill** pattern. (Bill, fill, Jill, pill, will)

High-Frequency Words

I, in, the, came

Point out **I, in, the,** and **came** in the poem. Ask volunteers to name the letters in each word. Clap and chant the spellings. Ask volunteers to find the words in the poem. Add the words to your word wall or to a list of words for writing.

ABC Using Manipulatives

Give six index cards or paper squares to each child. Model the formation of the letters **b, d, f, g, h,** and **i** and have children write one letter on each card. Allow children to use glue and glitter to decorate the **i** card. Invite them to use the cards to make words such as **big, fig, hid, fib,** and **if**.

Using the ABC Poem and Picture Charts: Ii Picture Chart

Phonemic Awareness

and

Sound-Symbol Awareness

Ii

Invite children to describe the scene on the chart. Children may wish to share their own experiences of being ill and getting well again.

Point to **Ii**. Ask what sound **i** makes in the word **igloo**. (short i) Use **Meeting Individual Needs** below to develop phonemic awareness and sound-symbol awareness according to the needs of the children in your class.

Note: If you wish to contrast **short i** with **long i,** also include the pictures identified for **long i**.

Pictured Words.....................

short i: igloo, iguana, ★inch, inchworm, ★ink, insects, invitation, ★pin, pig

long i: icicle, ice skates, ivy, iron

Meeting Individual Needs

Stage 0 Spellers
Prompt children to find pictures that contain /ĭ/. Ask, *"Do you see a bottle of ink? Ink begins with i."* Write each word, underlining the **i** that spells the **short i** sound.

Stage 1 Spellers
Ask children to find pictures whose names contain **short i**. Say and stretch each word, counting the sounds (e.g., **pin** = /p/ + /ĭ/ + /n/). Challenge children to provide letters for prominent consonant sounds.

Stage 2 Spellers
Ask a volunteer to point to a picture whose name contains **short i**. Say the word slowly and ask the volunteer to write a letter (or choose a magnetic letter) for each sound. Accept developmental spellings, such as **INGK** for **ink**.

Stage 3 Spellers
A few children may be ready for more spelling patterns. Ask children to find pictures whose names contain **short i** or **long i**. Compare and contrast the short and long vowel sounds.

For more information on the Stages of Spelling Development, see pages Z10–Z15.

ABC Poem and Picture Charts

Use dry erase markers on the laminated pages to highlight and emphasize words, pictures, and targeted sounds.

- Highlight letters on the **Poem Chart**.
- Underline high-frequency words on the **Poem Chart**.
- Circle pictures on the **Picture Chart**.
- Label objects on the **Picture Chart**.

Spelling and Writing

See page Z17 for more information.

Share experiences of going to the doctor. Provide a sheet of chart paper for each pair of children. Ask them to write and illustrate a sentence that gives advice for a child who is nervous about going to the doctor. Compile the sheets to make a nonfiction big book.

Using the Student Edition: Page 21

Phonemic Awareness and Sound-Symbol Awareness

Help children follow the directions on *Student Edition* page 21.

Use **Meeting Individual Needs** below to extend the practice activities according to the needs of children in your class.

One-Minute Handwriting Hint

The letter **i** should be written from top to bottom, never from bottom to top. It tosses a ball (dot) up over its head.

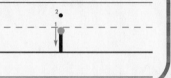

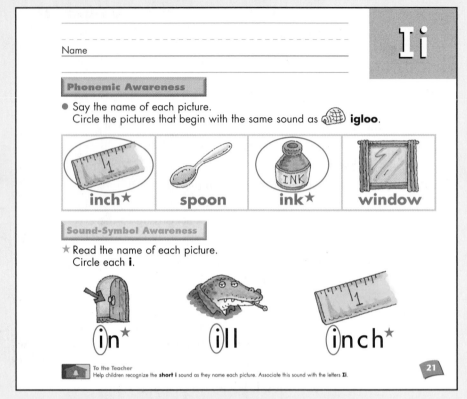

★**Note: Basic Words** are starred.

Meeting Individual Needs

Stage 0 Spellers

Make an inchworm from construction paper. Attach it to the chalkboard with tape. Draw a leaf shape on the chalkboard. Use a ruler to make inch marks between the worm and the leaf. Then say a number of words slowly. Use words from the unit and other words, such as **sad, big, sit, bun, fish, dot, win** and **if**. When children hear a word with **short i,** allow a volunteer to move the worm one inch closer to the leaf.

For more information on the Stages of Spelling Development, see pages Z10–Z15.

Stage 1 Spellers

Use the Stage 0 activity. Ask children to write the **short i** words on scrap paper. Encourage them to use developmental spelling to match sounds with letters they know (e.g., **IL** for **ill**).

Stage 2 Spellers

Ask volunteers to write words on chart paper that name the pictures in the **Phonemic Awareness** activity on *Student Edition* page 21. (inch, spoon, ink, window) Encourage children to use developmental spelling to write a letter for each sound.

Stage 3 Spellers

A few children may be ready for more spelling patterns. Start with **in, ill,** and **ink**. Challenge children to write new words with the **-in, -ill,** and **-ink** patterns. (pin, win; pill, fill; pink, sink, drink)

Spelling and Writing

See page Z17 for more information.

Invite children to draw a picture of something that is six inches tall and write about it. Provide rulers for measuring. Encourage the use of developmental spelling.

T56

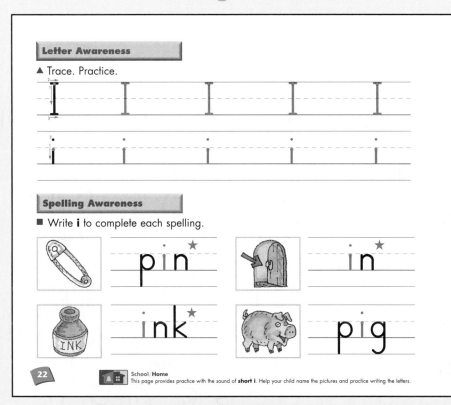

Letter Awareness and Spelling Awareness

Share these letter chants. Ask children to write the letters in the air as you chant together.

I

Pull down straight. Lift.
Slide right. Lift.
Slide right.
I's are so easy,
I could make them all night.

i

Pull down straight.
Lift, then dot.
Lowercase **i**
Is what you've got!

Point out the red directional arrows and the green dots that show where to begin each letter.

Guide children in tracing and writing **I** and **i** to complete the activities on *Student Edition* page 22.

Use **Meeting Individual Needs** below to extend the practice activities according to the needs of children in your class.

Meeting Individual Needs

Stage 0 Spellers

Have children sculpt **I** and **i** from clay. Encourage them to trace the clay letters with their fingers. Make sure children are following the correct stroke sequence.

Stage 1 Spellers

As you call out words from the **Spelling Awareness** activity on *Student Edition* page 22, have children sculpt letters from clay to match prominent sounds in the words.

Stage 2 Spellers

Write the words from the **Spelling Awareness** activity on large cards and laminate them. Allow children to use the cards as a base for building the words with clay.

Stage 3 Spellers

A few children may be ready to produce conventional (correct) spellings. Call out the words from the **Spelling Awareness** activity. Ask children to write them or sculpt them from clay. Have children check their spelling.

Building Words With Word Families
big, dig, jig, pig, wig

Point out the word part **-ig** in the **Spelling Awareness** activity on *Student Edition* page 22. Write **ig** on chart paper and say /ig/. Make cards for these letters: **b, d, j, p, w.** Give the cards to volunteers and ask each child to say the corresponding sound and hold the letter next to **ig**. Say the new words together. Add the **-ig** words to your word wall or to a list of words for writing.

Unit Assessment

See page Z16 for more information.

You may wish to check progress by having children write **I, i,** and one or more **Basic Words** (**in, pin, ink, inch**). Note spellings to determine each child's stage of spelling development.

Have children record one **i** word in their **My Words** book (following *Student Edition* page 56).

Ii

Mother, Mother

Mother, mother,
 I am ill.
Call the doctor
 over the hill.

In came the doctor,
In came the nurse,
In came the lion
With the itty-bitty
 purse.

School/Home

Read the poem with your child. Encourage him or her to chant the poem rhythmically while clapping, hopping, or jumping rope. Then look for words in the poem that begin with **I** or **i**. Read and write the **i** words together, emphasizing the **short i** sound heard at the beginning of **ill**.

MATERIALS

ABC Poem and Picture Charts

Jj Poem Chart: "Jack Be Nimble"
Jj Picture Chart

Student Edition

Pages 23–24

Teacher Edition

Pages T59–T64

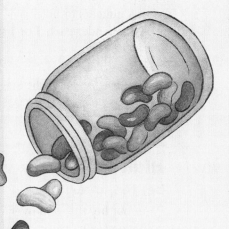

Basic Words

jump	jar
jam	jet

★**Note: Basic Words** are starred where they appear in this *Teacher Edition*.

High-Frequency Words

be	the
over	

Targeted Word Family

-ump

OBJECTIVES

ABC Poem and Picture Charts

Phonemic Awareness:
Identify the /j/ sound

Letter Recognition:
Recognize **J** and **j**

Sound-Symbol Awareness:
Associate the /j/ sound with the letters **Jj**

Early Reading:
Engage in repeated readings of the poem "Jack Be Nimble"

Early Writing:
Use developmental spelling to write *My Jumping Book*

Student Edition

Phonemic Awareness:
Identify the /j/ sound

Letter Recognition:
Recognize **J** and **j**

Sound-Symbol Awareness:
Associate the /j/ sound with the letters **Jj**

Early Reading:
Read a sentence from the poem "Jack Be Nimble"

Early Writing:
Write **Jj**; use developmental spelling to write directions for making a favorite food

---

Language and Cultural Differences

The letter **j** stands for a complex sound. The mouth actually produces /d/ and follows it immediately with /zh/, as in **pleasure**. Children may have difficulty making this sound.

Many languages do not have /j/. The closest related sound is /ch/, as in **chin**. Spanish has /ch/ but not /j/. Spanish-speaking children may pronounce **j** as /h/ if they have some knowledge of the alphabet in Spanish. As they acquire the /j/ sound, have children work with study buddies who are proficient English speakers.

Using the ABC Poem and Picture Charts:
Jj Poem Chart

Read "Jack Be Nimble" aloud, pointing to each word. Chant the words together, asking children to run in place and then jump up when they say **jump**.

Say **Jack**. Explain that **Jack** begins with **/j/**. (**Note:** Be sure to say **/j/,** not **/juh/,** to isolate the consonant sound.) Have children repeat **/j/,** noticing how the mouth looks and feels. Associate this sound with the letters **Jj** at the top of the chart.

Use **Meeting Individual Needs** below to develop phonemic awareness and sound-symbol awareness according to the needs of the children in your class.

School/Home
You may wish to duplicate the page that follows *Teacher Edition* page T63 so that children have their own copy of the poem.

Jj

Jack Be Nimble
Jack be nimble,
Jack be quick.
Jack jump* over
the candlestick.

★**Note: Basic Words** are starred.

Meeting Individual Needs

Stage 0 Spellers

Read the poem with the children, clapping to the rhythm. Read it again, asking children to clap only for words that begin with **/j/**. Invite volunteers to place a sticky note under each **J** or **j** in the poem.

For more information on the Stages of Spelling Development, see pages Z10–Z15.

Stage 1 Spellers

Use the Stage 0 activity. Stretch out and count the sounds in the **j** words (e.g., **Jack = /j/ + /ă/ + /k/**). Ask questions about prominent sounds in the words. For example, ask, *"What letter spells /j/ in Jack?"* (j)

Stage 2 Spellers

Use the Stage 0 activity. Ask children to write **jump,** giving one letter for each sound. Accept developmental spellings (e.g., **JOP**). Use the **Elkonin Boxes Practice Page** on page T173 to illustrate that **jump** has four sounds.

Stage 3 Spellers

A few children may be ready for more spelling patterns. Point out the **ck** spelling of the **/k/** sound in **Jack**. Ask children to listen carefully for the **/m/** sound in **jump** and remind them to include **m** in their spelling of the word.

High-Frequency Words
be, the, over

Point out **be, the,** and **over** in the poem. Ask volunteers to name the letters in each word. Clap and chant the spellings. Ask volunteers to find the words in the poem. Add the words to your word wall or to a list of words for writing.

ABC Using Manipulatives

Prepare a learning center with magnetic letters and fun dough or clay. Invite children to pound a lump of dough to make a flat surface. Show how to press the letters into the dough to make an impression. Have children use this technique to spell **j** words.

Using the ABC Poem and Picture Charts:
Jj Picture Chart

Invite children to describe the scene on the chart. Children may wish to tell about a time they built something with blocks.

Point to **Jj** and ask children to identify the letter and its sound. (/j/) Use **Meeting Individual Needs** below to develop phonemic awareness and sound-symbol awareness according to the needs of the children in your class.

Pictured Words.....................
Jack, ★jam, ★jar, jeep, juice, jelly beans, jewels, Jokes, ★jet

Meeting Individual Needs

Stage 0 Spellers

Prompt children to find pictures that begin with **/j/**. Ask, *"Do you see a box of juice? Juice begins with /j/."* Write the **/j/** words on chart paper and invite a volunteer to underline **j** in each word.

For more information on the Stages of Spelling Development, see pages Z10–Z15.

Stage 1 Spellers

Ask volunteers to find pictures that begin with **/j/**. Write each **j** word on chart paper, pausing to ask children to provide letters for prominent sounds, such as **/m/** in **jam**.

Stage 2 Spellers

Challenge children to find all nine items that begin with **/j/**. Count the sounds in each word (e.g., **jet** = /j/ + /ĕ/ + /t/). Ask a volunteer to write a letter (or choose a magnetic letter) for each sound. Accept developmental spellings.

Stage 3 Spellers

A few children may be ready for more spelling patterns. Write **j** words children identify as volunteers provide spellings. Underline the **-oke** pattern that spells the **long o** sound in **joke**.

ABC Poem and Picture Charts

Use dry erase markers on the laminated pages to highlight and emphasize words, pictures, and targeted sounds.

- Highlight letters on the **Poem Chart**.
- Underline high-frequency words on the **Poem Chart**.
- Circle pictures on the **Picture Chart**.
- Label objects on the **Picture Chart**.

Spelling and Writing

See page Z17 for more information.

For each child, duplicate a *My Jumping Book* cover and several pages with the sentence pattern "_____ jumps over the _____." Invite children to complete the sentences any way they like and to illustrate each page. Accept developmental spellings.

Phonemic Awareness and Sound-Symbol Awareness

Help children follow the directions on *Student Edition* page 23.

Use **Meeting Individual Needs** below to extend the practice activities according to the needs of children in your class.

One-Minute Handwriting Hint

Have children color a green stripe on the left edge of their paper. Say "curve toward the green" to help children avoid reversing **J** and **j**.

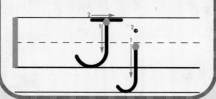

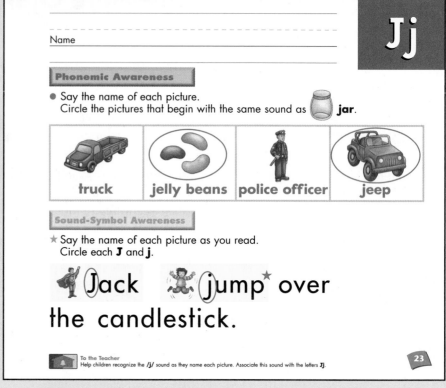

★Note: **Basic Words** are starred.

Meeting Individual Needs

Stage 0 Spellers

On an overhead projector, place paper silhouettes of a candle and Jack. Ask children to add **/j/** to the beginning of words you say: **am** (jam), **are** (jar), **aw** (jaw), **oak** (joke), **ugh** (jug), **ump** (jump). For each correct response, advance Jack's jump over the candlestick. Repeat the new words, emphasizing the initial **/j/** sound. Write the new words, underlining **j** in each one.

For more information on the Stages of Spelling Development, see pages Z10–Z15.

Stage 1 Spellers

Use the Stage 0 activity. Write each new **/j/** word, asking volunteers to provide letters for prominent sounds. Help children by asking questions such as *"What letter spells the /p/ sound in* **jump***?"* (p)

Stage 2 Spellers

Use the Stage 0 activity. Ask children to count the sounds in each new **/j/** word (e.g., **joke** = /j/ + /ō/ + /k/). Have volunteers provide a letter for each sound as you write developmental spellings.

Stage 3 Spellers

A few children may be ready for more spelling patterns. Use the Stage 0 activity. Ask volunteers to write each **j** word on the chalkboard. Award a **jelly bean** for each correct spelling.

Spelling and Writing

See page Z17 for more information.

Invite children to help you draw and write directions for making a jelly sandwich, fresh squeezed juice, or another food children like to eat. Model how to number each step.

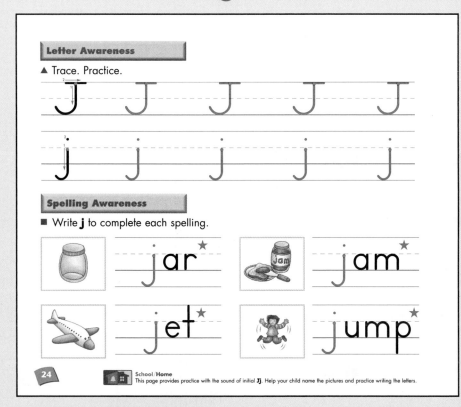

Letter Awareness

▲ Trace. Practice.

J J J J J

j j j j j

Spelling Awareness

■ Write **j** to complete each spelling.

j a r *

j a m *

j e t *

j ump *

24

School/Home
This page provides practice with the sound of initial **Jj**. Help your child name the pictures and practice writing the letters.

Letter Awareness and **Spelling Awareness**

Share these letter chants. Ask children to write the letters in the air as you chant together.

J
Pull down straight.
Then curve left back.
Do you know
the rhyme
About young Jack?
Lift. Slide right.
He went up a hill
To fetch some water
With his friend Jill.

j
Pull down straight.
Curve back left.
Lift but don't quit.
Your **j**'s not done yet.
Finished it's not
Because you've
still got
To put on a dot
Like a jaguar's spot.

Point out the red directional arrows and the green dots that show where to begin each letter.

Guide children in tracing and writing **J** and **j** to complete the activities on *Student Edition* page 24.

Use **Meeting Individual Needs** below to extend the practice activities according to the needs of children in your class.

Meeting Individual Needs

Stage 0 Spellers
Dispense a small amount of shaving cream on each child's tabletop. Show how to spread it out to make a "magic cloud" for finger-writing. Ask children to write **J** and **j,** following the correct stroke sequence.

Stage 1 Spellers
Use the Stage 0 activity. Slowly say words from the **Spelling Awareness** activity on *Student Edition* page 24. Ask children to finger-write letters for prominent sounds they hear.

Stage 2 Spellers
Use the Stage 0 activity. Pronounce the words from the **Spelling Awareness** activity and ask children to finger-write them, giving one letter for each sound they hear.

Stage 3 Spellers
A few children may be ready to produce conventional (correct) spellings. Call out words from the **Spelling Awareness** activity. Ask children to finger-write them in shaving cream and then check their spelling.

Building Words With Word Families
bump, dump, jump, lump, pump, thump

Point out the word part **-ump** on *Student Edition* page 24. Write **ump** on a large card and these letters on smaller cards: **b, d, j, l, p, th**. Say **/ump/**. Hold up each letter card and have children say the matching sound. Give the **ump** card to one child and a letter card to another. Ask the two to jump toward each other to make a new word. Say the new words together.

Unit Assessment
See page Z16 for more information.

You may wish to check progress by having children write **J, j,** and one or more **Basic Words (jump, jar, jam, jet)**. Note spellings to determine each child's stage of spelling development.

Have children record one **j** word in their **My Words** book (following *Student Edition* page 56).

Jj

Jack Be Nimble

Jack be nimble,
Jack be quick.
Jack jump over
   the candlestick.

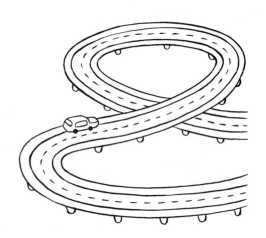

MATERIALS

ABC Poem and Picture Charts

Kk Poem Chart: "Kettle's for the Kitchen"

Kk Picture Chart

Student Edition

Pages 25–26

Teacher Edition

Pages T65–T70

OBJECTIVES

ABC Poem and Picture Charts	Student Edition
Phonemic Awareness: Identify the **/k/** sound	**Phonemic Awareness:** Identify the **/k/** sound
Letter Recognition: Recognize **K** and **k**	**Letter Recognition:** Recognize **K** and **k**
Sound-Symbol Awareness: Associate the **/k/** sound with the letters **Kk**	**Sound-Symbol Awareness:** Associate the **/k/** sound with the letters **Kk**
Early Reading: Engage in repeated readings of the poem "Kettle's for the Kitchen"	**Early Reading:** Read picture labels that begin with **k**
Early Writing: Use developmental spelling to complete a sentence pattern	**Early Writing:** Write **Kk;** use developmental spelling to write about a special key

Language and Cultural Differences

The letter **k** stands for only one sound in English, although it is usually silent when it precedes **n**. A difference between **/k/** in English and the corresponding sound in Spanish, French, and many other languages is that English **/k/** is accompanied by a puff of air (or aspiration). Some non-native English speakers pronounce **/k/** without aspiration, making it sound like **/g/**. For children acquiring English, bring to class some objects that are illustrated in the unit (e.g., a key, a kite, a kettle, a stuffed kitten). Allow children to pick them up and say their names.

Using the **ABC** Poem and Picture Charts: Kk Poem Chart

Read "Kettle's for the Kitchen" aloud, pointing to each word. Read it again, encouraging children to clap to the rhythm and/or march around the room.

Say **kid**. Explain that **kid** begins with **/k/**. (**Note:** Be sure to say **/k/,** not **/kuh/,** to isolate the consonant sound.) Have children repeat **/k/** several times, noticing how the mouth looks and feels. Associate this sound with the letters **Kk** at the top of the chart.

Use **Meeting Individual Needs** below to develop phonemic awareness and sound-symbol awareness according to the needs of the children in your class.

School/Home
You may wish to duplicate the page that follows *Teacher Edition* page T69 so that children have their own copy of the poem.

Kettle's for the Kitchen

A kettle's
for the kitchen,
A key* is
for the door,
A kitten* is
for playing with
And keeping
on the floor.

—Margaret and John Travers Moore

★**Note: Basic Words** are starred.

Meeting Individual Needs

Stage 0 Spellers

Sing "The ABC's," stopping at **k**. Point to **Kk** on the chart. Read the poem, asking children to clap when they hear a word with **/k/.** Allow a volunteer to underline **K** or **k** in each word or put a sticky note beside it.

For more information on the Stages of Spelling Development, see pages Z10–Z15.

Stage 1 Spellers

Provide a ring of keys. Chant the poem, asking a volunteer to shake the keys when he or she hears **/k/.** Repeat with other volunteers. Ask questions about each **k** word, such as *"What letter spells the /l/ sound in kettle?"* (l)

Stage 2 Spellers

Close the chart. Say and stretch the **k** words (e.g., **key** = /k/ + /ē/). Write the words, asking children to provide a letter for each sound. Accept developmental spellings, such as **KE** for **key**.

Stage 3 Spellers

A few children may be ready for more spelling patterns. Write **keep**. Challenge children to write new words using the **-eep** spelling pattern. (beep, deep, jeep, sheep)

High-Frequency Words
for, is, on, with

Point out **for, is, on,** and **with** in the poem. Ask volunteers to name the letters in each word. Clap and chant the spellings. Ask volunteers to find the words in the poem. Add the words to your word wall or to a list of words for writing.

ABC Using Manipulatives

Provide dry alphabet noodles or alphabet beads. Invite children to draw something that begins with **/k/** and glue on noodles or beads to spell the word. Accept developmental spellings. You may wish to give a chocolate *kiss* as a reward for each attempted spelling.

Using the ABC Poem and Picture Charts: Kk Picture Chart

Phonemic Awareness and Sound-Symbol Awareness

Invite children to describe the scene on the chart. Children may wish to tell about a game they like to play in the kitchen.

Point to **Kk** and ask children to identify the letter and its sound. (/k/) Use **Meeting Individual Needs** below to develop phonemic awareness and sound-symbol awareness according to the needs of the children in your class.

Pictured Words.....................
kangaroo, ketchup, kettle, *key, king, kiss, *kite, koala, *kitten, kitchen

Meeting Individual Needs

Stage 0 Spellers

Prompt children to find pictures that begin with **/k/**. Ask, *"Do you see a kite?* ***Kite begins with /k/."*** Write the **/k/** words on chart paper and invite a volunteer to underline **k** in each word.

Stage 1 Spellers

Ask volunteers to find pictures that begin with **/k/**. Write each **k** word on chart paper, pausing to ask children to provide letters for prominent sounds, such as **/g/** in **kangaroo**.

Stage 2 Spellers

Challenge children to find all ten pictures that begin with **/k/**. Help children count the sounds in each word (e.g., **kiss = /k/ + /ĭ/ + /s/**). Then ask a volunteer to write a letter (or choose a magnetic letter) for each sound.

Stage 3 Spellers

A few children may be ready for more spelling patterns. For each **/k/** picture, ask children to write the word on scrap paper and hold it up. Discuss spelling patterns such as **-ite** in **kite**.

For more information on the Stages of Spelling Development, see pages Z10–Z15.

ABC Poem and Picture Charts

Use dry erase markers on the laminated pages to highlight and emphasize words, pictures, and targeted sounds.

- Highlight letters on the **Poem Chart**.
- Underline high-frequency words on the **Poem Chart**.
- Circle pictures on the **Picture Chart**.
- Label objects on the **Picture Chart**.

Spelling and Writing

See page Z17 for more information.

On the chalkboard or chart paper, write the sentence pattern "A ____ is for ____." Ask each child to write the sentence, complete it any way he or she likes, and illustrate it. Make a book or bulletin board to publish children's writing.

Phonemic Awareness and Sound-Symbol Awareness

Help children follow the directions on *Student Edition* page 25.

Use **Meeting Individual Needs** below to extend the practice activities according to the needs of children in your class.

One-Minute Handwriting Hint

K and **k** each have two slant lines that "kick" out. Emphasize that the slant lines must touch the vertical line for good legibility.

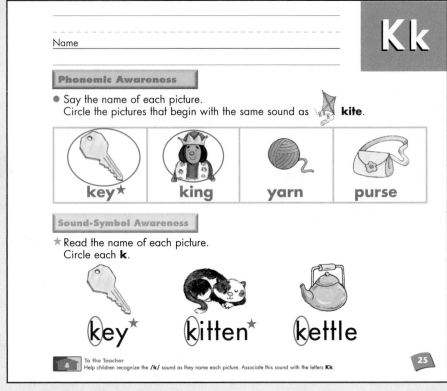

★**Note: Basic Words** are starred.

Meeting Individual Needs

Stage 0 Spellers

Have children write **k** on scrap paper. Pronounce groups of words. Ask children to hold up **k** for words that begin with /k/. Use these word sets:

- kitten, kite, bee
- girl, kind, good
- hat, king, kernel
- kangaroo, kick, dog
- hill, hand, kindergarten
- kitchen, fast, food
- goose, keep, give
- jump, kennel, kiss

Stage 1 Spellers

Use the Stage 0 activity. For each word set, have three children act out the words for the class. Ask the class to guess each word. For each word that begins with /k/, ask the actor to write **k** on the chalkboard.

Stage 2 Spellers

Use the Stage 0 activity. For each word set, choose one word to say slowly, stretching out the sounds (e.g., **kind** = /k/ + /ī/ + /n/ + /d/). Write the word, asking children to provide a letter for each sound.

Stage 3 Spellers

A few children may be ready for more spelling patterns. Choose several **k** words. Give clues to the word that include the number of letters. For example, say, *"This unlocks a door. It has three letters."* Challenge children to spell the word correctly.

Spelling and Writing

See page Z17 for more information.

Invite children to write words, a sentence, or a story about finding a key that opens an old box to reveal a treasure. Encourage the use of developmental spelling.

For more information on the Stages of Spelling Development, see pages Z10–Z15.

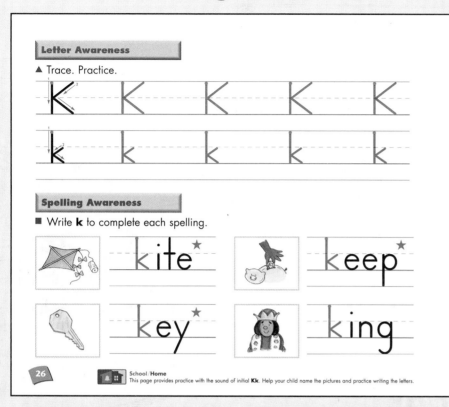

Letter Awareness and Spelling Awareness

Share these letter chants. Ask children to write the letters in the air as you chant together.

K
Pull down straight.
Lift. Let's go!
Slant left. Slant right.
It's big **K,** you know.

k
Follow those steps
To make small **k,** too.
Soon you'll write words
Like **king** and **kangaroo**.

Point out the red directional arrows and the green dots that show where to begin each letter.

Guide children in tracing and writing **K** and **k** to complete the activities on *Student Edition* page 26.

Use **Meeting Individual Needs** below to extend the practice activities.

Meeting Individual Needs

Stage 0 Spellers

Have children use their fingers to trace **K** and **k** in the air, on their tabletops, and on a partner's back. Check to make sure children are using the correct stroke sequence.

Stage 1 Spellers

Say a word from the **Spelling Awareness** activity. Ask, *"What is one sound you hear in the word? What letter spells that sound?"* After children respond with a letter, have them trace that letter on a partner's back.

Stage 2 Spellers

Have children work in pairs. The first child should choose a word from the **Spelling Awareness** activity and trace some or all of the letters on the second child's back. The second child should try to guess the word. Partners should then trade roles.

Stage 3 Spellers

A few children may be ready to produce conventional (correct) spellings. Use the Stage 2 activity. After the word is guessed, ask both partners to write it correctly on lined paper.

Building Words With Word Families
king, ring, sing, wing, bring, sting, thing

Point out the word part **-ing** in the **Spelling Awareness** activity on *Student Edition* page 26. Write **ing** on the chalkboard and say /ing/. Then say these sounds: /k/, /r/, /s/, /w/, /br/, /st/, /th/. Ask children to blend the sounds with /ing/ and say the new words. Write the **-ing** words on the chalkboard and read them together. Add them to your word wall or to a list of words for writing.

Unit Assessment

See page Z16 for more information.

You may wish to check progress by having children write **K, k,** and one or more **Basic Words** (**key, keep, kite, kitten**). Note spellings to determine each child's stage of spelling development.

Have children record one **k** word in their **My Words** book (following *Student Edition* page 56).

Kk

Kettle's for the Kitchen

A kettle's
for the kitchen,
A key is
for the door,
A kitten is
for playing with
And keeping
on the floor.

—Margaret and John Travers Moore

School/Home

Read the poem several times with your child. March around the room together, chanting the poem. Then look for words in the poem that begin with **k**. Read and write the **k** words together, emphasizing the **/k/** sound heard at the beginning of **keep**.

MATERIALS

ABC Poem and Picture Charts
Ll Poem Chart: "Lazy Little Alligator"
Ll Picture Chart

Student Edition
Pages 27–28

Teacher Edition
Pages T71–T76

Basic Words
lap	little
lock	ladder

★ Note: **Basic Words** are starred where they appear in this *Teacher Edition*.

High-Frequency Words
you	as
my	me

Targeted Word Family
-id

OBJECTIVES

ABC Poem and Picture Charts

Phonemic Awareness:
Identify the /l/ sound

Letter Recognition:
Recognize **L** and **l**

Sound-Symbol Awareness:
Associate the /l/ sound with the letters **Ll**

Early Reading:
Engage in repeated readings of the poem "Lazy Little Alligator"

Early Writing:
Write animal names from sound clues

Student Edition

Phonemic Awareness:
Identify the /l/ sound

Letter Recognition:
Recognize **L** and **l**

Sound-Symbol Awareness:
Associate the /l/ sound with the letters **Ll**

Early Reading:
Read a sentence related to the poem "Lazy Little Alligator"

Early Writing:
Write **Ll**; use developmental spelling to write a *Lunch List*

Language and Cultural Differences

The /l/ sound can be difficult for young children to master. Some children may substitute /w/ for /l/. Others may confuse /l/ with /r/, a related sound. Some languages, including Japanese, do not have separate sounds for /l/ and /r/. However, many languages around the world do have /l/, and it is usually similar to the English sound. The biggest difference is how far toward the upper front teeth the tongue is placed.

Encourage children who are acquiring English to draw and label pictures of objects whose names include /l/ in their native languages. Spanish-speaking children might choose **limón** (**lemon**) or **león** (**lion**).

Using the ABC Poem and Picture Charts: Ll Poem Chart

Phonemic Awareness and **Sound-Symbol Awareness**

Read "Lazy Little Alligator" aloud, pointing to each word. Read the poem again with children as they follow the rhythm by patting their knees and clapping.

Say **lap**. Explain that **lap** begins with the **/l/** sound. (**Note:** Be sure to say **/l/,** not **/luh/,** to isolate the consonant sound.) Have children repeat **/l/,** noticing how the mouth looks and feels. Associate this sound with **Ll** at the top of the chart.

Use **Meeting Individual Needs** below to develop phonemic awareness and sound-symbol awareness.

School/Home
You may wish to duplicate the page that follows *Teacher Edition* page T75 so that children have their own copy of the poem.

Ll

Lazy Little Alligator
Lazy little★alligator
Lying in my lap,★
Let me sit
   and stroke you
As you take
   a little nap.

—Tony Mitton

★**Note: Basic Words** are starred.

Meeting Individual Needs

Stage 0 Spellers
Show how to hold up your index finger to make an **l** shape (for lowercase **l**) and extend your index finger and thumb for an **L** shape. Read the poem, asking children to make **l** or **L** with their fingers for each word that begins with these letters.

Stage 1 Spellers
Use the Stage 0 activity. Ask questions about the sounds and letters in each **l** word. For example, ask, *"What letter spells the /l/ sound in* **little***?"* (l) *"What letter spells /p/ in* **lap***?"* (p)

Stage 2 Spellers
Say **l** words from the poem in "slow motion," stretching out the sounds (e.g., **let** = **/l/** + **/ĕ/** + **/t/**). Ask a volunteer to blend the sounds to pronounce the word and then write the word, giving one letter for each sound.

Stage 3 Spellers
A few children may be ready for more spelling patterns. Start with **let** and **lap**. Ask children how many words they can make with the **-et** and **-ap** spelling patterns. (get, net; map, clap)

For more information on the Stages of Spelling Development, see pages Z10–Z15.

High-Frequency Words
you, as, my, me

Point out **you, as, my,** and **me** in the poem. Ask volunteers to name the letters in each word. Clap and chant the spelling. Ask volunteers to find the words in the poem. Add the words to your word wall or to a list of words for writing.

ABC Using Manipulatives

Ask children to write an **l** word and cut the letters apart. Have them draw a picture clue on an envelope and put the letters inside. Invite children to "deliver" their envelopes to a partner who will use the letters to spell the word. The envelopes may be delivered again to continue the game.

T72

Using the ABC Poem and Picture Charts:
Ll Picture Chart

Phonemic Awareness and Sound-Symbol Awareness

Invite children to describe the scene on the chart. Children may wish to tell about a time they wore a costume.

Point to **Ll** and ask children what sound it makes. (/l/) Use **Meeting Individual Needs** below to develop phonemic awareness and sound-symbol awareness according to the needs of the children in your class.

Pictured Words.....................
leopard, lobster, ★lap, ★ladder, ★lock, ladybug, lamb, lamp, lemon, lemonade, lady, lion, lizard, lollipop, log

Meeting Individual Needs

Stage 0 Spellers
Prompt children to find pictures of items whose names begin with /l/. Ask, *"Do you see a lion? **Lion** begins with /l/."* Write each word on chart paper. Ask a volunteer to underline **l** in each word.

Stage 1 Spellers
As children find pictures whose names begin with /l/, stretch and count the sounds in several words (e.g., **lock** = /l/ + /ŏ/ + /k/). Write the words, asking children to provide letters for prominent sounds.

Stage 2 Spellers
Challenge children to find all 15 pictures that begin with /l/. Pronounce the words and ask children to write a letter (or choose a magnetic letter) for each sound. Accept developmental spellings (e.g., **LATR** for **ladder**).

Stage 3 Spellers
A few children may be ready for more spelling patterns. Write /l/ words children identify. Point out the **-er** ending in **ladder**. Circle **ock** in **lock** and ask for rhyming words. (sock, rock)

For more information on the Stages of Spelling Development, see pages Z10–Z15.

ABC Poem and Picture Charts
Use dry erase markers on the laminated pages to highlight and emphasize words, pictures, and targeted sounds.

- Highlight letters on the **Poem Chart**.
- Underline high-frequency words on the **Poem Chart**.
- Circle pictures on the **Picture Chart**.
- Label objects on the **Picture Chart**.

Spelling and Writing
See page Z17 for more information.

Ask children to name an **l** animal (e.g., lizard). Write the name, asking children to provide letters. Pick one sound (e.g., /z/ in **lizard**) and ask for an animal name beginning with that sound (e.g., **zebra**). Continue the game until all children have named an animal.

Phonemic Awareness and Sound-Symbol Awareness

Help children follow the directions on *Student Edition* page 27.

Use **Meeting Individual Needs** below to extend the practice activities according to the needs of the children in your class.

One-Minute Handwriting Hint

Remind children to begin **L** and **l** by pulling down straight from the top, never by pushing up from the bottom.

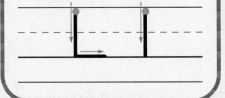

Note: Basic Words are starred.

Meeting Individual Needs

Stage 0 Spellers

Tell children they can make new words by adding /l/ to the beginning of words you say. Use these words: **ace** (lace), **aid** (laid), **and** (land), **ate** (late), **earn** (learn), **end** (lend), **it** (lit). Although many of the word pairs have different spelling patterns, children should be able to hear the sound relationship. You may wish to give a small treat, such as a **lemon** drop, for correct responses.

For more information on the Stages of Spelling Development, see pages Z10–Z15.

Stage 1 Spellers

Use the Stage 0 activity. Ask questions about sounds and letters in each /l/ word. For example, ask, *"What letter spells the /l/ sound in learn?"* (l) *"What letter spells /t/ in lit?"* (t)

Stage 2 Spellers

Use the Stage 0 activity. For several /l/ words, give a new consonant and ask children to substitute the corresponding sound for /l/. For example, for **land,** say *"b."* Children respond, *"band."* Write the rhyming words, underlining the shared spelling patterns.

Stage 3 Spellers

A few children may be ready for more spelling patterns. Use the Stage 0 activity. Then ask children to write words with the **-and** pattern as in **land** (e.g., **hand, sand**) and the **-ate** pattern as in **late** (e.g., **gate, date**).

Spelling and Writing

See page Z17 for more information.

Ask children to write "Lunch List" at the top of their papers. Ask them to write what they would like to have for lunch each day for the next week. Encourage the use of developmental spelling. Invite children to illustrate their lists.

Using the Student Edition: Page 28

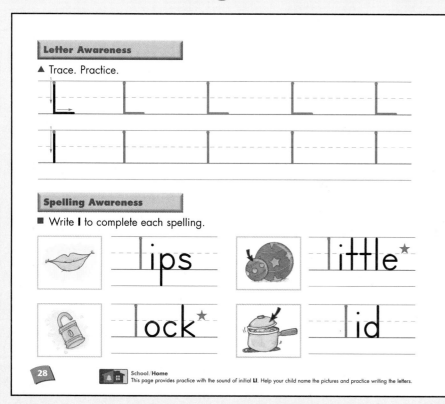

Letter Awareness

and

Spelling Awareness

Share these letter chants. Ask children to write the letters in the air as you chant together.

L

Pull down straight.
Slide right well.
That's how you write
Uppercase **L**!

l

Pull down straight,
Like a rope down a well.
That's all it takes
To write lowercase **l**.

Point out the red directional arrows and the green dots that show where to begin each letter.

Guide children in tracing and writing **L** and **l** to complete the activities on *Student Edition* page 28.

Use **Meeting Individual Needs** below to extend the practice activities according to the needs of the children in your class.

Meeting Individual Needs

Stage 0 Spellers
Dispense a small amount of shaving cream on each child's tabletop. Show how to spread it out to make a "magic cloud" for finger-writing. Ask children to write **L** and **l,** following the correct stroke sequence.

Stage 1 Spellers
Use the Stage 0 activity. Slowly say words from the **Spelling Awareness** activity on *Student Edition* page 28. Ask children to finger-write letters for prominent sounds they hear.

Stage 2 Spellers
Use the Stage 0 activity. Pronounce the words from the **Spelling Awareness** activity and ask children to finger-write them, giving one letter for each sound they hear. Accept developmental spellings.

Stage 3 Spellers
A few children may be ready to produce conventional (correct) spellings. Call out words from the **Spelling Awareness** activity. Ask children to finger-write them in shaving cream and then check their spelling.

Building Words With Word Families
did, hid, kid, lid, slid

Point out the word part **-id** in the **Spelling Awareness** activity on *Student Edition* page 28. Hold up a card with **id** and say /id/. Distribute self-sticking notes with these letters to volunteers: **d, h, k, l, sl**. Ask the volunteers to stick the notes to their shirts and stand, one at a time, beside the **id** card. Say the new words together. Add the **-id** words to your word wall or to a list of words for writing.

Unit Assessment
See page Z16 for more information.

You may wish to check progress by having children write **L, l,** and one or more **Basic Words** (**lap, little, lock, ladder**). Note spellings to determine each child's stage of spelling development.

Have children record one **l** word in their **My Words** book (following *Student Edition* page 56).

Ll

Lazy Little Alligator

Lazy little alligator
Lying in my lap,
Let me sit
    and stroke you
As you take
    a little nap.

—Tony Mitton

School/Home
Read the poem several times with your child. Recite the poem together, keeping the rhythm by patting your knees and clapping. Then look for words in the poem that begin with **L** or **l**. Read and write the **l** words together, emphasizing the **/l/** sound heard at the beginning of **little**.

MATERIALS

ABC Poem and Picture Charts

Mm Poem Chart: "The Muffin Man"
Mm Picture Chart

Student Edition

Pages 29–30

Teacher Edition

Pages T77–T82

OBJECTIVES

ABC Poem and Picture Charts

Phonemic Awareness:
Identify the /**m**/ sound

Letter Recognition:
Recognize **M** and **m**

Sound-Symbol Awareness:
Associate the /**m**/ sound with the letters **Mm**

Early Reading:
Engage in repeated readings of the poem "The Muffin Man"

Early Writing:
Write a silly muffin recipe

Student Edition

Phonemic Awareness:
Identify the /**m**/ sound

Letter Recognition:
Recognize **M** and **m**

Sound-Symbol Awareness:
Associate the /**m**/ sound with the letters **Mm**

Early Reading:
Read a sentence related to the poem "The Muffin Man"

Early Writing:
Write **Mm**; use developmental spelling to describe a special treat

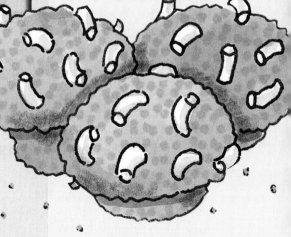

Language and Cultural Differences

The /**m**/ sound is widespread in languages around the world. (The Hawaiian language has only 13 sounds, but one of them is /**m**/.) In English, /**m**/ can be spelled **m, mm, lm** (**calm**), **mb** (**lamb**), and occasionally **mn** (**autumn**).

Several of the **m** words pictured in this unit also begin with **m** in Spanish. These include **montaña** (**mountain**), **macarrones** (**macaroni**), and **malvavisco** (**marshmallow**). Ask children to identify other things that begin with /**m**/ in their primary language.

Using the ABC Poem and Picture Charts: Mm Poem Chart

Read "The Muffin Man" aloud, pointing to each word. Sing the poem together, clapping to the rhythm.

Say **man**. Explain that **man** begins with the /m/ sound. (**Note:** Be sure to say /m/, not /muh/, to isolate the consonant sound.) Have children repeat /m/, noticing how the mouth looks and feels. Associate this sound with **Mm** at the top of the chart.

Use **Meeting Individual Needs** below to develop phonemic awareness and sound-symbol awareness according to the needs of children in your class.

School/Home
You may wish to duplicate the page that follows *Teacher Edition* page T81 so that children have their own copy of the poem.

Mm

The Muffin Man
Oh, do you know
    the muffin man,
The muffin man,
    the muffin man,
Oh, do you know
    the muffin man,
Who lives on
    Drury Lane?

★**Note: Basic Words** are starred.

Meeting Individual Needs

Stage 0 Spellers
Ask if any children have **M** or **m** in their names. If so, repeat the names together, emphasizing /m/. Read the poem together. Have children clap when they hear a word with /m/. Point out **M** or **m** in each word.

Stage 1 Spellers
Read the poem together. Have children clap when they hear a word with /m/. Stretch and count the sounds in each **m** word (e.g., **man** = /m/ + /ă/ + /n/). Ask questions such as *"What letter spells the /n/ sound in man?"* (n)

Stage 2 Spellers
Cover the poem. Say **man** and **muffin** slowly. Challenge a volunteer to write each word, giving one letter for each sound. Accept developmental spellings (e.g., **MOFN** for **muffin**).

Stage 3 Spellers
A few children may be ready for more spelling patterns. Start with **man**. Challenge children to write new words by changing only the last letter. (map, mat, mad, mam)

For more information on the Stages of Spelling Development, see pages Z10–Z15.

High-Frequency Words
do, you, on, the

Point out **do, you, on,** and **the** in the poem. Ask volunteers to name the letters in each word. Clap and chant the spellings. Ask volunteers to find the words in the poem. Add the words to your word wall or to a list of words for writing.

ABC Using Manipulatives
Ask each child to glue mini-marshmallows to a sheet of construction paper in the shape of **m**. Invite volunteers to tape their marshmallow **m**'s to the chalkboard and write letters before or after to spell words.

Using the ABC Poem and Picture Charts: Mm Picture Chart

Phonemic Awareness *and* **Sound-Symbol Awareness**

Mm

Invite children to describe the scene on the chart. Children may wish to tell which kind of muffin they would like to try.

Point to **Mm** and ask children what sound it makes. (/m/) Use **Meeting Individual Needs** below to develop phonemic awareness and sound-symbol awareness according to the needs of the children in your class.

Pictured Words............................

muffin, ★man, macaroni, meatball, mirror, ★mop, mountain, mushroom, marshmallow,★mud, ★milk

Meeting Individual Needs

Stage 0 Spellers

Prompt children to notice the bakery signs and find pictures of items whose names begin with **/m/**. Ask, *"Do you see a mop? Mop begins with /m/."* Write each word on chart paper. Ask a volunteer to underline **m** in each word.

Stage 1 Spellers

Help children read the bakery signs and find other pictures that begin with **/m/**. Stretch and count the sounds in each word (e.g., **mop = /m/ + /ŏ/ + /p/**). Write the words, asking children to provide letters for prominent sounds.

Stage 2 Spellers

Challenge children to find all the words and pictures that begin with **/m/**. Pronounce the words and ask children to write a letter (or choose a magnetic letter) for each sound. Accept developmental spellings (e.g., **MLK** for **milk**).

Stage 3 Spellers

A few children may be ready for more spelling patterns. Write **/m/** words children identify. Point out the four different short vowel sounds and corresponding letters in **man, mop, mud,** and **milk**.

For more information on the Stages of Spelling Development, see pages Z10–Z15.

ABC Poem and Picture Charts

Use dry erase markers on the laminated pages to highlight and emphasize words, pictures, and targeted sounds.

- Highlight letters on the **Poem Chart**.
- Underline high-frequency words on the **Poem Chart**.
- Circle pictures on the **Picture Chart**.
- Label objects on the **Picture Chart**.

Spelling and Writing

See page Z17 for more information.

Work as a class to write a silly muffin recipe on chart paper. Invite each child to suggest an ingredient and its quantity. As you write the words, ask children to provide letters for prominent sounds they hear. If you wish, ask children to copy and illustrate the recipe.

Using the Student Edition: Page 29

Phonemic Awareness and Sound-Symbol Awareness

Help children follow the directions on *Student Edition* page 29.

Use **Meeting Individual Needs** below to extend the practice activities according to the needs of children in your class.

One-Minute Handwriting Hint

Remind children to bring the pencil all the way down to touch the baseline before beginning the second "hump" in **M** and **m**.

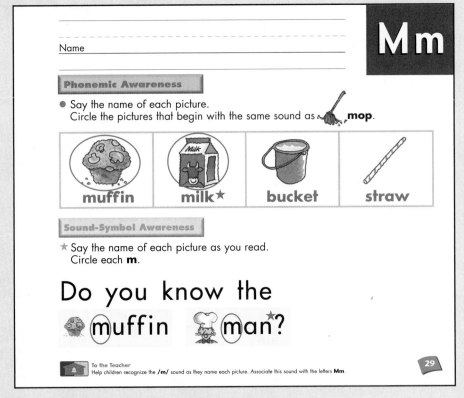

Name _____

Mm

Phonemic Awareness

● Say the name of each picture.
  Circle the pictures that begin with the same sound as **mop**.

| muffin | milk★ | bucket | straw |

Sound-Symbol Awareness

★ Say the name of each picture as you read.
  Circle each **m**.

Do you know the muffin man?

To the Teacher
Help children recognize the /m/ sound as they name each picture. Associate this sound with the letters **Mm**.

29

★ **Note: Basic Words** are starred.

Meeting Individual Needs

Stage 0 Spellers

Say **man**. Ask children to hold up a magic marker to show that **man** begins with /m/. Continue the game (i.e., children hold up a marker when a word begins with /m/) with these words: **muffin, rat, fox, mop, mud, mad, milk, dog, mine, man, map, make, run, pig, tree, mom**. Write several of the words, underlining **m** in each.

Stage 1 Spellers

Use the Stage 0 activity. Pause during the activity to ask questions about letters and sounds in some of the words. Ask, *"What letter spells the /n/ sound in man?"* (n) *"What letter spells the /p/ sound in mop?"* (p)

Stage 2 Spellers

Use the Stage 0 activity. Repeat several of the /m/ words slowly. Challenge volunteers to provide a letter for each sound. Accept developmental spellings (e.g., **MOFEN** for **muffin**).

Stage 3 Spellers

A few children may be ready for more spelling patterns. Use the Stage 0 activity. Start with **mud, mad,** and **mop**. Ask children to write new words with the **-ud, -ad,** and **-op** patterns. (bud, thud; had, bad; hop, stop)

Spelling and Writing

See page Z17 for more information.

Invite children to draw a picture of a special cookie, muffin, cupcake, or cake. It may be a birthday treat just for them. Ask children to write a description of their drawing that includes details about color, shape, size, and taste. Accept developmental spelling.

For more information on the Stages of Spelling Development, see pages Z10–Z15.

Using the Student Edition: Page 30

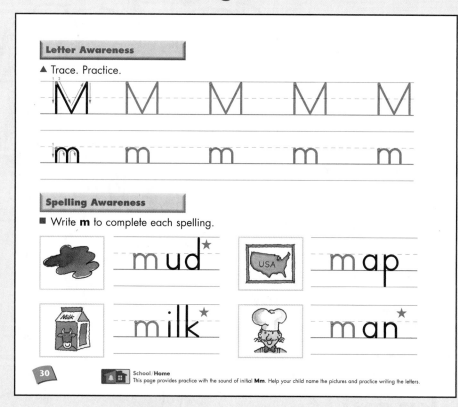

Letter Awareness

▲ Trace. Practice.

M M M M M

m m m m m

Spelling Awareness

■ Write **m** to complete each spelling.

mud★   map

milk★   man★

30 School/Home
This page provides practice with the sound of initial **Mm.** Help your child name the pictures and practice writing the letters.

Letter Awareness *and* **Spelling Awareness**

Share these letter chants. Ask children to write the letters in the air as you chant together.

M

Pull down straight. Lift. Slant right.
Slant up, and pull down.
If you write your ups and downs
Smooth and light, then uppercase **M**
Is sure to be right!

m

Pull down straight. Push up. Curve right.
Pull down straight. Push up. Curve right.
Pull down straight.
You've reached the end of the steps it takes
To make lowercase **m.**

Point out the red directional arrows and the green dots that show where to begin each letter.

Guide children in tracing and writing **M** and **m** to complete the activities.

Use **Meeting Individual Needs** below to extend the practice activities.

Meeting Individual Needs

Stage 0 Spellers

Provide a zip-top bag for each child. Spread a small amount of washable paint in each bag and seal it. Ask children to lay the bags flat and use them as "magic slates" for finger-tracing **M** and **m.** Check to make sure they are following the correct stroke sequence.

Stage 1 Spellers

Use the Stage 0 activity. Slowly say words from the **Spelling Awareness** activity on *Student Edition* page 30. Ask children to trace letters for prominent sounds they hear in the words.

Stage 2 Spellers

Use the Stage 0 activity. Slowly say words from the **Spelling Awareness** activity. Ask children to trace a letter for each sound they hear. Accept developmental spellings (e.g., **MED** for **mud**).

Stage 3 Spellers

A few children may be ready to produce conventional (correct) spellings. Call out words from the **Spelling Awareness** activity. Ask children to trace them on the "magic slates" and then check their spelling.

Building Words With Word Families
can, fan, man, pan, ran, tan, than

Point out the word part -**an** in the **Spelling Awareness** activity on *Student Edition* page 30. Write **an** on the chalkboard and say /an/. Challenge volunteers to suggest letters to combine with **an** to form new words. If needed, suggest these letters: **c, f, m, p, r, t, th.** Point out combinations children suggest, such as **han,** which do not form English words. Say the new words together. Add the -**an** words to your word wall or to a list of words for writing.

Unit Assessment

See page Z16 for more information.

You may wish to check progress by having children write **M, m,** and one or more **Basic Words** (**man, mop, mud, milk**). Note spellings to determine each child's stage of spelling development.

Have children record one **m** word in their **My Words** book (following *Student Edition* page 56).

Mm

The Muffin Man

Oh, do you know
    the muffin man,
The muffin man,
    the muffin man,
Oh, do you know
    the muffin man,
Who lives on
    Drury Lane?

School/Home
Read the poem several times with your child. Sing the poem together. Then look for words in the poem that begin with **M** or **m**. Read and write the **m** words together, emphasizing the /**m**/ sound heard at the beginning of **man**.

MATERIALS

ABC Poem and Picture Charts

Nn Poem Chart: "Oodles of Noodles"
Nn Picture Chart

Student Edition

Pages 31–32

Teacher Edition

Pages T83–T88

OBJECTIVES

ABC Poem and Picture Charts

Phonemic Awareness:
Identify the /**n**/ sound

Letter Recognition:
Recognize **N** and **n**

Sound-Symbol Awareness:
Associate the /**n**/ sound with the letters **Nn**

Early Reading:
Engage in repeated readings of the poem "Oodles of Noodles"

Early Writing:
Design a flag for your class and use developmental spelling to write about it

Student Edition

Phonemic Awareness:
Identify the /**n**/ sound

Letter Recognition:
Recognize **N** and **n**

Sound-Symbol Awareness:
Associate the /**n**/ sound with the letters **Nn**

Early Reading:
Read picture labels that begin with **n**

Early Writing:
Write **Nn**; use developmental spelling to write about making "nest cookies"

Language and Cultural Differences

The /**n**/ sound is easy for children to make, and they learn to produce it at a young age. It is one of the most widespread sounds in languages around the world. Even languages with few distinct sounds have /**n**/. The Hawaiian language has only 13 sounds, but one of them is /**n**/! For children who are acquiring English, make use of the pictures in this unit. Point to a pictured object (such as a nest), say its name, and ask children to repeat the word.

Using the **ABC** Poem and Picture Charts:
Nn Poem Chart

Phonemic Awareness and **Sound-Symbol Awareness**

Read "Oodles of Noodles" aloud, pointing to each word. Read it again, pausing to allow children to shout the rhyming words **noodles, oodles,** and **foodles.**

Say **now.** Explain that **now** begins with the **/n/** sound. (**Note:** Be sure to say **/n/,** not **/nuh/,** to isolate the consonant sound.) Have children repeat **/n/,** noticing how the mouth looks and feels. Associate this sound with **Nn** at the top of the chart.

Use **Meeting Individual Needs** below to develop phonemic awareness and sound-symbol awareness according to the needs of children in your class.

Oodles of Noodles
I love noodles.
   Give me oodles.
Make a mound up
   to the sun.
Noodles are my
   favorite foodles.
I eat noodles by
   the ton.

—Lucia and James L. Hymes, Jr.

School/Home
You may wish to duplicate the page that follows *Teacher Edition* page T87 so that children have their own copy of the poem.

Meeting Individual Needs

Stage 0 Spellers

Talk about the nonsense words **oodles** and **foodles.** Have children make rhyming words by adding sounds before **oodles:** **/b/** (boodles), **/d/** (doodles), **/n/** (noodles), **/p/** (poodles). Read the poem, having children clap when they hear **/n/.**

Stage 1 Spellers

Use the Stage 0 activity. Write **oodles** on chart paper five times. Ask children to supply the correct beginning letter as you say the following: **noodles, boodles, doodles, foodles, poodles.** Complete each word.

Stage 2 Spellers

Use these words: **not, nut, nap, Nat.** Say each word slowly, stretching the sounds (e.g., **nut** = **/n/** + **/ŭ/** + **/t/**). Have children provide a letter for each sound.

Stage 3 Spellers

A few children may be ready for more spelling patterns. Have children write **not, nut, nap,** and **Nat.** See how many new words they can write by changing the beginning letter of each word.

For more information on the Stages of Spelling Development, see pages Z10–Z15.

High-Frequency Words
up, love, make, my

Point out **up, love, make,** and **my** in the poem. Ask volunteers to name the letters in each word. Clap and chant the spellings. Ask volunteers to find the words in the poem. Add the words to your word wall or to a list of words for writing.

ABC Using Manipulatives

Place a variety of dry noodles in a shallow tub or sand table. Also provide sheets of construction paper. Allow children to experiment with forming letters and words from the noodle shapes. Ask them to glue noodles in place to spell a word that begins with **n.**

Using the **ABC** Poem and Picture Charts:
Nn Picture Chart

Phonemic Awareness
and
Sound-Symbol Awareness

Invite children to describe the scene on the chart. Children may wish to tell about a time they visited a restaurant.

Point to **Nn** and ask children what sound it makes. (/n/) Use **Meeting Individual Needs** below to develop phonemic awareness and sound-symbol awareness according to the needs of the children in your class.

Pictured Words..................
necklace, nurse, ★nuts, newspaper, napkin, ★nine, ★nest, nail, ★net, nickel, nose

Meeting Individual Needs

Stage 0 Spellers
Prompt children to find pictures of items whose names begin with /n/. Ask, *"Do you see a napkin? Napkin begins with /n/."* Write each word on chart paper. Ask a volunteer to underline **n** in each word.

Stage 1 Spellers
As children find pictures whose names begin with /n/, stretch and count the sounds in each word (e.g., **nuts** = /n/ + /ŭ/ + /t/ + /s/). Write the words, asking children to provide letters for prominent sounds.

Stage 2 Spellers
Challenge children to find all 11 pictures that begin with /n/. Pronounce the words and ask children to write a letter (or choose a magnetic letter) for each sound. Accept developmental spellings (e.g., **NOZ** for **nose**).

Stage 3 Spellers
A few children may be ready for more spelling patterns. Invite children to write the names of pictures they see that begin with /n/. Show how to write a longer word, such as **napkin,** one syllable at a time.

For more information on the Stages of Spelling Development, see pages Z10–Z15.

ABC Poem and Picture Charts
Use dry erase markers on the laminated pages to highlight and emphasize words, pictures, and targeted sounds.

- Highlight letters on the **Poem Chart**.
- Underline high-frequency words on the **Poem Chart**.
- Circle pictures on the **Picture Chart**.
- Label objects on the **Picture Chart**.

Spelling and Writing
See page Z17 for more information.

Talk about how flags represent groups of people. Provide paper and drawing materials and ask children to design a flag that represents your class. Have children write a few words or sentences about their flags. Accept developmental spelling.

Phonemic Awareness and Sound-Symbol Awareness

Help children follow the directions on *Student Edition* page 31.

Use **Meeting Individual Needs** below to extend the practice activities according to the needs of children in your class.

One-Minute Handwriting Hint

Model how to retrace the vertical line carefully to avoid looping **n**.

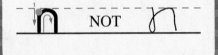

NOT

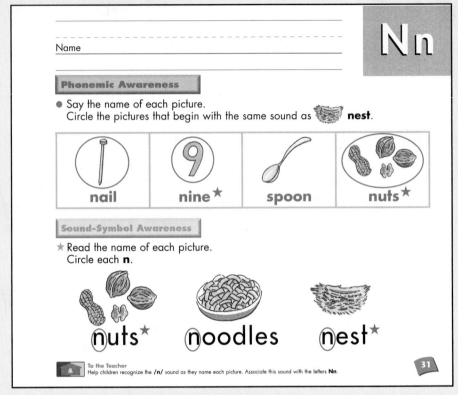

★**Note: Basic Words** are starred.

Meeting Individual Needs

Stage 0 Spellers

Ask children to say the **/n/** sound. Have them look around the classroom for objects whose names begin with **/n/**. (nails, necklaces, necks, noses, numbers, etc.) Have children repeat each word, emphasizing the initial **/n/** sound. Write the words, underlining **n** in each one.

Stage 1 Spellers

Say words that contain **/n/**. Have children repeat each word, exaggerating the **/n/** sound at the beginning or the ending of the word. Use these words: **nap, nail, ran, nose, spoon, name, never, nuts, win, nest, mine, nice, bone, need**.

Stage 2 Spellers

Use the Stage 1 activity. Choose several of the **n** words. Say each word, stretching out its sounds (e.g., **nuts** = /n/ + /ŭ/ + /t/ + /s/). Write the words, asking children to give a letter for each sound. Accept developmental spellings.

Stage 3 Spellers

A few children may be ready for more spelling patterns. Start with **nest** and **nine**. Challenge children to write new words with the **-est** and **-ine** patterns. (best, pest; mine, fine)

Spelling and Writing

See page Z17 for more information.

Make "nest cookies" by shaping 2 cups chow mein noodles mixed with 2 cups melted butterscotch chips. Place jelly bean eggs in each nest and allow to dry on wax paper. Ask children to write about the experience. Accept developmental spelling.

For more information on the Stages of Spelling Development, see pages Z10–Z15.

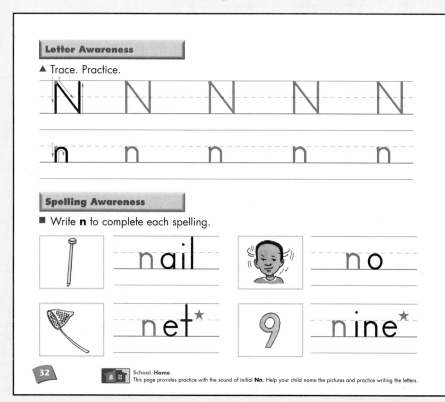

Letter Awareness
and
Spelling Awareness

Share these letter chants. Ask children to write the letters in the air as you chant together.

N

Pull down straight.
Lift. Slant right.
Push up straight.
Uppercase **N** is in sight!

n

Pull down straight.
Push up. Curve right.
Pull down straight
To write **no** and **night**.

Point out the red directional arrows and the green dots that show where to begin each letter.

Guide children in tracing and writing **N** and **n** to complete the activities on *Student Edition* page 32.

Use **Meeting Individual Needs** below to extend the practice activities according to the needs of children in your class.

Meeting Individual Needs

Stage 0 Spellers

Provide cups of water and clean paintbrushes. Allow groups of children to go to the chalkboard and paint with water. Have them paint **N** and **n**. Check to make sure children are following the correct stroke sequence.

Stage 1 Spellers

Use the Stage 0 activity. Slowly say words from the **Spelling Awareness** activity on *Student Edition* page 32. Ask children to paint letters for prominent sounds they hear in the words.

Stage 2 Spellers

Use the Stage 0 activity. Write words from the **Spelling Awareness** activity in a large size on the chalkboard. Invite children to either paint over your words or paint the words directly below your model.

Stage 3 Spellers

A few children may be ready to produce conventional (correct) spellings. Call out words from the **Spelling Awareness** activity. Ask children to paint them with water and then check their spelling.

Building Words With Word Families
dine, fine, line, mine, nine, pine

Point out the word part **-ine** in the **Spelling Awareness** activity on *Student Edition* page 32. Make a grid on chart paper with six squares. Write one of the following letters in each square and ask children to say its corresponding sound: **d, f, l, m, n, p.** Below the grid, write **ine.** Say /ine/. Ask children to throw a beanbag at the grid and to say the word formed by blending the letter hit with **ine**.

Unit Assessment

See page Z16 for more information.

You may wish to check progress by having children write **N, n,** and one or more **Basic Words** (**net, nuts, nest, nine**). Note spellings to determine each child's stage of spelling development.

Have children record one **n** word in their **My Words** book (following *Student Edition* page 56).

Nn

Oodles of Noodles

I love noodles.
   Give me oodles.
Make a mound up
   to the sun.
Noodles are my
   favorite foodles.
I eat noodles by
   the ton.

—Lucia and James L. Hymes, Jr.

From *Oodles of Noodles* by Lucia and James Hymes, Jr. Reprinted by permission of Pearson Education, Inc. pg. 7. © 1964 by Lucia and James Hymes, Jr.

School/Home

Read the poem several times with your child. Say it together while pretending to stack up a pile of noodles. Then look for words in the poem that begin with **N** and **n**. Read and write the **n** words together, emphasizing the **/n/** sound heard in **nest**.

MATERIALS

ABC Poem and Picture Charts

Oo Poem Chart: "O Is Very Useful"
Oo Picture Chart

Student Edition

Pages 33–34

Teacher Edition

Pages T89–T94

Basic Words

ox	on
off	dock

★**Note: Basic Words** are starred where they appear in this *Teacher Edition*.

High-Frequency Words

very	you
say	only

Targeted Word Family

-ock

OBJECTIVES

ABC Poem and Picture Charts

Phonemic Awareness:
Identify the **short o** sound

Letter Recognition:
Recognize **O** and **o**

Sound-Symbol Awareness:
Associate the **short o** sound with the letters **Oo**

Early Reading:
Engage in repeated readings of the poem "O Is Very Useful"

Early Writing:
Write a poem with **o** words

Student Edition

Phonemic Awareness:
Identify the **short o** sound

Letter Recognition:
Recognize **O** and **o**

Sound-Symbol Awareness:
Associate the **short o** sound with the letters **Oo**

Early Reading:
Read picture labels that begin with **o**

Early Writing:
Write **Oo**; use developmental spelling to write about a new invention

Language and Cultural Differences

This unit focuses on **short o**. It is a low vowel, meaning that the jaw is dropped. Vowel sounds differ from region to region. The major variation in **short o** has to do with how low the jaw drops. This shouldn't cause any special problems in teaching **short o** words.

For children who are acquiring English, ask "yes/no" questions about the poem "O Is Very Useful." For example, ask, *"Does Oscar have an ostrich?"* (yes) Next, ask questions that require a one-word answer. For example, ask, *"What is orange?"* (owl)

T89

Using the ABC Poem and Picture Charts: Oo Poem Chart

Read "O Is Very Useful" aloud, pointing to each word. Have half of the children stand on each side of the room. Ask the first group to shout the first line in the poem, the second group to shout the next line, and so on.

Say **ostrich**. Isolate the initial sound and explain that this is the **short o** sound. (This unit focuses primarily on **short o**.) Have children repeat **/ŏ/**, noticing how the mouth looks and feels.

Use **Meeting Individual Needs** below to develop phonemic awareness and sound-symbol awareness according to the needs of children in your class.

School/Home
You may wish to duplicate the page that follows *Teacher Edition* page T93 so that children have their own copy of the poem.

Oo

O Is Very Useful
O is very useful.
You use it when
   you say:
"Oscar's only ostrich
   oiled an orange
   owl today."

—Dr. Seuss

Meeting Individual Needs

Stage 0 Spellers
Sing "The ABC's," stopping at **o**. Read the poem, asking children to trace **o** in the air when they see a word that begins with **o**. Write a list of the words, underlining **o** in each one.

Stage 1 Spellers
Use the Stage 0 activity. As children identify each **o** word, ask them to write it using developmental, or "sound" spelling. Help children include letters for prominent sounds.

Stage 2 Spellers
Use the Stage 0 activity. Count the sounds in **only** and **Oscar** (e.g., **only** = /ŏ/ + /n/ + /l/ + /ē/). Help children write the words, giving one sound for each letter. Accept developmental spellings (e.g., **ONLE** for **only; OSCR** for **Oscar**).

Stage 3 Spellers
A few children may be ready for more spelling patterns. See how many words children can write using the **consonant-o-consonant** pattern seen in **hot**. (pop, top, dog, fog, job)

For more information on the Stages of Spelling Development, see pages Z10–Z15.

High-Frequency Words
very, you, say, only

Point out **very, you, say,** and **only** in the poem. Ask volunteers to name the letters in each word. Clap and chant the spellings. Ask volunteers to find the words in the poem. Add the words to your word wall or to a list of words for writing.

Using Manipulatives

Provide short lengths of yarn, blank cards, and glue. Ask each child to glue the yarn in a circle to make a tactile **o** card. Additional tactile letter cards may be made for word building, or children may use their tactile **o** cards in combination with plain letter cards.

Using the ABC Poem and Picture Charts: Oo Picture Chart

Invite children to describe the scene on the chart. Children may wish to talk about their experiences using remote-controlled toys.

Point to **Oo**. Ask what sound **o** makes in the word **ostrich**. (short o) Use **Meeting Individual Needs** below to develop phonemic awareness and sound-symbol awareness according to the needs of the children in your class.

Note: If you wish to contrast **short o** with **long o,** also include the pictures identified for **long o**.

Pictured Words...................

short o: ostrich, octopus, otter, ★ox, ★on, ★off, olives, Oscar, ★dock

long o: ocean, oatmeal, overalls, boat

Meeting Individual Needs

Stage 0 Spellers

Prompt children to find pictures of items whose names contain **short o**. Ask, *"Do you see an off switch? Off begins with /ŏ/."* Write each word on chart paper. Ask a volunteer to underline **o** in each word.

Stage 1 Spellers

As children find pictures whose names contain /ŏ/, stretch and count the sounds in each word (e.g., **on** = /ŏ/ + /n/). Write the words, asking children to provide letters for prominent sounds.

Stage 2 Spellers

Challenge children to find all nine pictures whose names contain /ŏ/. Pronounce the words and ask children to write a letter (or choose a magnetic letter) for each sound. Accept developmental spellings (e.g., **OTR** for **otter**).

Stage 3 Spellers

A few children may be ready for more spelling patterns. Ask children to find pictures whose names contain **short o** or **long o**. Write each word, pointing out patterns such as the **oa** spelling of **long o** in **oatmeal** and **boat**.

For more information on the Stages of Spelling Development, see pages Z10–Z15.

ABC Poem and Picture Charts

Use dry erase markers on the laminated pages to highlight and emphasize words, pictures, and targeted sounds.

- Highlight letters on the **Poem Chart**.
- Underline high-frequency words on the **Poem Chart**.
- Circle pictures on the **Picture Chart**.
- Label objects on the **Picture Chart**.

Spelling and Writing

See page Z17 for more information.

Make a word bank of **o** words, including words from this unit. Ask each child to use the word bank words to complete a new poem that begins "O is very useful. You use it when you say…." Invite children to illustrate and share their poems.

Using the Student Edition: Page 33

Help children follow the directions on *Student Edition* page 33.

Use **Meeting Individual Needs** below to extend the practice activities according to the needs of children in your class.

One-Minute Handwriting Hint

Have children practice beginning **O** and **o** at the upper right (at approximately "one o'clock"). This habit will help children with other circle letters, such as **a** and **d**.

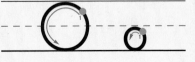

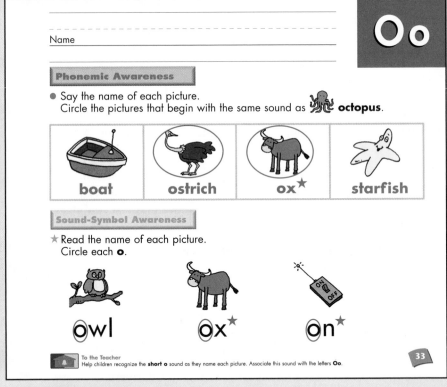

★**Note: Basic Words** are starred.

Meeting Individual Needs

Stage 0 Spellers

Draw the head of an octopus on the chalkboard or on chart paper. Remind children that **octopus** begins with the **short o** or **/ŏ/** sound. Tell the children you will say a word in slow motion and ask them to say it normally. For example, if you say **/ŏ/-/n/,** they would respond *"on."* Each time they blend a word correctly, draw a tentacle on the octopus. Use these words: **odd, Oz, ox, on, off, of, octopus, ostrich**.

For more information on the Stages of Spelling Development, see pages Z10–Z15.

Stage 1 Spellers

Use **short o** words that have two phonemes, such as **odd, Oz, ox, on,** and **off**. Say each word slowly, stretching out the two sounds. For each word, ask, *"What letter spells the first sound?"* (o) *"What letter spells the second sound?"* (Answers will vary.)

Stage 2 Spellers

Use the Stage 0 activity. Ask a volunteer to write each **short o** word on a tentacle. Accept developmental spellings (e.g., **OD** for **odd**).

Stage 3 Spellers

A few children may be ready for more spelling patterns. Start with **ox, hot,** and **top**. Ask children to write new words with the **-ox, -ot,** and **-op** patterns. (box, fox; dot, got; pop, hop)

Spelling and Writing

See page Z17 for more information.

Provide blank paper and drawing materials. Invite children to draw a new invention. It can be silly or serious. It should include an on/off switch with labels. Have children write about their inventions. Accept developmental spelling.

Using the Student Edition: Page 34

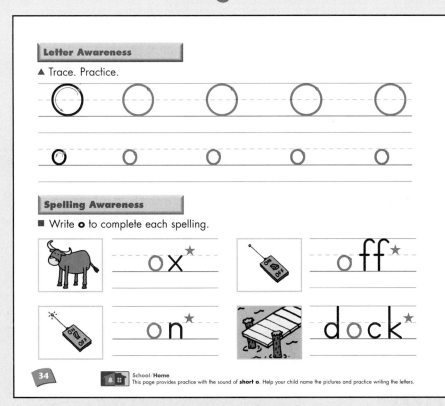

Letter Awareness and Spelling Awareness

Share this letter chant. Ask children to write the letters in the air as you chant together.

Oo
Circle back left.
Go all the way.
O and **o** are easy.
We can go all day!

Point out the red directional arrows and the green dots that show where to begin each letter.

Guide children in tracing and writing **O** and **o** to complete the activities on *Student Edition* page 34.

Use **Meeting Individual Needs** below to extend the practice activities according to the needs of children in your class.

Meeting Individual Needs

Stage 0 Spellers

Have children sculpt **o** and **O** from clay. Encourage them to trace the clay letters with their fingers, using the correct starting point.

Stage 1 Spellers

Use the Stage 0 activity. Slowly say words from the **Spelling Awareness** activity on *Student Edition* page 34. Ask children to sculpt letters from clay to match prominent sounds they hear.

Stage 2 Spellers

Write the words from the **Spelling Awareness** activity on large cards and laminate them. Allow children to use them as a base for building the words with clay.

Stage 3 Spellers

A few children may be ready to produce conventional (correct) spellings. Call out words from the **Spelling Awareness** activity and ask children to write them or sculpt them with clay. Have children use their books to check spelling.

Building Words With Word Families
dock, lock, rock, sock, clock

Point out the word part **-ock** in the **Spelling Awareness** activity on *Student Edition* page 34. Write **ock** on the chalkboard and say /ock/. Then hide cards with these letters around the room: **d, l, r, s, cl**. Invite volunteers to spot a letter, retrieve it, say its sound, and place it in front of **ock**. Say the new words together. Add the **-ock** words to your word wall or to a list of words for writing.

Unit Assessment

See page Z16 for more information.

You may wish to check progress by having children write **O, o,** and one or more **Basic Words** (**ox, on, off, dock**). Note spellings to determine each child's stage of spelling development.

Have children record one **o** word in their **My Words** book (following *Student Edition* page 56).

O Is Very Useful

O is very useful.
You use it when
you say:
"Oscar's only ostrich
oiled an orange
owl today."

—Dr. Seuss

From *Dr. Seuss' ABC* by Dr. Seuss, ™ & copyright © by Dr. Seuss Enterprises, L.P. 1963, renewed 1981. Used by permission of Random House Children's Books, a division of Random House, Inc.

 School/Home
Read the poem several times with your child. See how quickly you and your child can say the final, tongue-twister portion of the poem. Then look for words in the poem that begin with **O** and **o**. Read and write the **o** words together, emphasizing the **short o** sound heard at the beginning of **ostrich**.

MATERIALS

ABC Poem and Picture Charts

Pp Poem Chart: "Mix a Pancake"
Pp Picture Chart

Student Edition

Pages 35–36

Teacher Edition

Pages T95–T100

Basic Words

pop	pan
pig	pen

★ **Note: Basic Words** are starred where they appear in this *Teacher Edition*.

High-Frequency Words

you	if
can	a

Targeted Word Family

-en

OBJECTIVES

ABC Poem and Picture Charts

Phonemic Awareness:
Identify the **/p/** sound

Letter Recognition:
Recognize **P** and **p**

Sound-Symbol Awareness:
Associate the **/p/** sound with the letters **Pp**

Early Reading:
Engage in repeated readings of the poem "Mix a Pancake"

Early Writing:
Write a class story about pretending to be kernels of popcorn

Student Edition

Phonemic Awareness:
Identify the **/p/** sound

Letter Recognition:
Recognize **P** and **p**

Sound-Symbol Awareness:
Associate the **/p/** sound with the letters **Pp**

Early Reading:
Read a sentence related to the poem "Mix a Pancake"

Early Writing:
Write **Pp**; use developmental spelling to write about things to put in pockets

Language and Cultural Differences

The /p/ sound is spelled **p** in English words. It is common in languages around the world, and one of the first sounds that babies produce. The /**b**/ sound is closely related. The Arabic language has /**b**/, but not /**p**/. (Arabic speakers are likely to pronounce **plastic** as /**bi-las-tik**/). Korean /**p**/ is pronounced /**b**/ between vowels.

In English, /**p**/ is pronounced with a puff of air (or aspiration), similar to /**h**/. Speakers of Spanish, French, and other languages may pronounce /**p**/ without the aspiration. To native English speakers, this sounds a bit like /**b**/.

Using the **ABC** Poem and Picture Charts:
Pp Poem Chart

Read "Mix a Pancake" aloud, pointing to each word. Ask children to recite the poem while acting out the steps for cooking pancakes. Have them clap for the word **pop**.

Say **pan**. Explain that **pan** begins with the /p/ sound. (**Note:** Be sure to say /p/, not /puh/, to isolate the consonant sound.) Have children repeat /p/, noticing how the mouth looks and feels. Associate this sound with **Pp** at the top of the chart.

Use **Meeting Individual Needs** below to develop phonemic awareness and sound-symbol awareness.

School/Home
You may wish to duplicate the page that follows *Teacher Edition* page T99 so that children have their own copy of the poem.

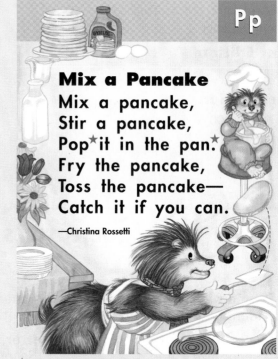

Pp

Mix a Pancake
Mix a pancake,
Stir a pancake,
Pop★it in the pan.★
Fry the pancake,
Toss the pancake—
Catch it if you can.

—Christina Rossetti

★**Note: Basic Words** are starred.

Meeting Individual Needs

Stage 0 Spellers
Sing "The ABC's," stopping at **p**. Ask if any children have **P** or **p** in their names. If so, repeat the names, emphasizing the /p/ sound. Read the poem. Ask children to raise their hands when they hear a word that begins with /p/.

Stage 1 Spellers
Say **pop, pan,** and **pancake** slowly, stretching the sounds (e.g., **pan** = /p/ + /ă/ + /n/). Ask children to count the number of sounds in each word and to blend them together to say the word.

Stage 2 Spellers
Distribute these letter cards to volunteers: **p, a, o, n**. Read the poem. Say **pop** and **pan** slowly, stretching out the sounds (e.g., **pop** = /p/ + /ŏ/ + /p/). Invite the volunteers to raise a letter card for each sound you say.

Stage 3 Spellers
A few children may be ready for more spelling patterns. Write **pop** and **pan**. Challenge children to write new words by changing the last letter in each word. (pot, pat, pad, paw)

For more information on the Stages of Spelling Development, see pages Z10–Z15.

High-Frequency Words
a, if, you, can

Point out **a, if, you,** and **can** in the poem. Ask volunteers to name the letters in each word. Clap and chant the spellings. Ask volunteers to find the words in the poem. Add the words to your word wall or to a list of words for writing.

Using Manipulatives

Purchase small flowerpots. Write a **p** word, such as **pig,** on each. Inside, place the letters in the word plus a few extra. (Use small letter tiles or cards.) For **pig,** you might include **p, b, e, i,** and **g**. In a center, allow children to use the letters in each pot to spell a word.

Using the ABC Poem and Picture Charts: Pp Picture Chart

Invite children to describe the scene on the chart. Children may wish to talk about breakfast time at their house.

Point to **Pp** and ask children what sound it makes. (/p/) Use **Meeting Individual Needs** below to develop phonemic awareness and sound-symbol awareness according to the needs of the children in your class.

Pictured Words ·················
pancake, pajamas, ★pan, peanut butter, porcupine, ★pig, parachute, pink, plate, paint, parrot, pillow, pencil, purple, ★pen, peas

Meeting Individual Needs

Stage 0 Spellers

Prompt children to find pictures of items whose names begin with **/p/**. Ask, *"Do you see a parachute? **Parachute** begins with /p/."* Write each word on chart paper. Ask a volunteer to underline **p** in each word.

Stage 1 Spellers

As children find pictures whose names begin with **/p/,** stretch and count the sounds in several words (e.g., **pig** = /p/ + /ĭ/ + /g/). Write the words, asking children to provide letters for prominent sounds.

Stage 2 Spellers

Challenge children to find all 16 pictures that begin with **/p/**. Pronounce the words and ask children to write a letter (or choose a magnetic letter) for each sound. Accept developmental spellings (e.g., **PIN** for **pen**).

Stage 3 Spellers

A few children may be ready for more spelling patterns. Write **/p/** words children identify. Point out the consonant cluster **pl** in **plate**. Underline the **a-consonant-silent e** pattern in **pancake**.

For more information on the Stages of Spelling Development, see pages Z10–Z15.

ABC Poem and Picture Charts

Use dry erase markers on the laminated pages to highlight and emphasize words, pictures, and targeted sounds.

- Highlight letters on the **Poem Chart**.
- Underline high-frequency words on the **Poem Chart**.
- Circle pictures on the **Picture Chart**.
- Label objects on the **Picture Chart**.

Spelling and Writing

See page Z17 for more information.

Ask children to pretend they are popcorn kernels being poured in a pan, heated up, and beginning to pop! After they act it out, ask them to dictate a sentence about each stage of the experience. Write the story on chart paper. Ask children to provide letters for prominent sounds.

Help children follow the directions on *Student Edition* page 35.

Use **Meeting Individual Needs** below to extend the practice activities according to the needs of the children in your class.

One-Minute Handwriting Hint

To write **p**, retrace the vertical line from bottom to top before making the circle. Help children practice retracing, or "walking on the same line," with their pencils.

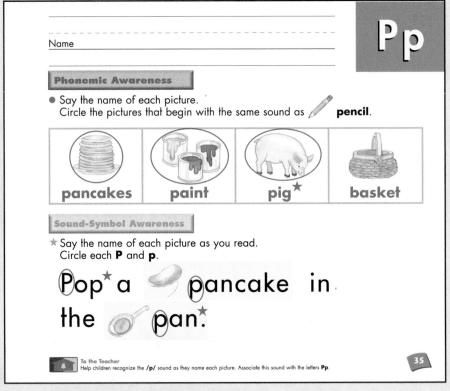

★**Note: Basic Words** are starred.

Meeting Individual Needs

Stage 0 Spellers

Say **pat**, emphasizing the initial /**p**/ sound. Tell children that you will say some words. If they hear /**p**/ at the beginning of a word, they should **pat** their heads. Use these words: **pat, pan, pet, bag, tan, pig, hid, nail, pen, sit, pill, fan, crayon, pencil, pop**.

Stage 1 Spellers

Use the Stage 0 activity. Ask questions about each /**p**/ word. For example, ask, *"What letter spells the /**p**/ sound in **pig**?"* (p) *"What letter spells the /**n**/ sound in **pan**?"* (n)

Stage 2 Spellers

Use the Stage 0 activity. Say several of the /**p**/ words slowly, stretching the sounds (e.g., **pop** = /**p**/ + /ŏ/ + /**p**/). Invite volunteers to write the words. Accept developmental spellings (e.g., **PINSL** for **pencil**).

Stage 3 Spellers

A few children may be ready for more spelling patterns. Use the Stage 0 activity. Write **pig, pan, pop,** and **pen**. Point out the **consonant-vowel-consonant** pattern in each word. Circle the letters that spell the short vowel sounds.

Spelling and Writing

See page Z17 for more information.

Invite children to draw pictures of things they might put in their pockets. Have them write labels for their drawings or write a few sentences about a time they had something special in their pockets. Encourage the use of developmental spelling.

For more information on the Stages of Spelling Development, see pages Z10–Z15.

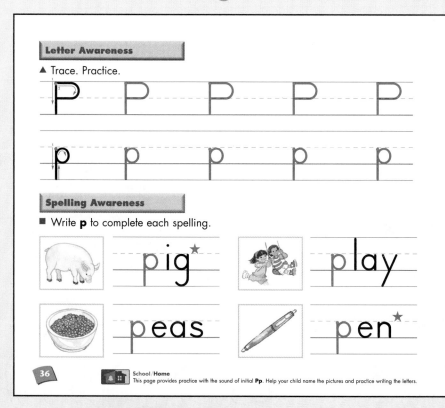

Letter Awareness

▲ Trace. Practice.

P P P P P

p p p p p

Spelling Awareness

■ Write **p** to complete each spelling.

pig★

play

peas

pen★

36 School/**Home** This page provides practice with the sound of initial **Pp**. Help your child name the pictures and practice writing the letters.

Letter Awareness
and
Spelling Awareness

Share these letter chants. Ask children to write the letters in the air as you chant together.

P

Pull down straight.
Lift and slide.
Curve, slide left.
Write **P** with pride.

p

Pull down straight,
Then push up.
Circle right all the way,
Like a sideways cup.

Point out the red directional arrows and the green dots that show where to begin each letter.

Guide children in tracing and writing **P** and **p** to complete the activities on *Student Edition* page 36.

Use **Meeting Individual Needs** below to extend the practice activities according to the needs of children in your class.

Meeting Individual Needs

Stage 0 Spellers

Provide pipe cleaners and show children how to use them to form the letters **P** and **p**. Invite children to trace their pipe cleaner letters with their fingers, following the correct stroke sequence.

Stage 1 Spellers

Use the Stage 0 activity. Then say words from the **Spelling Awareness** activity on *Student Edition* page 36. For prominent sounds, such as **/g/** in **pig,** ask children to make a corresponding letter out of pipe cleaners.

Stage 2 Spellers

Use the Stage 0 activity. Then invite children to choose one or more words from the **Spelling Awareness** activity and model it with pipe cleaners.

Stage 3 Spellers

A few children may be ready to produce conventional (correct) spellings. Call out words from the **Spelling Awareness** activity. Ask children to write the words (or model them with pipe cleaners) and check their spelling.

Building Words With Word Families

den, hen, men, pen, ten, then, when

Point out the word part **-en** in the **Spelling Awareness** activity on *Student Edition* page 36. Write **en** on the chalkboard and say **/en/**. Then say these sounds: **/d/, /h/, /m/, /p/, /t/, /th/,** and **/wh/**. For each sound, invite a volunteer to provide the corresponding letter, write it beside **en,** and say the new word. Add the **-en** words to your word wall or to a list of words for writing.

Unit Assessment

See page Z16 for more information.

You may wish to check progress by having children write **P, p,** and one or more **Basic Words** (**pop, pan, pig, pen**). Note spellings to determine each child's stage of spelling development.

Have children record one **p** word in their **My Words** book (following *Student Edition* page 56).

Pp

Mix a Pancake

Mix a pancake,
Stir a pancake,
Pop it in the pan.
Fry the pancake,
Toss the pancake—
Catch it if you can.

—Christina Rossetti

School/Home
Read the poem with your child. Recite the poem together while acting out the cooking motions. Then have your child point to words in the poem that begin with **P** or **p**. Read and write the **p** words together, emphasizing the /**p**/ sound heard at the beginning of **pan**.

MATERIALS

ABC Poem and Picture Charts

Qq Poem Chart: "Big Q, Little q"

Qq Picture Chart

Student Edition

Pages 37–38

Teacher Edition

Pages T101–T106

Basic Words

queen	quack
quilt	quiet

★**Note: Basic Words** are starred where they appear in this *Teacher Edition*.

High-Frequency Words

big	little
what	and

Targeted Word Family

-ack

OBJECTIVES

ABC Poem and Picture Charts

Phonemic Awareness:
Identify the **/kw/** sound

Letter Recognition:
Recognize **Q** and **q**

Sound-Symbol Awareness:
Associate the **/kw/** sound with the letters **Qu** and **qu**

Early Reading:
Engage in repeated readings of the poem "Big Q, Little q"

Early Writing:
Write a class list of rules for the Duck Queen's castle

Student Edition

Phonemic Awareness:
Identify the **/kw/** sound

Letter Recognition:
Recognize **Q** and **q**

Sound-Symbol Awareness:
Associate the **/kw/** sound with the letters **Qu** and **qu**

Early Reading:
Read picture labels that begin with **q**

Early Writing:
Write **Qq;** use developmental spelling to write on quilt squares

Quack!

Quack!

Language and Cultural Differences

In English spelling, the letter **q** is almost always followed by **u**; **qu** is pronounced **/kw/**. While not all languages have this blend, it is fairly easy to pronounce.

In Spanish, **qu** has a **silent u**. It is pronounced **/k/**. This spelling for **/k/** occurs before **i** or **e**. Before **a, o,** and **u, /k/** is spelled **c**. A Spanish equivalent for **/kw/** might be **cu + vowel,** as in **cuidado (caution), cuidadora (babysitter), cuando (when),** and **cuesta (hill).** Use these examples to help children master the **/kw/** sound.

Using the ABC Poem and Picture Charts: Qq Poem Chart

BIG Q, little q
BIG Q
little q
What begins with Q?

The quick
Queen★ of Quincy
And her
Quacking quacker-oo.

—Dr. Seuss

Quack! Quack! Quack!

Read "Big Q, Little q" aloud, pointing to each word. Act as the queen and ask children to act as ducks as you parade around the room, reciting the poem.

Say **quiet**. Explain that **quiet** begins with the **/kw/** sound. (**Note:** Explain that this sound is made by **q** and **u** together.) Have children repeat **/kw/,** noticing how the mouth looks and feels. Associate this sound with **Qq** at the top of the chart.

Use **Meeting Individual Needs** below to develop phonemic awareness and sound-symbol awareness according to the needs of the children in your class.

School/Home
You may wish to duplicate the page that follows *Teacher Edition* page T105 so that children have their own copy of the poem.

★**Note: Basic Words** are starred.

Meeting Individual Needs

Stage 0 Spellers
Ask half the class to write **q** on a sticky note and stick it to their shirts. Ask the other half to wear **u** notes. Partner **q**'s and **u**'s. Read the poem, asking partners to clap hands together when they hear a word with **/kw/**.

Stage 1 Spellers
Use the Stage 0 activity. For each **/kw/** word in the poem, choose one pair of children and ask them what letters they think are in that word. Help by asking questions such as *"What letter spells /n/ in queen?"* (n)

Stage 2 Spellers
Use the Stage 0 activity. Say each **/kw/** word slowly, stretching its sounds. Ask a pair of children to use magnetic letters to arrive at a developmental spelling (e.g., **QUIK** for **quick**).

Stage 3 Spellers
A few children may be ready for more spelling patterns. Start with **quick** and **quack**. Ask children to write new words with the **-ick** and **-ack** patterns. (kick, pick; back, pack)

For more information on the Stages of Spelling Development, see pages Z10–Z15.

High-Frequency Words
big, little, what, and

Point out **big, little, what,** and **and** in the poem. Ask volunteers to name the letters in each word. Clap and chant the spellings. Ask volunteers to find the words in the poem. Add the words to your word wall or to a list of words for writing.

ABC Using Manipulatives

Make a duck puppet from a sock or a paper bag. Write **qu** inside its mouth. Then write these word parts on cards or on chart paper: **ack, arter, ilt, een, ail, estion**. Invite children to open the puppet's mouth beside the letters to make these **qu** words: **quack, quarter, quilt, queen, quail, question**.

Using the ABC Poem and Picture Charts:
Qq Picture Chart

Invite children to describe the scene on the chart. Children may wish to invent a story to go along with the picture.

Point to **Qq** and ask children what sound this letter makes with **u**. (/kw/) Use **Meeting Individual Needs** below to develop phonemic awareness and sound-symbol awareness according to the needs of the children in your class.

Pictured Words.....................
★quilt, ★queen, quarter, quail, question mark, quills, ★quack, ★quiet

Meeting Individual Needs

Stage 0 Spellers

Prompt children to find pictures of items whose names begin with **/kw/**. Ask, *"Do you see a porcupine quill? Quill begins with /kw/."* Write each word on chart paper. Ask a volunteer to underline **qu** in each word.

Stage 1 Spellers

Ask children to find pictures whose names begin with **/kw/**. Stretch and count the sounds in each word (e.g., **queen** = /kw/ + /ē/ + /n/). Write the words, asking children to provide letters for prominent sounds.

Stage 2 Spellers

Challenge children to find all eight pictures that begin with **/kw/**. Pronounce the words and ask children to write a letter for each sound. Accept developmental spellings (e.g., **QUELT** for **quilt**).

Stage 3 Spellers

A few children may be ready for more spelling patterns. Write **/kw/** words children identify. Point out the **-er** ending in **quarter** and the **-tion** ending in **question**.

For more information on the Stages of Spelling Development, see pages Z10–Z15.

ABC Poem and Picture Charts

Use dry erase markers on the laminated pages to highlight and emphasize words, pictures, and targeted sounds.

- Highlight letters on the **Poem Chart**.
- Underline high-frequency words on the **Poem Chart**.
- Circle pictures on the **Picture Chart**.
- Label objects on the **Picture Chart**.

Spelling and Writing

See page Z17 for more information.

Display the **Qq Picture Chart** and talk about the ducklings' activities. Then write a list of rules for the Duck Queen's castle. The first rule might be *"Quack quietly."* Write the rules on chart paper, asking children to provide letters for prominent sounds.

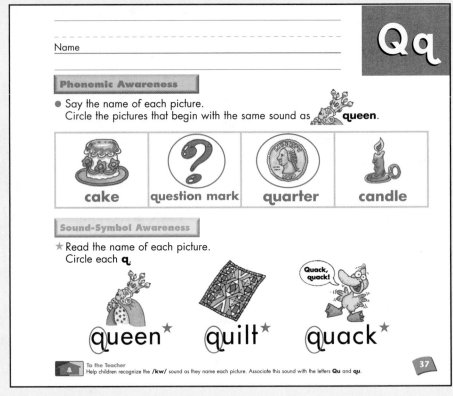

Phonemic Awareness
and
Sound-Symbol Awareness

Help children follow the directions on *Student Edition* page 37.

Use **Meeting Individual Needs** below to extend the practice activities according to the needs of the children in your class.

One-Minute Handwriting Hint

Tell children to write a complete circle first for **Q** and **q**. To complete **Q**, add the slanted "tail." For **q**, retrace carefully and curve to the right.

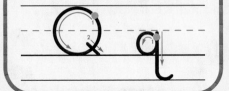

★**Note: Basic Words** are starred.

Meeting Individual Needs

Stage 0 Spellers

Provide a rubber duck toy that squeaks. Tell children they can make the duck quack by adding **/kw/** to the beginning of word parts you say. Use these word parts: **ick** (quick), **een** (queen), **iet** (quiet), **ilt** (quilt), **it** (quit), **estion** (question), **arter** (quarter). For each correct response, allow a child to squeeze the duck. Continue until all have had a turn. Ask what letters begin each word. (qu)

For more information on the Stages of Spelling Development, see pages Z10–Z15.

Stage 1 Spellers

Use the Stage 0 activity. After children say each **/kw/** word, ask one child to make the toy duck quack and then tell what letters match sounds heard in the word. Help by asking questions such as *"What letter spells the /t/ sound in quilt?"* (t)

Stage 2 Spellers

Use the Stage 0 activity. After children say each **/kw/** word, ask one child to make the toy duck quack and then write the word, giving one letter for each sound. Accept developmental spellings (e.g., **QUELT** for **quilt**).

Stage 3 Spellers

A few children may be ready for more spelling patterns. Write **queen** and point out the **ee** spelling of **long e**. Write words that rhyme with **queen** such as **seen, green, bean,** and **clean**. Ask children to sort the words according to the **ee** and **ea** patterns.

Spelling and Writing

See page Z17 for more information.

Ask each child to write a sentence on a square of paper about something that is quiet. Encourage developmental spelling. Ask children to decorate their squares and tape them in a grid on the wall to make a "quiet quilt."

Using the Student Edition: Page 38

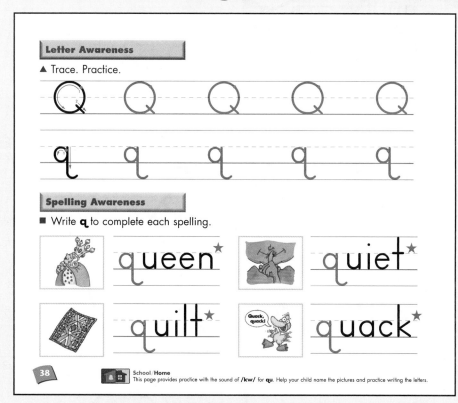

Letter Awareness and Spelling Awareness

Share these letter chants. Ask children to write the letters in the air as you chant together.

Q

Circle back left, all the way around.
Lift. Slant right.
Take that tail to the ground.

q

Circle back left, all the way around.
Keep little **q** quite close to the ground.
Push up straight.
Pull down straight, too.
Curve forward right.
That's lowercase **q**.

Point out the red directional arrows and the green dots that show where to begin each letter.

Guide children in tracing and writing **Q** and **q** to complete the activities.

Use **Meeting Individual Needs** below to extend the practice activities.

Meeting Individual Needs

Stage 0 Spellers
Allow children to write **Q** and **q** in a large size on the chalkboard. Alternately, allow them to paint with a wide brush on an easel. Make sure children are following the correct stroke sequence.

Stage 1 Spellers
Use the Stage 0 activity. Slowly say words from the **Spelling Awareness** activity on *Student Edition* page 38. Ask children to write or paint letters for prominent sounds they hear in the words.

Stage 2 Spellers
Use the Stage 0 activity. Slowly say words from the **Spelling Awareness** activity. Ask children to write a letter for each sound they hear. Accept developmental spellings (e.g., **QUAK** for **quack**).

Stage 3 Spellers
A few children may be ready to produce conventional (correct) spellings. Call out words from the **Spelling Awareness** activity. Ask children to write or paint them and then check their spelling.

Building Words With Word Families
back, pack, rack, sack, tack, black, quack, stack

Point out the word part **-ack** in the **Spelling Awareness** activity on *Student Edition* page 38. Write **ack** on a large card and give it to a volunteer. Make smaller cards for the letters **b, p, r, s, t, bl, qu,** and **st**. Ask volunteers to choose a letter, say the corresponding sound, and hold the card beside **ack**. Say the new words together. Add the **-ack** words to your word wall or to a list of words for writing.

Unit Assessment
See page Z16 for more information.

You may wish to check progress by having children write **Q, q,** and one or more **Basic Words** (**queen, quack, quilt, quiet**). Note spellings to determine each child's stage of spelling development.

Have children record one **q** word in their **My Words** book (following *Student Edition* page 56).

BIG Q, Little q

Big Q
little q
What begins with Q?

The quick
Queen of Quincy
And her
Quacking quacker-oo.

—Dr. Seuss

School/Home
Read the poem several times with your child. Ask your child to say the poem while waddling and pretending to be a duck. Then look for words in the poem that begin with **Qu** and **qu**. Read and write the **q** words together, emphasizing the **/kw/** sound heard at the beginning of **quiet**.

MATERIALS

ABC Poem and Picture Charts
Rr Poem Chart: "R Is for Ribbon"
Rr Picture Chart

Student Edition
Pages 39–40

Teacher Edition
Pages T107–T112

OBJECTIVES

ABC Poem and Picture Charts	Student Edition
Phonemic Awareness: Identify the /r/ sound	**Phonemic Awareness:** Identify the /r/ sound
Letter Recognition: Recognize **R** and **r**	**Letter Recognition:** Recognize **R** and **r**
Sound-Symbol Awareness: Associate the /r/ sound with the letters **Rr**	**Sound-Symbol Awareness:** Associate the /r/ sound with the letters **Rr**
Early Reading: Engage in repeated readings of the poem "R Is for Ribbon"	**Early Reading:** Read picture labels that begin with **r**
Early Writing: Write a class poem with **r** words	**Early Writing:** Write **Rr**; use developmental spelling to write about things that are red

Language and Cultural Differences

The letter **r** stands for a sound that is difficult for many children to make. At first, young children may substitute another sound, such as **/w/,** so that **red** is pronounced **/wed/.**

Many sounds are represented by **r** in languages around the world, including tongue flaps and trills, as in Spanish **perro** (**dog**). Some languages do not distinguish between /l/ and /r/. In Japanese and Korean, whether a sound is /r/-like or /l/-like depends on its position in a word. Many British, Australian, South African, and East Coast American speakers of English don't pronounce /r/ after a vowel so that **court** sounds like **caught.**

Using the ABC Poem and Picture Charts:
Rr Poem Chart

R Is for Ribbon
R is for ribbon,
a rose★
and a ring,★
a ruby,
a raindrop
and a robin in spring!

—Margaret and John Travers Moore

★**Note: Basic Words** are starred.

Phonemic Awareness and **Sound-Symbol Awareness**

Read "R Is for Ribbon" aloud, pointing to each word. Read the poem again, omitting the pictured words that begin with **r**. Point to the pictures and ask children to supply the missing words.

Say **rose**. Explain that **rose** begins with the **/r/** sound. (**Note:** Be sure to say **/r/,** not **/ruh/,** to isolate the consonant sound.) Have children repeat **/r/,** noticing how the mouth looks and feels. Associate this sound with **Rr** at the top of the chart.

Use **Meeting Individual Needs** below to develop phonemic awareness and sound-symbol awareness.

School/Home
You may wish to duplicate the page that follows *Teacher Edition* page T111 so that children have their own copy of the poem.

Meeting Individual Needs

Stage 0 Spellers
Ask if any children have **R** or **r** in their names. If so, repeat the names, emphasizing **/r/**. Have children stand and recite the poem. Ask them to run in place when they say a word that begins with **/r/**.

Stage 1 Spellers
Give clues about sounds and letters in **r** words from the poem. For example, say, *"This word begins with /r/. It ends with /g/."* (ring) As each word is guessed, have a volunteer point to the picture and the word on the chart.

Stage 2 Spellers
Tape a blank card over each **r** word in the poem. Say each word, stretching its sounds. Ask a volunteer to write the word on the card, giving one letter for each sound. Accept developmental spellings (e.g., **ROZ** for **rose**).

Stage 3 Spellers
A few children may be ready for more spelling patterns. Use the Stage 2 activity. Raise each card and compare developmental spellings to correct spellings. Point out **ing** in **ring** and **spring**.

For more information on the Stages of Spelling Development, see pages Z10–Z15.

High-Frequency Words
in, and, is, for

Point out **in, and, is,** and **for** in the poem. Ask volunteers to name the letters in each word. Clap and chant the spellings. Ask volunteers to find the words in the poem. Add the words to your word wall or to a list of words for writing.

Using Manipulatives

Cut raindrop shapes from blue paper. Write one of these letters on each: **r, e, a, i, o, d, g, n, t, y, s, c, k.** Attach them to a vertical surface with magnets, Velcro, felt, or tape. Allow children to use the pieces to build **r** words such as **red, rain, rock,** and **rag**.

Using the ABC Poem and Picture Charts: Rr Picture Chart

Invite children to describe the scene on the chart. Children may wish to tell about a time they roller-skated or raked leaves.

Point to **Rr** and ask children what sound it makes. (/r/) Use **Meeting Individual Needs** below to develop phonemic awareness and sound-symbol awareness according to the needs of the children in your class.

Pictured Words..................
robin, ★rose, ★ring, ruby, ★rain, rainbow, rabbit, rocket, rake, ★red, raincoat, rocks, roller skates, river, rowboat

Meeting Individual Needs

Stage 0 Spellers

Prompt children to find pictures of items whose names begin with /r/. Ask, *"Do you see a rocket? Rocket begins with /r/."* Write each word on chart paper. Ask a volunteer to underline **r** in each word.

Stage 1 Spellers

As children find pictures whose names begin with **/r/,** stretch and count the sounds in several words (e.g., **red = /r/ + /ĕ/ + /d/**). Write the words, asking children to provide letters for prominent sounds.

Stage 2 Spellers

Challenge children to find all 15 pictures that begin with **/r/**. Pronounce the words and ask children to write a letter (or choose a magnetic letter) for each sound. Accept developmental spellings (e.g., **RAN** for **rain**).

Stage 3 Spellers

A few children may be ready for more spelling patterns. Write **/r/** words children identify. Point out the **consonant-vowel-vowel-consonant** pattern in **rain**. Model other words that have this pattern. (read, road)

For more information on the Stages of Spelling Development, see pages Z10–Z15.

ABC Poem and Picture Charts

Use dry erase markers on the laminated pages to highlight and emphasize words, pictures, and targeted sounds.

- Highlight letters on the **Poem Chart**.
- Underline high-frequency words on the **Poem Chart**.
- Circle pictures on the **Picture Chart**.
- Label objects on the **Picture Chart**.

Spelling and Writing

See page Z17 for more information.

Write the poem "R Is for Ribbon" on chart paper, substituting a blank for each **r** word. Ask children to suggest a new **r** word for each blank. Have children help spell each **r** word by providing letters for prominent sounds. Children may copy and illustrate the new poem.

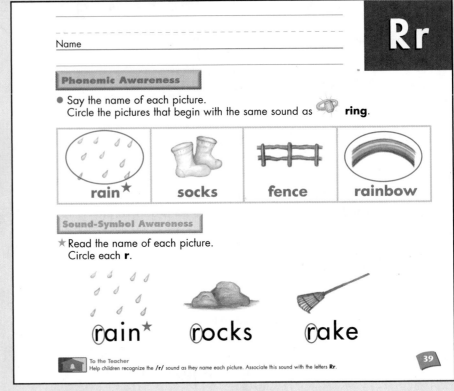

Phonemic Awareness and Sound-Symbol Awareness

Help children follow the directions on *Student Edition* page 39.

Use **Meeting Individual Needs** below to extend the practice activities according to the needs of the children in your class.

One-Minute Handwriting Hint

Show how **R** begins like **B**, but ends with a slant line. Provide practice in carefully retracing the vertical line in lowercase **r**.

★**Note: Basic Words** are starred.

Meeting Individual Needs

Stage 0 Spellers

Share these riddles. Explain that each answer begins with /r/.

- It is a color that means "stop." (red)
- It circles a finger. (ring)
- It rhymes with **socks**. (rocks)
- It rhymes with **cake**. (rake)
- It falls on your umbrella. (rain)

Write children's answers in a list. Ask a volunteer to underline **r** in each word.

For more information on the Stages of Spelling Development, see pages Z10–Z15.

Stage 1 Spellers

Use the Stage 0 activity. After each response, ask a child to tell what letters he or she hears in the word (e.g., **d** for /d/ in **red**). On chart paper, write these letters. Fill in missing letters to complete the word.

Stage 2 Spellers

Use the Stage 0 activity. Say each **r** word, stretching its sounds. Ask a volunteer to write each word on chart paper. Accept developmental spellings (e.g., **ROKS** for **rocks**).

Stage 3 Spellers

A few children may be ready for more spelling patterns. Use the Stage 0 activity. Write each **r** word. Beside each word, write another word that shares its spelling pattern. For example, write **bed** beside **red** and **stain** beside **rain**.

Spelling and Writing

See page Z17 for more information.

Invite children to think of things that might be red. (fire truck, stop sign, rose, traffic light, apple) Ask them to draw things that are red and label them or write something about them. Encourage the use of developmental spelling.

T110

Using the Student Edition: Page 40

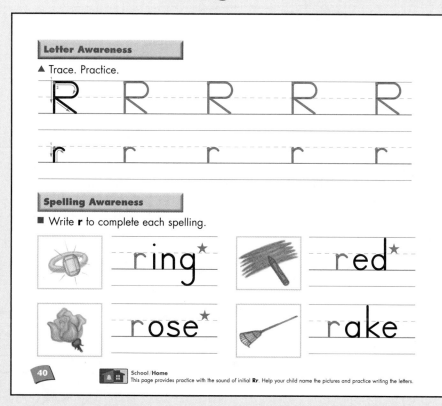

Letter Awareness and Spelling Awareness

Share these letter chants. Ask children to write the letters in the air as you chant together.

R

Pull down and lift.
Then slide right.
There are three more steps.
Don't hold your pencil too tight!
Curve forward right. Slide left. Slant right.
For uppercase **R,**
These steps are just right!

r

First thing you do
Is pull down straight.
Then push up and curve right.
Lowercase **r** is great!

Point out the red directional arrows and the green dots that show where to begin each letter.

Guide children in tracing and writing **R** and **r** to complete the activities on *Student Edition* page 40.

Meeting Individual Needs

Stage 0 Spellers
Provide a zip-top bag for each child. Spread a small amount of washable paint in each bag and seal it. Ask children to lay the bags flat and use them as "magic slates" for finger-tracing **R** and **r**. Check to make sure they are following the correct stroke sequence.

Stage 1 Spellers
Use the Stage 0 activity. Slowly say words from the **Spelling Awareness** activity on *Student Edition* page 40. Ask children to trace letters for prominent sounds they hear in the words.

Stage 2 Spellers
Use the Stage 0 activity. Slowly say words from the **Spelling Awareness** activity. Ask children to write a letter for each sound they hear. Accept developmental spellings (e.g., **RAK** for **rake**).

Stage 3 Spellers
A few children may be ready to produce conventional (correct) spellings. Call out words from the **Spelling Awareness** activity. Ask children to trace them on the "magic slates" and then check their spelling.

Building Words With Word Families
bake, cake, lake, make, rake, take, wake, snake

Point out the word part **-ake** in the **Spelling Awareness** activity on *Student Edition* page 40. Ask children to think of words that rhyme with **rake**. For each response (e.g., **cake**) isolate the initial sound (e.g., /k/) and ask children to provide the corresponding letter. Write the **-ake** words in a list. Add them to your word wall or to a list of words for writing.

Unit Assessment
See page Z16 for more information.

You may wish to check progress by having children write **R, r,** and one or more **Basic Words** (**rain, ring, red, rose**). Note spellings to determine each child's stage of spelling development.

Have children record one **r** word in their **My Words** book (following *Student Edition* page 56).

Rr

R Is for Ribbon

R is for ribbon,
a rose
and a ring,
a ruby,
a raindrop
and a robin in spring!

—Margaret and John Travers Moore

School/Home
Read the poem several times with your child. Make up a tune for the poem and sing it together. Then look
for words in the poem that begin with **R** or **r**. Read and write the **r** words together, emphasizing the /**r**/
sound heard at the beginning of **rain**.

MATERIALS

ABC Poem and Picture Charts

Ss Poem Chart: "Way Down Deep"
Ss Picture Chart

Student Edition

Pages 41–42

Teacher Edition

Pages T113–T118

Basic Words

sun	sand
six	sock

★**Note: Basic Words** are starred where they appear in this *Teacher Edition*.

High-Frequency Words

in	way
down	the

Targeted Word Family

-ail

OBJECTIVES

ABC Poem and Picture Charts

Phonemic Awareness:
Identify the **/s/** sound

Letter Recognition:
Recognize **S** and **s**

Sound-Symbol Awareness:
Associate the **/s/** sound with the letters **Ss**

Early Reading:
Engage in repeated readings of the poem "Way Down Deep"

Early Writing:
Make and label objects for a beach bulletin board

Student Edition

Phonemic Awareness:
Identify the **/s/** sound

Letter Recognition:
Recognize **S** and **s**

Sound-Symbol Awareness:
Associate the **/s/** sound with the letters **Ss**

Early Reading:
Read picture labels that begin with **s**

Early Writing:
Write **Ss**; use developmental spelling to write a description of life under the sea

Language and Cultural Differences

This unit focuses on /s/ spelled **s**. The /z/ sound is closely related. If you whisper **zebra,** you will hear voiceless /s/ instead of /z/. Some languages, such as Spanish, have only voiceless /s/ and lack /z/. Spanish-speaking children may have trouble pronouncing /z/ for **s** at the end of a word like **seals.** Hawaiian has no /s/ or /z/. In Japanese, /s/ becomes /sh/ before some vowels. Japanese learners may pronounce a word such as **season** as /sheed-zun/.

Ask children to identify words in the unit that also begin with /s/ in Spanish. These include **seis (six), siete (seven),** and **sol (sun).**

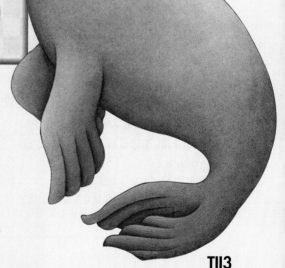

Using the ABC Poem and Picture Charts:
Ss Poem Chart

Read "Way Down Deep" aloud, pointing to each word. Ask children to recite the poem as they "swim" around the room, pretending to be sea creatures.

Say **sand**. Explain that **sand** begins with the /s/ sound. (**Note:** Be sure to say /s/, not /suh/, to isolate the consonant sound.) Have children repeat /s/, noticing how the mouth looks and feels. Associate this sound with **Ss** at the top of the chart.

Use **Meeting Individual Needs** below to develop phonemic awareness and sound-symbol awareness.

School/Home
You may wish to duplicate the page that follows *Teacher Edition* page T117 so that children have their own copy of the poem.

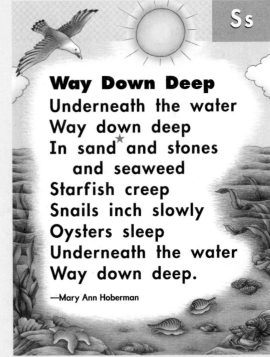

Way Down Deep
Underneath the water
Way down deep
In sand* and stones
   and seaweed
Starfish creep
Snails inch slowly
Oysters sleep
Underneath the water
Way down deep.

—Mary Ann Hoberman

★**Note: Basic Words** are starred.

Meeting Individual Needs

Stage 0 Spellers

Have children repeat /s/. Ask them to look around the room and find things that begin with /s/. (seats, sink, soap, signs, socks) Read the poem, asking children to clap when they hear a word that begins with /s/.

Stage 1 Spellers

Read the poem. Ask children to clap when they hear a word that begins with /s/. Ask questions about sounds and letters in the **s** words. For example, ask, *"What letter spells the /d/ sound in sand?"* (d)

Stage 2 Spellers

Say each **s** word from the poem slowly, stretching its sounds (e.g., **sand** = /s/ + /ă/ + /n/ + /d/). Ask a volunteer to choose a magnetic letter for each sound. Accept developmental spellings (e.g., **SNAL** for **snail**).

Stage 3 Spellers

A few children may be ready for more spelling patterns. Use the Stage 2 activity. Compare the developmental spellings to correct spellings. Point out **nd** in **sand** and **st** in **starfish** and **stones**.

For more information on the Stages of Spelling Development, see pages Z10–Z15.

High-Frequency Words
in, way, down, the

Point out **in, way, down,** and **the** in the poem. Ask volunteers to name the letters in each word. Clap and chant the spellings. Ask volunteers to find the words in the poem. Add the words to your word wall or to a list of words for writing.

ABC Using Manipulatives

Make a class set of tactile letter cards. Assign several letters to each group of children. Show how to use stencils to trace a letter shape on sandpaper, cut it out, and glue it onto a blank index card. Put the card set in a center for ongoing spelling practice.

Using the **ABC** Poem and Picture Charts:
Ss Picture Chart

Invite children to describe the scene on the chart. Children may wish to talk about a time they visited a beach or lakeshore.

Point to **Ss** and ask children what sound it makes. (/s/) Use **Meeting Individual Needs** below to develop phonemic awareness and sound-symbol awareness according to the needs of the children in your class.

Pictured Words • • • • • • • • • • • • • • • • •
★sun, ★sand, sea, sail, seal, shell, shovel, ★six, seven, snail, starfish, shoes, ★sock

Meeting Individual Needs

Stage 0 Spellers
Prompt children to find pictures of items whose names begin with **/s/**. Ask, *"Do you see sand? **Sand** begins with **/s/**."* Write each word on chart paper. Ask a volunteer to underline **s** in each word.

For more information on the Stages of Spelling Development, see pages Z10–Z15.

Stage 1 Spellers
As children find pictures whose names begin with **/s/**, stretch and count the sounds in each word (e.g., **sun** = /s/ + /ŭ/ + /n/). Write the words, asking children to provide letters for prominent sounds.

Stage 2 Spellers
Challenge children to find all 13 pictures that begin with **/s/**. Pronounce the words and ask children to write a letter (or choose a magnetic letter) for each sound. Accept developmental spellings (e.g., **SIKS** for **six**).

Stage 3 Spellers
A few children may be ready for more spelling patterns. Write **/s/** words children identify. Point out the four different short vowel sounds in **sun** (**short u**), **sand** (**short a**), **six** (**short i**), and **sock** (**short o**).

ABC Poem and Picture Charts
Use dry erase markers on the laminated pages to highlight and emphasize words, pictures, and targeted sounds.

• Highlight letters on the **Poem Chart**.
• Underline high-frequency words on the **Poem Chart**.
• Circle pictures on the **Picture Chart**.
• Label objects on the **Picture Chart**.

Spelling and Writing
See page Z17 for more information.

Make a beach-themed bulletin board. Invite children to cut something from construction paper that begins with **s** and belongs at the beach. Ask children to label their creations and add them to the scene. Accept developmental spellings.

Phonemic Awareness and Sound-Symbol Awareness

Help children follow the directions on *Student Edition* page 41.

Use **Meeting Individual Needs** below to extend the practice activities according to the needs of the children in your class.

One-Minute Handwriting Hint

To guide children's practice, draw a green starting dot and a red ending dot for each letter. This will help them avoid reversing **S**.

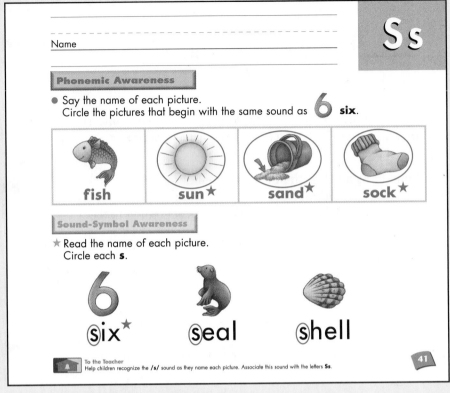

★ **Note: Basic Words** are starred.

Meeting Individual Needs

Stage 0 Spellers

Draw a large circle on the chalkboard. Explain that children can make the sun shine by adding /s/ to the beginning of words you say. Use these words: **and** (sand), **Ed** (said), **alley** (Sally), **aim** (same), **at** (sat), **elf** (self), **end** (send), **oh** (so), **it** (sit), **ink** (sink), and **I** (sigh). Help children hear the /s/ sound at the beginning of each new word. For each correct response, invite a volunteer to draw a ray from the sun.

For more information on the Stages of Spelling Development, see pages Z10–Z15.

Stage 1 Spellers

Use the Stage 0 activity. After each volunteer has drawn a ray, ask him or her a question about the **s** word. For example, ask, *"What letter spells the /s/ sound in sand?"* (s) *"What letter spells /t/ in sit?"* (t)

Stage 2 Spellers

Use the Stage 0 activity. Say each /s/ word slowly, stretching the sounds (e.g., **sand** = /s/ + /ă/ + /n/ + /d/). Invite volunteers to write the words beside the sun. Accept developmental spellings (e.g., **SANT** for **sand**).

Stage 3 Spellers

Use the Stage 0 activity. Have children write the **s** words. To check their spelling, make an **s** card and a set of rime cards (e.g., an **at** card for **sat**). Hold the **s** card next to each rime card and blend the sounds to say the word.

Spelling and Writing

See page Z17 for more information.

Invite children to imagine they are starfish at the bottom of the sea. Have them write words or sentences to describe their surroundings. They should include details about sights, sounds, and feelings. Encourage the use of developmental spelling.

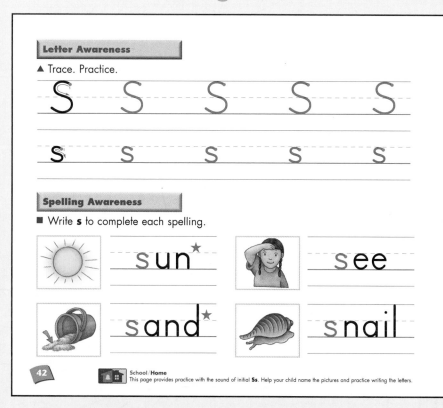

Letter Awareness

▲ Trace. Practice.

S S S S S

s s s s s

Spelling Awareness

■ Write **s** to complete each spelling.

sun★

see

sand★

snail

42

School/Home
This page provides practice with the sound of initial **Ss**. Help your child name the pictures and practice writing the letters.

Letter Awareness

and

Spelling Awareness

Share these letter chants. Ask children to write the letters in the air as you chant together.

S

Curve back left.
Curve forward right.
That's how uppercase **S**
Is made just right.

s

Curve back left.
Curve forward right.
Write lowercase **s**—
But not too tight!

Point out the red directional arrows and the green dots that show where to begin each letter.

Guide children in tracing and writing **S** and **s** to complete the activities on *Student Edition* page 42.

Use **Meeting Individual Needs** below to extend the practice activities according to the needs of the children in your class.

Meeting Individual Needs

Stage 0 Spellers
Have children sculpt **S** and **s** from clay. Encourage them to trace the clay letters with their fingers, using the correct starting point.

Stage 1 Spellers
Use the Stage 0 activity. Slowly say words from the **Spelling Awareness** activity on *Student Edition* page 42. Ask children to sculpt letters from clay to match prominent sounds they hear.

Stage 2 Spellers
Write the words from the **Spelling Awareness** activity on large cards and laminate them. Allow children to use them as a base for building the words with clay.

Stage 3 Spellers
A few children may be ready to produce conventional (correct) spellings. Call out words from the **Spelling Awareness** activity and ask children to write them or sculpt them with clay. Have children use their books to check spelling.

Building Words With Word Families
fail, hail, mail, pail, rail, sail, tail, trail, snail

Point out the word part **-ail** in the **Spelling Awareness** activity. Write **ail** on chart paper and say /ail/. Ask children to look at an alphabet chart and suggest letters that will make words when added to **-ail**. Challenge children to blend **tr** and **sn** and add the letters to **ail** to make **trail** and **snail**. Write the new words and say them together. Add the **-ail** words to your word wall or to a list of words for writing.

Unit Assessment
See page Z16 for more information.

You may wish to check progress by having children write **S, s,** and one or more **Basic Words** (**sun, sand, six, sock**). Note spellings to determine each child's stage of spelling development.

Have children record one **s** word in their **My Words** book (following *Student Edition* page 56).

Ss

Way Down Deep

Underneath the water
Way down deep
In sand and stones
    and seaweed
Starfish creep
Snails inch slowly
Oysters sleep
Underneath the water
Way down deep.

—Mary Ann Hoberman

School/Home
Read the poem several times with your child. Read the poem again as your child pretends to "swim" around the room. Then look for words in the poem that begin with **S** or **s**. Read and write the **s** words together, emphasizing the /**s**/ sound heard at the beginning of **sand**.

MATERIALS

ABC Poem and Picture Charts

Tt Poem Chart: "Teddy Bear,
Teddy Bear"
Tt Picture Chart

Student Edition

Pages 43–44

Teacher Edition

Pages T119–T124

OBJECTIVES

ABC Poem and Picture Charts

Phonemic Awareness:
Identify the /t/ sound

Letter Recognition:
Recognize **T** and **t**

Sound-Symbol Awareness:
Associate the /t/ sound with
the letters **Tt**

Early Reading:
Engage in repeated readings
of the poem "Teddy Bear,
Teddy Bear"

Early Writing:
Write a *Teddy Bear, Teddy
Bear* class big book

Student Edition

Phonemic Awareness:
Identify the /t/ sound

Letter Recognition:
Recognize **T** and **t**

Sound-Symbol Awareness:
Associate the /t/ sound with
the letters **Tt**

Early Reading:
Read a sentence from
the poem "Teddy Bear,
Teddy Bear"

Early Writing:
Write **Tt**; use developmental
spelling to write about the
adventures of a stuffed
animal

Basic Words

ten	tent
turn	top

★**Note: Basic Words** are
starred where they appear
in this *Teacher Edition*.

High-Frequency Words

your	will
do	the

Targeted Word Family

-op

Language and Cultural Differences

This unit focuses on the **/t/** sound. Like **/k/** and **/p/**, **/t/** is a "stop" (i.e., air is
completely blocked in the mouth as air pressure builds up and is then released
all at once). American English speakers tend to pronounce **/t/** and **/d/** the same
between vowels, so that the words **ladder** and **latter** sound the same.

Arrange for children who are acquiring English to work with an English-proficient
study buddy. Ask the buddies to say and write simple sentences that include the **t**
words pictured in this unit.

Using the ABC Poem and Picture Charts: Tt Poem Chart

Read "Teddy Bear, Teddy Bear" aloud, pointing to each word. Have children stand and sing the poem, acting out the motions.

Say **turn**. Explain that **turn** begins with the **/t/** sound. (**Note:** Be sure to say **/t/,** not **/tuh/,** to isolate the consonant sound.) Have children repeat **/t/,** noticing how the mouth looks and feels. Associate this sound with **Tt** at the top of the chart.

Use **Meeting Individual Needs** below to develop phonemic awareness and sound-symbol awareness according to the needs of the children in your class.

School/Home
You may wish to duplicate the page that follows *Teacher Edition* page T123 so that children have their own copy of the poem.

Teddy Bear, Teddy Bear

Tt

Teddy bear, teddy bear,
    turn★ around.
Teddy bear, teddy bear,
    touch the ground.
Teddy bear, teddy bear,
    tie your shoe.
Teddy bear, teddy bear,
    that will do!

★**Note: Basic Words** are starred.

Meeting Individual Needs

Stage 0 Spellers

Ask children to look around for things that begin with **/t/**. (tape, TV, table, teacher, teeth, tissue) Read the poem, asking children to tap their toes when they hear a word that begins with **/t/**. Point out **t** in each word.

Stage 1 Spellers

Read the poem. Ask children to tap their toes when they hear a word that begins with **/t/**. For each **t** word, ask questions such as *"What letter spells the /t/ sound in turn?"* (t) *"Does **Teddy** start with /t/?"* (yes)

Stage 2 Spellers

Tape a blank card over each **t** word in the poem. Read the poem and ask children to shout each missing word. Have a volunteer write the word on the blank card. Accept developmental spellings (e.g., **TRN** for **turn**).

Stage 3 Spellers

A few children may be ready for more spelling patterns. Use the Stage 2 activity. Lift the cards and compare the developmental spellings with the adult spellings.

For more information on the Stages of Spelling Development, see pages Z10–Z15.

High-Frequency Words
your, will, do, the

Point out **your, will, do,** and **the** in the poem. Ask volunteers to name the letters in each word. Clap and chant the spellings. Ask volunteers to find the words in the poem. Add the words to your word wall or to a list of words for writing.

ABC Using Manipulatives

Provide two craft sticks for each child. Show how to hold up the craft sticks to make a **t** shape. Then say a variety of words, including **pen, ten, dream, turn, top, tent, kite, day, tie, pie.** Ask children to make a **t** with their sticks and hold it up when they hear a word that begins with **/t/**.

Using the ABC Poem and Picture Charts: Tt Picture Chart

Invite children to describe the scene on the chart. Children may wish to talk about things they bring to your classroom to share.

Point to **Tt** and ask children what sound it makes. (/t/) Use **Meeting Individual Needs** below to develop phonemic awareness and sound-symbol awareness according to the needs of the children in your class.

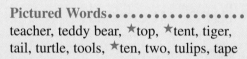

Pictured Words.....................
teacher, teddy bear, ★top, ★tent, tiger, tail, turtle, tools, ★ten, two, tulips, tape

Meeting Individual Needs

Stage 0 Spellers

Prompt children to find pictures of items whose names begin with /t/. Ask, *"Do you see a tent? Tent begins with /t/."* Write each word on chart paper. Ask a volunteer to underline **t** in each word.

For more information on the Stages of Spelling Development, see pages Z10–Z15.

Stage 1 Spellers

Ask children to find pictures whose names begin with /t/. Stretch and count the sounds in each word (e.g., **ten** = /t/ + /ĕ/ + /n/). Write the words, asking children to provide letters for prominent sounds.

Stage 2 Spellers

Challenge children to find all 12 pictures that begin with /t/. Pronounce the words and ask children to write a letter (or choose a magnetic letter) for each sound. Accept developmental spellings (e.g., **TRTL** for **turtle**).

Stage 3 Spellers

A few children may be ready for more spelling patterns. Write /t/ words children identify. Underline the **consonant-vowel-consonant** pattern in **top** and **ten**.

ABC Poem and Picture Charts

Use dry erase markers on the laminated pages to highlight and emphasize words, pictures, and targeted sounds.

- Highlight letters on the **Poem Chart**.
- Underline high-frequency words on the **Poem Chart**.
- Circle pictures on the **Picture Chart**.
- Label objects on the **Picture Chart**.

Spelling and Writing

See page Z17 for more information.

On each page of a blank big book, write *"Teddy bear, teddy bear...."* Ask children to suggest an action that begins with **t** to complete each sentence (e.g., **taste, touch, tell, talk**). Ask children to provide letters for prominent sounds as you write. Illustrate the book.

Using the Student Edition: Page 43

See page Z17 for more information.

Phonemic Awareness and Sound-Symbol Awareness

Help children follow the directions on *Student Edition* page 43.

Use **Meeting Individual Needs** below to extend the practice activities according to the needs of the children in your class.

One-Minute Handwriting Hint

Remind children to begin **T** at the top, then go back to put on the "hat." Lowercase **t** crosses at the midline.

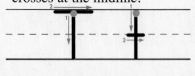

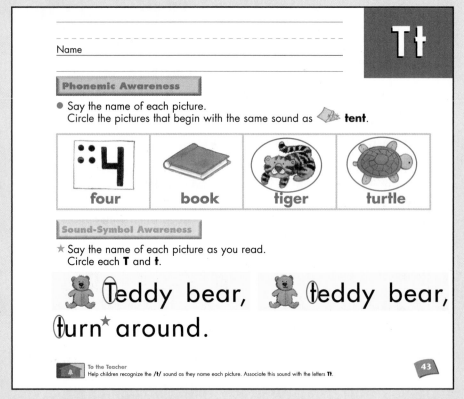

★ **Note: Basic Words** are starred.

Meeting Individual Needs

Stage 0 Spellers

Say **ten**. Elongate the /t/ sound and point out that it is heard at the beginning of the word. Appoint a volunteer artist. Tell children that the artist will draw part of a teddy bear (e.g., head, ears) for each correct response. Then say these words and ask children to tell if they hear /t/ at the beginning of the word: **boat, write, cat, tiger, coat, ten, tool, boot, time, pit, top, tent.**

For more information on the Stages of Spelling Development, see pages Z10–Z15.

Stage 1 Spellers

Use the Stage 0 activity. Choose several of the /t/ words and ask questions about letters and sounds. For example, ask, *"What letter spells the /t/ sound in* ten*?"* (t) *"What letter spells the /n/ sound in* ten*?"* (n)

Stage 2 Spellers

Use the Stage 0 activity. Pronounce several of the /t/ words slowly, stretching the sounds. Invite volunteers to write the words beside the teddy bear drawing. Accept developmental spellings (e.g., **TINT** for **tent**).

Stage 3 Spellers

A few children may be ready for more spelling patterns. Use the Stage 0 activity. Write **ten, pit, cat,** and **top**. Point out the four different short vowel sounds. Have a volunteer circle the letter that spells the vowel sound in each word.

Spelling and Writing

See page Z17 for more information.

Invite children to write words or sentences about the adventures of a teddy bear or other stuffed animal. Ask them to use the word **I** to write from the toy's point of view. Encourage the use of developmental spelling.

Using the Student Edition: Page 44

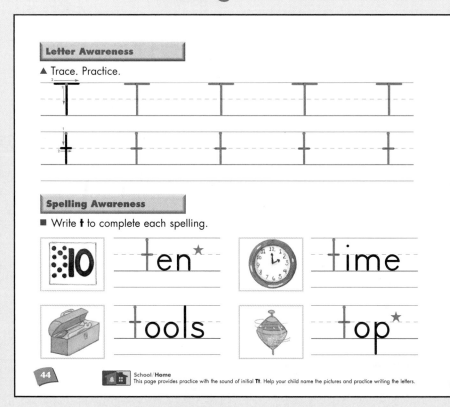

Letter Awareness and Spelling Awareness

Share this letter chant. Ask children to write the letters in the air as you chant together.

Tt

Pull down straight.
Lift. Slide right.
One **T** is for **Tom,**
And the other is for **tight**.

Point out the red directional arrows and the green dots that show where to begin each letter.

Guide children in tracing and writing **T** and **t** to complete the activities on *Student Edition* page 44.

Use **Meeting Individual Needs** below to extend the practice activities according to the needs of the children in your class.

Meeting Individual Needs

Stage 0 Spellers

Dispense a small amount of shaving cream on each child's tabletop. Show how to spread it out to make a "magic cloud" for finger-writing. Ask children to write **T** and **t,** following the correct stroke sequence.

Stage 1 Spellers

Use the Stage 0 activity. Slowly say words from the **Spelling Awareness** activity on *Student Edition* page 44. Ask children to finger-write letters for prominent sounds they hear.

Stage 2 Spellers

Use the Stage 0 activity. Pronounce the words from the **Spelling Awareness** activity and ask children to finger-write them, giving one letter for each sound they hear. Accept developmental spellings.

Stage 3 Spellers

A few children may be ready to produce conventional (correct) spellings. Call out words from the **Spelling Awareness** activity. Ask children to finger-write them in shaving cream and then check their spelling.

Building Words With Word Families

hop, mop, pop, top, stop

Point out the word part **-op** in the **Spelling Awareness** activity on *Student Edition* page 44. Display the magnetic letters **op** and say /op/. Invite children to add other magnetic letters as they say the corresponding sounds—/h/, /m/, /p/, /t/, and /st/. Say the new words together. Add the **-op** words to your word wall or to a list of words for writing.

Unit Assessment

See page Z16 for more information.

You may wish to check progress by having children write **T, t,** and one or more **Basic Words** (**ten, tent, turn, top**). Note spellings to determine each child's stage of spelling development.

Have children record one **t** word in their **My Words** book (following *Student Edition* page 56).

TI23

Tt

Teddy Bear, Teddy Bear

Teddy bear, teddy bear,
    turn around.
Teddy bear, teddy bear,
    touch the ground.
Teddy bear, teddy bear,
    tie your shoe.
Teddy bear, teddy bear,
    that will do!

School/Home
Read the poem several times with your child. Ask your child to sing the poem while jumping back and forth over a rope or a line on the floor. Then look for words in the poem that begin with **T** or **t**. Read and write the **t** words together, emphasizing the **/t/** sound heard at the beginning of **two**.

MATERIALS

ABC Poem and Picture Charts
Uu Poem Chart: "Umbrellas"
Uu Picture Chart

Student Edition
Pages 45–46

Teacher Edition
Pages T125–T130

Basic Words

up	under
umbrellas	bug

★**Note: Basic Words** are starred where they appear in this *Teacher Edition*.

High-Frequency Words

the	my
I	why

Targeted Word Family
-ug

OBJECTIVES

ABC Poem and Picture Charts

Phonemic Awareness:
Identify the **short u** sound

Letter Recognition:
Recognize **U** and **u**

Sound-Symbol Awareness:
Associate the **short u** sound with the letters **Uu**

Early Reading:
Engage in repeated readings of the poem "Umbrellas"

Early Writing:
Use developmental spelling to write about "Upside Down Town"

Student Edition

Phonemic Awareness:
Identify the **short u** sound

Letter Recognition:
Recognize **U** and **u**

Sound-Symbol Awareness:
Associate the **short u** sound with the letters **Uu**

Early Reading:
Read a sentence related to the poem "Umbrellas"

Early Writing:
Write **Uu;** use developmental spelling to write about things that are up high

Language and Cultural Differences

This unit focuses on the /ŭ/, or **short u,** sound. This sound does not exist in Spanish. Have children practice /ŭ/ several times. Then add consonants (e.g., **up, pup, cup**). Ask children to repeat each word until they have mastered the pronunciation.

You may wish to introduce **long u,** as in **unicorn.** Be aware that to Spanish-speaking children, **long u** will sound like **iu,** as in **ciudad** (**city**). Japanese and Korean speakers may tend to pronounce **long u** with the lips spread rather than rounded.

Using the ABC Poem and Picture Charts:
Uu Poem Chart

Phonemic Awareness and Sound-Symbol Awareness

Read "Umbrellas" aloud, pointing to each word. Ask children to recite the poem while pretending to hold umbrellas and splash in puddles.

Say **up**. Isolate the initial sound and explain that this is the **short u** sound. (This unit focuses on **short u**.) Have children repeat /ŭ/, noticing how the mouth looks and feels. Associate this sound with **Uu** at the top of the chart.

Use **Meeting Individual Needs** below to develop phonemic awareness and sound-symbol awareness according to the needs of the children in your class.

School/Home
You may wish to duplicate the page that follows *Teacher Edition* page T129 so that children have their own copy of the poem.

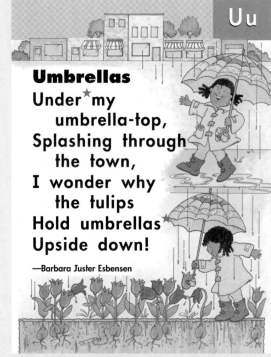

Umbrellas
Under★my
    umbrella-top,
Splashing through
    the town,
I wonder why
    the tulips
Hold umbrellas★
Upside down!

—Barbara Juster Esbensen

★**Note: Basic Words** are starred.

Meeting Individual Needs

Stage 0 Spellers

Sing "The ABC's," stopping at **u**. Point to **Uu** at the top of the chart and ask children to practice making the /ŭ/, or **short u,** sound. Read the poem, asking children to hold up a pretend umbrella when they hear a word with the /ŭ/ sound.

Stage 1 Spellers

Use the Stage 0 activity. Say several words from the poem, stretching the sounds (e.g., **upside** = /ŭ/ + /p/ + /s/ + /ī/ + /d/). Ask volunteers to blend the sounds to say the complete words and point to them in the poem.

Stage 2 Spellers

Write each letter in the word **umbrellas** on a card and give it to a volunteer. Ask each volunteer to make the sound that corresponds to his or her letter. Have the rest of the class help you arrange the volunteers to spell **umbrellas**.

Stage 3 Spellers

A few children may be ready for more spelling patterns. Ask children to write new words by adding consonant letters before **-up, -un,** and **-um**. (cup, pup; sun, fun; gum, hum)

For more information on the Stages of Spelling Development, see pages Z10–Z15.

High-Frequency Words
the, my, I, why

Point out **the, my, I,** and **why** in the poem. Ask volunteers to name the letters in each word. Clap and chant the spellings. Ask volunteers to find the words in the poem. Add the words to your word wall or to a list of words for writing.

Using Manipulatives

Have partners play a word-building game. Put these letter cards in a bag: **p, p, s, d, m, g, t, b, r, j**. Give one **u** card to each partner. Players should take turns drawing letters from the bag until they can make a **u** word. They earn one point for each word.

Using the **ABC** Poem and Picture Charts:
Uu Picture Chart

Invite children to describe the scene on the chart. Children may wish to talk about a time they walked in the rain.

Point to **Uu**. Ask what sound **u** makes in the word **up**. (/ŭ/) Use **Meeting Individual Needs** below to develop phonemic awareness and sound-symbol awareness according to the needs of the children in your class.

Note: If you wish to contrast **short u** with **long u,** also include the pictures identified for **long u.**

Pictured Words..................

short u: umbrella, umpire, ★up, ★under, ★bug

long u: unicorn, unicycle

Meeting Individual Needs

Stage 0 Spellers

Prompt children to find pictures of items whose names contain /ŭ/. Ask, *"Do you see an umpire? Umpire has /ŭ/."* Write each word on chart paper. Ask a volunteer to underline **u** in each word.

Stage 1 Spellers

As children find pictures with /ŭ/, stretch and count the sounds in each word (e.g., **up** = /ŭ/ + /p/). Write the words, asking children to provide letters for prominent sounds.

Stage 2 Spellers

Challenge children to find all five pictures with /ŭ/. Pronounce the words and ask children to write a letter (or choose a magnetic letter) for each sound. Accept developmental spellings (e.g., **UNDR** for **under**).

Stage 3 Spellers

A few children may be ready for more spelling patterns. Ask children to find pictures whose names contain **short u** or **long u**. Write each word, pointing out patterns such as the **vowel-consonant-silent e** spelling of **long i** in **umpire**.

For more information on the Stages of Spelling Development, see pages Z10–Z15.

ABC Poem and Picture Charts

Use dry erase markers on the laminated pages to highlight and emphasize words, pictures, and targeted sounds.

- Highlight letters on the **Poem Chart**.
- Underline high-frequency words on the **Poem Chart**.
- Circle pictures on the **Picture Chart**.
- Label objects on the **Picture Chart**.

Spelling and Writing

See page Z17 for more information.

Invite children to draw a picture of "Upside Down Town." Encourage them to include a sign with the town's name, buildings, vehicles, people, and plants. Ask children to write a few words or sentences about their drawings. Accept developmental spelling.

Phonemic Awareness
and
Sound-Symbol Awareness

Help children follow the directions on *Student Edition* page 45.

Use **Meeting Individual Needs** below to extend the practice activities according to the needs of the children in your class.

One-Minute Handwriting Hint

Show how to make **U**, and the first stroke of **u**, with one, fluid stroke.

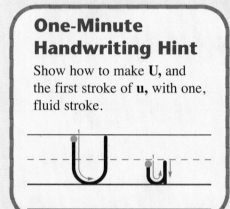

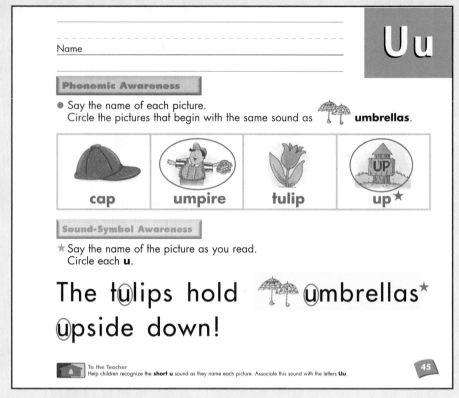

Name

Uu

Phonemic Awareness

● Say the name of each picture.
  Circle the pictures that begin with the same sound as ☂ **umbrellas**.

| cap | umpire | tulip | up ★ |

Sound-Symbol Awareness

★ Say the name of the picture as you read.
  Circle each **u**.

The t(u)lips hold ☂ (u)mbrellas★
(u)pside down!

🏠 **To the Teacher**
Help children recognize the **short u** sound as they name each picture. Associate this sound with the letters **Uu**.

45

★**Note: Basic Words** are starred.

Meeting Individual Needs

Stage 0 Spellers

Draw an umbrella and raindrops on chart paper. Tell children that you will say words in slow motion and ask them to say them in a normal way (e.g., for **fun,** say, *"/f/ - /ŭ/ - /n/"*). Each time they say a word correctly, ask a volunteer to color one part of the drawing with markers. Use these **short u** words: **up, us, bug, bus, run, duck, sun, cut, cup, puff, hum.** Write the words, underlining **u** in each one.

For more information on the Stages of Spelling Development, see pages Z10–Z15.

Stage 1 Spellers

Use the Stage 0 activity. After children say each word correctly, ask questions about prominent sounds. For example, ask, *"What letter spells the /ŭ/ sound in up?"* (u) *"What letter spells the /g/ sound in bug?"* (g)

Stage 2 Spellers

Use the Stage 0 activity. After each volunteer colors part of the drawing, repeat the **short u** word and ask him or her to write it, giving one letter for each sound. Accept developmental spellings (e.g., **DUK** for **duck**).

Stage 3 Spellers

A few children may be ready for more spelling patterns. Use the Stage 0 activity. Have children write each **short u** word. Ask volunteers to share their spellings. Point out the **consonant-vowel-consonant** pattern in words such as **bug** and **sun**.

Spelling and Writing

See page Z17 for more information.

Have children make an *Up* book by completing this sentence pattern on several pages: "Look up to see ___." (Possible responses: a balloon, birds, clouds, the moon) Encourage the use of developmental spelling. Have children compile and illustrate their books.

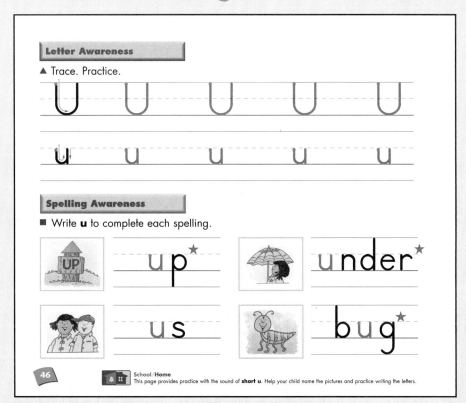

Letter Awareness
and
Spelling Awareness

Share these letter chants. Ask children to write the letters in the air as you chant together.

U

Pull down straight. Curve right. Push up.
An uppercase **U** looks like a big cup.

u

Pull down straight.
Get ready to curve.
Curve right. Push up.
Pull down. Don't swerve!
If lowercase **u** keeps its head below the line,
Then your **ups** and **umbrellas** will look just fine.

Point out the red directional arrows and the green dots that show where to begin each letter.

Guide children in tracing and writing U and **u** to complete activities on *Student Edition* page 46.

Use **Meeting Individual Needs** below to extend the practice activities.

Meeting Individual Needs

Stage 0 Spellers

Provide pipe cleaners and show children how to use them to form the letters **U** and **u**. Invite children to trace their pipe cleaner letters with their fingers, following the correct stroke sequence.

Stage 1 Spellers

Use the Stage 0 activity. Then say words from the **Spelling Awareness** activity on *Student Edition* page 46. For prominent sounds, such as /s/ in **us,** ask children to make a corresponding letter out of pipe cleaners.

Stage 2 Spellers

Use the Stage 0 activity. Then invite children to choose one or more words from the **Spelling Awareness** activity and model it with pipe cleaners.

Stage 3 Spellers

A few children may be ready to produce conventional (correct) spellings. Call out words from the **Spelling Awareness** activity. Ask children to write the words (or model them with pipe cleaners) and check their spelling.

Building Words With Word Families

bug, dug, hug, jug, mug, rug, tug

Point out the word part **-ug** in the **Spelling Awareness** activity on *Student Edition* page 46. Write **ug** on the chalkboard and say /ug/. Hide cards with these letters around the room: **b, d, h, j, m, r, t**. Invite volunteers to spot a letter, retrieve it, say the corresponding sound, and place it in front of **ug**. Say the new words together. Add the **-ug** words to your word wall or to a list of words for writing.

Unit Assessment

See page Z16 for more information.

You may wish to check progress by having children write **U, u,** and one or more **Basic Words** (**up, under, umbrellas, bug**). Note spellings to determine each child's stage of spelling development.

Have children record one **u** word in their **My Words** book (following *Student Edition* page 56).

Uu

Umbrellas

Under my
umbrella-top,
Splashing through
the town,
I wonder why
the tulips
Hold umbrellas
Upside down!

—Barbara Juster Esbensen

School/Home
Read the poem several times with your child. If possible, allow your child to stand under an umbrella while reciting the poem. Then look for words in the poem that begin with **U** or **u**. Read and write the **u** words together, emphasizing the **short u** sound heard at the beginning of **up**.

From *Swing Around the Sun* by Barbara Juster Esbensen. Text copyright © 1965 by Lerner Publications Co., text copyright © 2003 by Carolrhoda Books, Inc., imprints of Lerner Publishing Group. Used by permission. All rights reserved.

MATERIALS

ABC Poem and Picture Charts
Vv Poem Chart: "Roses Are Red"
Vv Picture Chart

Student Edition
Pages 47–48

Teacher Edition
Pages T131–T136

OBJECTIVES

ABC Poem and Picture Charts

Phonemic Awareness:
Identify the **/v/** sound

Letter Recognition:
Recognize **V** and **v**

Sound-Symbol Awareness:
Associate the **/v/** sound with the letters **Vv**

Early Reading:
Engage in repeated readings of the poem "Roses Are Red"

Early Writing:
Write words to make a class "vine" of **v** words

Student Edition

Phonemic Awareness:
Identify the **/v/** sound

Letter Recognition:
Recognize **V** and **v**

Sound-Symbol Awareness:
Associate the **/v/** sound with the letters **Vv**

Early Reading:
Read a sentence related to the poem "Roses Are Red"

Early Writing:
Write **Vv**; use developmental spelling to write about a visitor from Venus

Language and Cultural Differences

The /v/ sound is made by narrowing the space through which air exits the mouth. The lower lip curls under the upper teeth. The Arabic and Korean languages do not have /v/. Spanish, Japanese, and other languages have a similar sound that is produced by bringing the lips close together. Spanish speakers learning English frequently substitute this sound for English /v/. Children who are missing lower front teeth will temporarily have trouble making /v/.

Using the ABC Poem and Picture Charts:
Vv Poem Chart

Phonemic Awareness and **Sound-Symbol Awareness**

Vv

Roses Are Red
Roses are red.
Violets are blue.
Sugar is sweet,
And so are you.

Be my valentine.

Read "Roses Are Red" aloud, pointing to each word. Read the poem again. For the last word in each line, say only the initial sound as a clue. For example, say, *"Roses are /r/."* Ask children to shout the word to complete each line.

Say **van**. Explain that **van** begins with the **/v/** sound. (**Note:** Be sure to say **/v/,** not **/vuh/,** to isolate the consonant sound.) Have children repeat **/v/,** noticing how the mouth looks and feels. Associate this sound with **Vv** at the top of the chart.

Use **Meeting Individual Needs** below to develop phonemic awareness and sound-symbol awareness.

School/Home
You may wish to duplicate the page that follows *Teacher Edition* page T135 so that children have their own copy of the poem.

Meeting Individual Needs

Stage 0 Spellers

Ask children to repeat the **/v/** sound. Show how to hold up two fingers to make a **V** shape. Read the poem. Ask children to hold up **V** fingers when you read a word that begins with **/v/.**

Stage 1 Spellers

Read the poem, asking children to hold up **V** fingers for words that begin with **/v/.** Cover **violets** and **valentine** and say the words slowly, stretching the sounds. Ask children to name letters they hear in the words.

Stage 2 Spellers

Use the Stage 1 activity. Write **violets** and **valentine** on chart paper, asking children to provide a letter for each sound they hear. Accept developmental spellings (e.g., **VALNTIN** for **valentine**).

Stage 3 Spellers

A few children may be ready for more spelling patterns. Point out the **i-consonant-silent e** spelling of **long i** in **valentine.** Ask children to write new words that end in **-ine.** (mine, pine, porcupine)

For more information on the Stages of Spelling Development, see pages Z10–Z15.

High-Frequency Words
are, red, blue, you

Point out **are, red, blue,** and **you** in the poem. Ask volunteers to name the letters in each word. Clap and chant the spellings. Ask volunteers to find the words in the poem. Add the words to your word wall or to a list of words for writing.

ABC Using Manipulatives

Provide drinking straws, glue, scissors, and construction paper. Invite children to cut the straws to various lengths. Show how to position and glue the pieces to form **V, v,** and pictures of volcanoes, mountains, fence posts, sailboats, etc.

Using the ABC Poem and Picture Charts:
Vv Picture Chart

Phonemic Awareness and Sound-Symbol Awareness

Invite children to describe the scene on the chart. Children may wish to talk about ways they celebrate Valentine's Day.

Point to **Vv** and ask children what sound it makes. (/v/) Use **Meeting Individual Needs** below to develop phonemic awareness and sound-symbol awareness according to the needs of the children in your class.

Pictured Words.....................
violets, valentine, Valentine's Day, violin, ★vase, ★vest, ★vine, vacuum cleaner, ★van, vegetables

Meeting Individual Needs

Stage 0 Spellers
Prompt children to find pictures of items whose names begin with **/v/**. Say, *"Do you see a vest? **Vest** begins with /v/."* Write each word on chart paper. Ask a volunteer to underline **v** in each word.

Stage 1 Spellers
As children find pictures whose names begin with **/v/**, stretch and count the sounds in each word (e.g., **van = /v/ + /ă/ + /n/**). Write the words, asking children to provide letters for prominent sounds.

Stage 2 Spellers
Challenge children to find all ten pictures that begin with **/v/**. Pronounce the words and ask children to write a letter (or choose a magnetic letter) for each sound. Accept developmental spellings (e.g., **VIN** for **vine**).

Stage 3 Spellers
A few children may be ready for more spelling patterns. Write **/v/** words children identify. Point out the **vowel-consonant-silent e** pattern that spells the long vowel sounds in **vase** and **vine**.

For more information on the Stages of Spelling Development, see pages Z10–Z15.

ABC Poem and Picture Charts

Use dry erase markers on the laminated pages to highlight and emphasize words, pictures, and targeted sounds.

- Highlight letters on the **Poem Chart**.
- Underline high-frequency words on the **Poem Chart**.
- Circle pictures on the **Picture Chart**.
- Label objects on the **Picture Chart**.

Spelling and Writing

See page Z17 for more information.

Have children cut leaf shapes from green paper. Ask them to write **v** words on the leaves. Suggest words from this unit as well as **volcano, visit, very,** and **vacation**. Make a class "vine" of **v** words by attaching the leaves to a length of green yarn with tape or clothespins.

Help children follow the directions on *Student Edition* page 47.

Use **Meeting Individual Needs** below to extend the practice activities according to the needs of the children in your class.

One-Minute Handwriting Hint

Show how to pause (without lifting the pencil) after the first slant stroke in **v** and **V**. The letters should be wide open at the top like a vanilla ice cream cone.

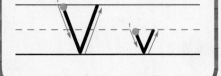

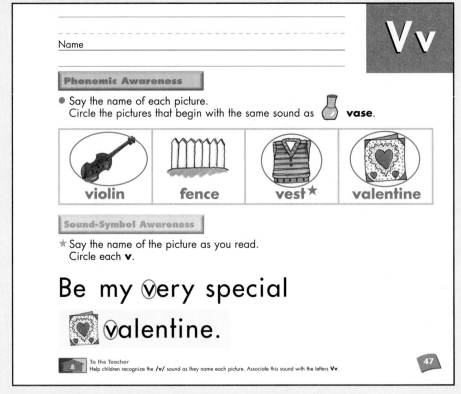

Name

Phonemic Awareness

● Say the name of each picture.
   Circle the pictures that begin with the same sound as 🏺 **vase**.

| violin | fence | vest ★ | valentine |

Sound-Symbol Awareness

★ Say the name of the picture as you read.
   Circle each **v**.

Be my ⓥery special
🂠 ⓥalentine.

To the Teacher
Help children recognize the /v/ sound as they name each picture. Associate this sound with the letters **Vv**.

47

★**Note: Basic Words** are starred.

Meeting Individual Needs

Stage 0 Spellers

Share these riddles. Explain that each answer begins with /v/.

• You can put a flower in it. (vase)

• It is a plant that can grow up a pole. (vine)

• It is a vehicle with a big door on its side. (van)

• You wear it to keep warm. It has no sleeves. (vest)

• It could be a heart-shaped card from someone who loves you. (valentine)

For more information on the Stages of Spelling Development, see pages Z10–Z15.

Stage 1 Spellers

Use the Stage 0 activity. As children answer the riddles, say each **v** word slowly, stretching the sounds. Ask volunteers to provide letters for prominent sounds (e.g., **a** for **long a** in **vase**).

Stage 2 Spellers

Use the Stage 0 activity. Invite volunteers to write answers to the riddles on the chalkboard. Encourage them to give one letter for each sound. Accept developmental spellings (e.g., **VAS** for **vase**).

Stage 3 Spellers

A few children may be ready for more spelling patterns. Use the Stage 0 activity. Point out the **vowel-consonant-silent e** pattern that spells **long a** in **vase** and **long i** in **vine**. Make new words using the **-ase** and **-ine** patterns. (base, nine)

Spelling and Writing

See page Z17 for more information.

Ask children to write "A Visitor From Venus" on their papers. Invite them to draw a picture of the visitor from another planet and to write about why the visitor has come to Earth. Encourage the use of developmental spelling.

Using the Student Edition: Page 48

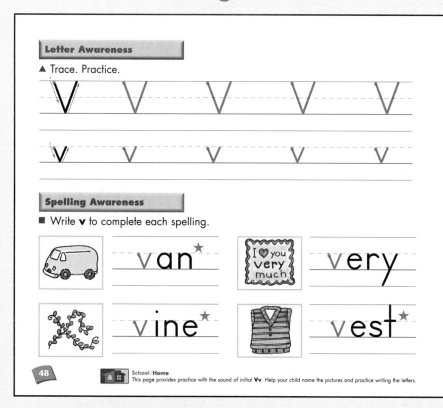

Letter Awareness
and
Spelling Awareness

Share these letter chants. Ask children to write the letters in the air as you chant together.

V

Slant right and slant up
For uppercase **V**.
It's really quite easy,
Don't you agree?

v

Slant right and slant up
For lowercase **v**.
It's just half as tall
As uppercase **V**.

Point out the red directional arrows and the green dots that show where to begin each letter.

Guide children in tracing and writing **V** and **v** to complete the activities on *Student Edition* page 48.

Use **Meeting Individual Needs** below to extend the practice activities according to the needs of the children in your class.

Meeting Individual Needs

Stage 0 Spellers

Have children use their fingers to trace **V** and **v** in the air, on their tabletops, and on a partner's back. Check to make sure children are using the correct stroke sequence.

Stage 1 Spellers

Say a word from the **Spelling Awareness** activity on *Student Edition* page 48. Ask, *"What is one sound you hear? What letter spells the sound?"* After children respond with a letter, have them trace it on a partner's back.

Stage 2 Spellers

Have children work in pairs. The first child should choose a word from the **Spelling Awareness** activity and trace some or all of the letters on the second child's back. The second child should try to guess the word. Partners should then trade roles.

Stage 3 Spellers

A few children may be ready to produce conventional (correct) spellings. Use the Stage 2 activity. After the word is guessed, ask both partners to write it correctly on lined paper.

Building Words With Word Families
best, nest, pest, rest, test, vest, west

Point out the word part **-est** in the **Spelling Awareness** activity on *Student Edition* page 48. Write **est** on the chalkboard and say /est/. Hide cards with these letters around the room: **b, n, p, r, t, v, w**. Invite volunteers to find a letter, retrieve it, say the corresponding sound, and hold it next to **est**. Say the new words together. Add the **-est** words to your word wall or to a list of words for writing.

Unit Assessment

See page Z16 for more information.

You may wish to check progress by having children write **V, v,** and one or more **Basic Words** (**van, vest, vase, vine**). Note spellings to determine each child's stage of spelling development.

Have children record one **v** word in their **My Words** book (following *Student Edition* page 56).

Vv

Roses Are Red

Roses are red.
Violets are blue.
Sugar is sweet,
And so are you.

Be my valentine.

School/Home
Read the poem several times with your child. Invent a hand-clapping game to play together as you recite the poem. Then look for words in the poem that begin with **V** or **v**. Read and write the **v** words together, emphasizing the /v/ sound heard at the beginning of **van**.

MATERIALS

ABC Poem and Picture Charts

Ww Poem Chart: "Fingers Like to
Wiggle, Waggle"
Ww Picture Chart

Student Edition

Pages 49–50

Teacher Edition

Pages T137–T142

Basic Words

web	water
wing	worm

★Note: **Basic Words** are
starred where they appear
in this *Teacher Edition*.

High-Frequency Words

like	to
in	me

Targeted Word Family

-ing

OBJECTIVES

ABC Poem and Picture Charts

Phonemic Awareness:
Identify the **/w/** sound

Letter Recognition:
Recognize **W** and **w**

Sound-Symbol Awareness:
Associate the **/w/** sound
with the letters **Ww**

Early Reading:
Engage in repeated readings
of the poem "Fingers Like to
Wiggle, Waggle"

Early Writing:
Write finger pantomimes
that include **w** words

Student Edition

Phonemic Awareness:
Identify the **/w/** sound

Letter Recognition:
Recognize **W** and **w**

Sound-Symbol Awareness:
Associate the **/w/** sound with
the letters **Ww**

Early Reading:
Read picture labels that
begin with **w**

Early Writing:
Write **Ww;** use developmental spelling to write about
taking a walk

Language and Cultural Differences

This unit focuses on the **/w/** sound spelled **w**. German and a number of other languages use **w** to stand for **/v/**. In French, **w** usually occurs only in words that have
been borrowed from English or German. You may find that children acquiring
English substitute **/v/** for **/w/**. Provide practice in pronouncing **/w/**.

Many languages do not have **/w/**. Some of these do have a similar sound: **/oo/**
followed by another vowel. An example from Spanish is **huevo** (**egg**) pronounced
/oo-ay-voh/. If you pronounce **/oo/** and glide into **/ay/,** you will hear what sounds
like **/w/**.

Using the ABC Poem and Picture Charts:
Ww Poem Chart

Read "Fingers Like to Wiggle, Waggle" aloud, pointing to each word. Ask children to chant the poem while wiggling their fingers behind their backs. They should bring their wiggly fingers to the front when they say, *"right in front of me."*

Say **wiggle**. Explain that **wiggle** begins with the /w/ sound. (**Note:** Be sure to say /w/, not /wuh/, to isolate the consonant sound.) Have children repeat /w/, noticing how the mouth looks and feels. Associate this sound with **Ww** at the top of the chart.

Use **Meeting Individual Needs** below to develop phonemic awareness and sound-symbol awareness.

School/Home
You may wish to duplicate the page that follows *Teacher Edition* page T141 so that children have their own copy of the poem.

Ww

**Fingers Like to
Wiggle, Waggle**
Fingers like to
  wiggle, waggle,
Wiggle, waggle,
  wiggle, waggle,
Fingers like to
  wiggle, waggle,
Right in front of me.

Meeting Individual Needs

Stage 0 Spellers
Ask children to look for things that begin with /w/. (wall, window, watch, words) Read the poem, asking children to wiggle their fingers and then extend the first and second fingers of each hand in a **W** shape.

For more information on the Stages of Spelling Development, see pages Z10–Z15.

Stage 1 Spellers
Read the poem, omitting /w/ (e.g., say, *"fingers like to iggle, aggle"*). Invite children to add /w/ and repeat the words back to you. Continue the game by asking children to add /w/ to the beginning of **all, indow, atch,** and **ords**.

Stage 2 Spellers
Distribute these letter cards to volunteers: **w, a, i, g, l.** Read the poem. Say **wiggle** and **waggle** slowly, stretching out the sounds (e.g., **waggle** = /w/ + /ă/ + /g/ + /l/). Invite the volunteers to raise a letter card for each sound you say.

Stage 3 Spellers
A few children may be ready for more spelling patterns. Start with **wall**. Ask children to write new words using the **-all** pattern. (fall, ball, mall, small)

High-Frequency Words
like, to, in, me

Point out **like, to, in,** and **me** in the poem. Ask volunteers to name the letters in each word. Clap and chant the spellings. Ask volunteers to find the words in the poem. Add the words to your word wall or to a list of words for writing.

ABC Using Manipulatives

Use plastic peel-off paint (available in craft stores) to make a set of window cling letters. Apply the clings to a window in your classroom. Invite children to work alone or in small groups to use the clings to spell **w** words such as **water, web,** and **window**.

Using the ABC Poem and Picture Charts:
Ww Picture Chart

Invite children to describe the scene on the chart. Children may wish to talk about a time they visited a lakeshore or played with a wagon.

Point to **Ww** and ask children what sound it makes. (/w/) Use **Meeting Individual Needs** below to develop phonemic awareness and sound-symbol awareness according to the needs of the children in your class.

Pictured Words.................
★worm, ★water, wagon, ★web, watermelon, wristwatch, window, ★wing, waterfall, white, woods, woodpecker

Meeting Individual Needs

Stage 0 Spellers
Prompt children to find pictures of items whose names begin with **/w/**. Ask, *"Do you see a window? **Window** begins with /w/."* Write each word on chart paper. Ask a volunteer to underline **w** in each word.

Stage 1 Spellers
As children find pictures whose names begin with **/w/,** stretch and count the sounds in each word (e.g., **web** = /w/ + /ĕ/ + /b/). Write the words, asking children to provide letters for prominent sounds.

Stage 2 Spellers
Challenge children to find all 12 pictures that begin with **/w/**. Pronounce the words and ask children to write a letter (or choose a magnetic letter) for each sound. Accept developmental spellings (e.g., **WATR** for **water**).

Stage 3 Spellers
A few children may be ready for more spelling patterns. Write **/w/** words children identify. Point out that a vowel letter comes before **r** in **water** and **worm**. Explain that long words, such as **watermelon,** include a vowel in each syllable.

For more information on the Stages of Spelling Development, see pages Z10–Z15.

ABC Poem and Picture Charts
Use dry erase markers on the laminated pages to highlight and emphasize words, pictures, and targeted sounds.

- Highlight letters on the **Poem Chart**.
- Underline high-frequency words on the **Poem Chart**.
- Circle pictures on the **Picture Chart**.
- Label objects on the **Picture Chart**.

Spelling and Writing
See page Z17 for more information.

Write finger pantomimes with **w** words. Include actions such as *waving in the wind, sprinkling water, opening a window, winding a kite string,* and *eating watermelon.* As you write, ask children to provide letters for sounds they hear. Perform the actions together.

Using the Student Edition: Page 49

Phonemic Awareness and Sound-Symbol Awareness

Help children follow the directions on *Student Edition* page 49.

Use **Meeting Individual Needs** below to extend the practice activities according to the needs of children in your class.

One-Minute Handwriting Hint

Remind children to pause (without lifting the pencil) after each slant stroke in **W** and **w**.

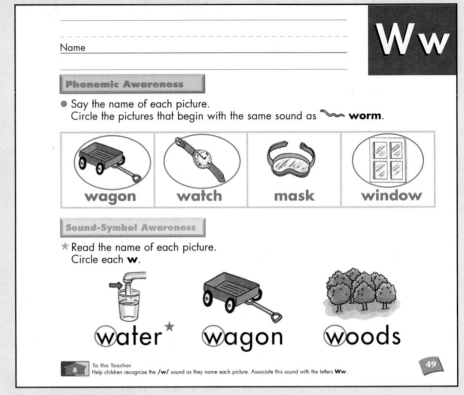

★**Note: Basic Words** are starred.

Meeting Individual Needs

Stage 0 Spellers

Say **bag**. Model how to change the beginning sound to /w/ to make **wag**. Ask children to follow your model with these words: **say** (way), **talk** (walk), **sing** (wing), **call** (wall), **heard** (word), **fill** (will), **bear** (wear), **sent** (went), **need** (weed), **rake** (wake), **good** (wood), **paste** (waste), **giggle** (wiggle). For each correct response, invite children to wiggle their arms and legs.

For more information on the Stages of Spelling Development, see pages Z10–Z15.

Stage 1 Spellers

Use the Stage 0 activity. Ask questions about each /w/ word children say. For example, ask, *"What letter spells the /g/ sound in wiggle?"* (g) *"What letter spells the /ă/ sound in wag?"* (a)

Stage 2 Spellers

Use the Stage 0 activity. Say several of the /w/ words slowly, stretching the sounds (e.g., **wing** = /w/ + /ĭng/). Invite volunteers to write the words. Accept developmental spellings (e.g., **WENG** for **wing**).

Stage 3 Spellers

A few children may be ready for more spelling patterns. Use the Stage 0 activity. Then write words for the pictures on *Student Edition* page 49 and discuss their spellings.

Spelling and Writing

See page Z17 for more information.

Write **walk** on the chalkboard. Invite children to write a few words or sentences about a taking a walk around the school or around their neighborhood. Encourage the use of developmental spelling. Ask children to illustrate their work.

Using the Student Edition: Page 50

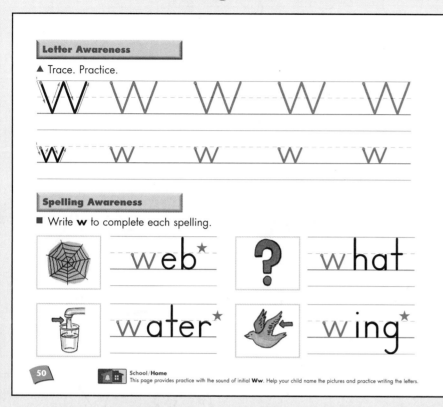

Letter Awareness and Spelling Awareness

Share these letter chants. Ask children to write the letters in the air as you chant together.

W

Slant down right
And slant up, too.
Now make these strokes again,
To write a **W**.

w

Slant down right
And then slant up.
Do this twice,
And your **w** will be nice!

Point out the red directional arrows and the green dots that show where to begin each letter.

Guide children in tracing and writing **W** and **w** to complete the activities on *Student Edition* page 50.

Use **Meeting Individual Needs** below to extend the practice activities according to the needs of children in your class.

Meeting Individual Needs

Stage 0 Spellers

Provide cups of water and clean paintbrushes. Allow groups of children to go to the chalkboard and paint **W** and **w** with water. Check to make sure children are using the correct starting point and stroke sequence.

Stage 1 Spellers

Use the Stage 0 activity. Slowly say words from the **Spelling Awareness** activity on *Student Edition* page 50. Ask children to paint letters for prominent sounds they hear in the words.

Stage 2 Spellers

Use the Stage 0 activity. Write words from the **Spelling Awareness** activity in a large size on the chalkboard. Invite children to either paint over your words or paint the words directly below your model.

Stage 3 Spellers

A few children may be ready to produce conventional (correct) spellings. Call out words from the **Spelling Awareness** activity. Ask children to paint them with water and then check their spelling.

Building Words With Word Families

king, ring, sing, wing, bring, thing, spring

Point out the word part **-ing** in the **Spelling Awareness** activity on *Student Edition* page 50. Display magnetic letters **ing** and say /ing/. Invite volunteers to select other magnetic letters that will yield new words when placed in front of **ing**. Discuss letter combinations that don't yield new words. Say the new words together. Add the **-ing** words to your word wall or to a list of words for writing.

Unit Assessment

See page Z16 for more information.

You may wish to check progress by having children write **W, w,** and one or more **Basic Words** (**web, water, wing, worm**). Note spellings to determine each child's stage of spelling development.

Have children record one **w** word in their **My Words** book (following *Student Edition* page 56).

Fingers Like to Wiggle, Waggle

Fingers like to
    wiggle, waggle,
Wiggle, waggle,
    wiggle, waggle,
Fingers like to
    wiggle, waggle,
Right in front of me.

School/Home
Read the poem several times with your child. Read the poem again as you wiggle your fingers and make a **W** shape by extending the first and second fingers of each hand. Then look for words in the poem that begin with **W** or **w**. Read and write the **w** words together, emphasizing the **/w/** sound heard at the beginning of **water**.

MATERIALS

ABC Poem and Picture Charts

Xx Poem Chart: "Fox in a Box"
Xx Picture Chart

Student Edition

Pages 51–52

Teacher Edition

Pages T143–T148

Basic Words

ox	fox
box	six

★**Note: Basic Words** are starred where they appear in this *Teacher Edition*.

High-Frequency Words

one	red
big	go

Targeted Word Family

-ix

OBJECTIVES

ABC Poem and Picture Charts	Student Edition
Phonemic Awareness: Identify the **/ks/** sound	**Phonemic Awareness:** Identify the **/ks/** sound
Letter Recognition: Recognize **X** and **x**	**Letter Recognition:** Recognize **X** and **x**
Sound-Symbol Awareness: Associate the **/ks/** sound with the letters **Xx**	**Sound-Symbol Awareness:** Associate the **/ks/** sound with the letters **Xx**
Early Reading: Engage in repeated readings of the poem "Fox in a Box"	**Early Reading:** Read picture labels that contain **x**
Early Writing: Write a class big book titled *What's in the Box?*	**Early Writing:** Write **Xx**; use developmental spelling to write about being six years old

Language and Cultural Differences

This unit focuses on the use of **x** to stand for **/ks/,** the blended sound **x** usually represents at the end of English words such as **box**. English language learners may need practice in making the **/ks/** sound smoothly. It begins with **/k/,** which is produced by blocking air at the soft palate. The air is then released suddenly and the tongue immediately moves to form **/s/**. For children acquiring English, point to pictures in the unit and have children say their names.

Using the ABC Poem and Picture Charts:
Xx Poem Chart

Read "Fox in a Box" aloud, pointing to each word. Sing the poem together, using the tune to "The Farmer in the Dell."

Ask children who are six years old to raise their hands. Explain that **six** ends with the sound **/ks/**. Have children repeat **/ks/,** noticing how the mouth looks and feels. Point to **Xx** at the top of the chart and explain that **x** often makes the **/ks/** sound at the end of words.

Use **Meeting Individual Needs** below to develop phonemic awareness and sound-symbol awareness according to the needs of children in your class.

School/Home
You may wish to duplicate the page that follows *Teacher Edition* page T147 so that children have their own copy of the poem.

Xx

Fox in a Box
A-walking we will go.
A-walking we will go.

First we'll catch
  one red fox.★
Then we'll catch
  one brown ox.★

We'll put them in a
  great big box,★
And then we'll let
  them go.

★**Note: Basic Words** are starred.

Meeting Individual Needs

Stage 0 Spellers

Have volunteers point to each **x**. Ask where **x** is in the words. (at the end) Show children how to cross their index fingers to make **x** as they say **/ks/**. Read the poem, asking children to hold up **x** fingers when they hear a word with **/ks/**.

Stage 1 Spellers

Use the Stage 0 activity. Stretch out and count the sounds in each **x** word (e.g., **fox** = **/f/ + /ŏ/ + /ks/**). Ask questions such as *"What letter spells the /b/ sound in box?"* (b)

Stage 2 Spellers

Use the Stage 0 activity. Read the poem again, stretching and counting the sounds in each **x** word, as in the Stage 1 activity. Write the words, asking children to provide a letter for each sound and an **x** for **/ks/**.

Stage 3 Spellers

A few children may be ready for more spelling patterns. Explain that some words rhyme with **ox** but end with **cks** (e.g., **socks, clocks, blocks**). Ask children to write more words with the **-ox** and **-ocks** patterns.

For more information on the Stages of Spelling Development, see pages Z10–Z15.

High-Frequency Words
one, red, big, go

Point out **one, red, big,** and **go** in the poem. Ask volunteers to name the letters in each word. Clap and chant the spellings. Ask volunteers to find the words in the poem. Add the words to your word wall or to a list of words for writing.

ABC Using Manipulatives

Give two craft sticks to each child. Show how to hold them up while crossing them to make an **X** shape. Then say a number of words such as **keys, buzz, box, kick, fox, ox, ax, freeze,** and **wax.** Ask children to hold up **X** when they hear a word with **/ks/**.

Using the **ABC** Poem and Picture Charts:
Xx Picture Chart

Invite children to describe the scene on the chart. Children may wish to tell about a time they had an adventure in the woods.

Point to **Xx** and ask children what sound it makes at the end of words. (/ks/) Use **Meeting Individual Needs** below to develop phonemic awareness and sound-symbol awareness according to the needs of the children in your class.

Pictured Words....................
★box, ★fox, ax, ★six, ★ox, mix, wax, exit

Meeting Individual Needs

Stage 0 Spellers

Prompt children to find pictures of items whose names end with **/ks/**. Ask, *"Do you see the number six? Six ends with /ks/."* Write each word on chart paper. Ask a volunteer to underline **x** in each word.

Stage 1 Spellers

Ask children to find pictures whose names end with **/ks/**. Stretch and count the sounds in each word (e.g., **ax = /ă/ + /ks/**). Write the words, asking children to provide letters for prominent sounds.

Stage 2 Spellers

Challenge children to find all eight pictures whose names contain **x**. Pronounce the words and ask children to write a letter (or choose a magnetic letter) for each sound. Accept developmental spellings (e.g., **BAX** for **box**).

Stage 3 Spellers

A few children may be ready for more spelling patterns. Focus on the vowel sounds and letters in the **x** words. Ask for rhyming words that end with **-ox**. (box, fox, ox) With **-ix**? (six, mix, fix) With **-ax**? (ax, sax, tax, wax)

For more information on the Stages of Spelling Development, see pages Z10–Z15.

ABC Poem and Picture Charts

Use dry erase markers on the laminated pages to highlight and emphasize words, pictures, and targeted sounds.

- Highlight letters on the **Poem Chart**.
- Underline high-frequency words on the **Poem Chart**.
- Circle pictures on the **Picture Chart**.
- Label objects on the **Picture Chart**.

Spelling and Writing

See page Z17 for more information.

Write a *What's in the Box?* big book. Place a small item in a shoebox and write three clues about it. Ask children to guess, and then reveal the item and write its name on the next page. Continue with several items. Ask groups of children to illustrate the pages.

Phonemic Awareness and Sound-Symbol Awareness

Help children follow the directions on *Student Edition* page 51.

Use **Meeting Individual Needs** below to extend the practice activities according to the needs of children in your class.

One-Minute Handwriting Hint

Remind children to begin each slant line in **X** and **x** at the top. The lines should cross halfway.

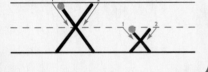

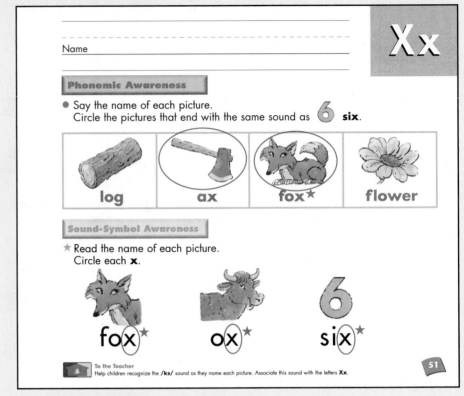

★**Note: Basic Words** are starred.

Meeting Individual Needs

Stage 0 Spellers

Find a fox puppet or make one from a sock and felt scraps. In a small cardboard box, cut a hole the size of your hand so you can make the puppet hide in the box or pop out. Tell children they can see the fox by saying whether a word ends with **/ks/**. Say these words slowly: **fix, rat, fox, cap, mix, sat, six, pop, miss, bear, ox, ax.** For each correct response, make the fox pop out of the box.

For more information on the Stages of Spelling Development, see pages Z10–Z15.

Stage 1 Spellers

Use the Stage 0 activity. Repeat **x** words from the activity and from *Student Edition* page 51. Ask children to provide letters for prominent sounds as you write the words on chart paper.

Stage 2 Spellers

Use the Stage 0 activity. Give a clue to one of the words from the activity or from *Student Edition* page 51. For **six,** the clue might be "more than five." Ask children to write the words. Accept developmental spellings (e.g., **MEX** for **mix**).

Stage 3 Spellers

A few children may be ready for more spelling patterns. Continue the Stage 2 activity by asking children to check their spelling after they write words based on your clues.

Spelling and Writing

See page Z17 for more information.

Ask children to write and illustrate several words or sentences that tell what they think will happen during the year that they are six years old. Encourage the use of developmental spelling.

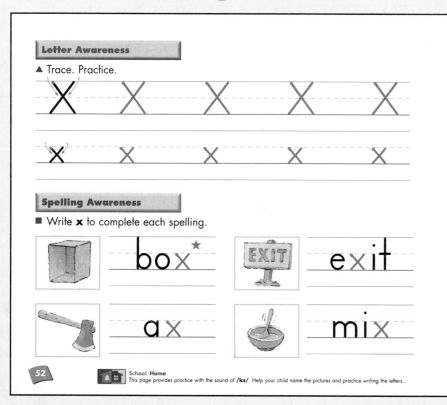

Letter Awareness and Spelling Awareness

Share this letter chant. Ask children to write the letters in the air as you chant together.

Xx

Slant right. Lift.
Now quick like a fox,
Slant left, and
Get ready to finish **ox**.

Point out the red directional arrows and the green dots that show where to begin each letter.

Guide children in tracing and writing **X** and **x** to complete the activities on *Student Edition* page 52.

Use **Meeting Individual Needs** below to extend the practice activities according to the needs of children in your class.

Meeting Individual Needs

Stage 0 Spellers
Allow children to practice writing **X** and **x** in a large size on the chalkboard or on an easel. Watch to make sure children are following the correct stroke sequence.

Stage 1 Spellers
Use the Stage 0 activity. As children are standing at the chalkboard or easel, slowly say words from the **Spelling Awareness** activity on *Student Edition* page 52. Ask children to write letters for prominent sounds they hear.

Stage 2 Spellers
Use the Stage 0 activity. Spell words from the **Spelling Awareness** activity aloud (e.g., e-x-i-t for **exit**). Ask children to write the words in a large size.

Stage 3 Spellers
A few children may be ready to produce conventional (correct) spellings. Call out words from the **Spelling Awareness** activity and ask children to write them on the chalkboard or easel. Help children check their spelling.

Building Words With Word Families
fix, mix, six

Point out the word part **-ix** in the **Spelling Awareness** activity on *Student Edition* page 52. On chart paper, write "To fix the pudding mix, add six drops of milk." Ask a volunteer to underline the words that end in **ix**. Say the words together. Add the **-ix** words to your word wall or to a list of words for writing.

Unit Assessment
See page Z16 for more information.

You may wish to check progress by having children write **X, x,** and one or more **Basic Words (ox, fox, box, six)**. Note spellings to determine each child's stage of spelling development.

Have children record one **x** word in their **My Words** book (following *Student Edition* page 56).

Xx

Fox in a Box

A-walking we will go.
A-walking we will go.

First we'll catch
 one red fox.
Then we'll catch
 one brown ox.

We'll put them in a
 great big box,
And then we'll let
 them go.

School/Home
Read the poem several times with your child. Sing it together to the tune of "The Farmer in the Dell." Then look for words in the poem that end with **x**. Read and write the **x** words together, emphasizing the **/ks/** sound heard at the end of **box**.

MATERIALS

ABC Poem and Picture Charts

Yy Poem Chart: "When I Get Up in the Morning"

Yy Picture Chart

Student Edition

Pages 53–54

Teacher Edition

Pages T149–T154

Basic Words

yawn	yarn
yell	yellow

★Note: **Basic Words** are starred where they appear in this *Teacher Edition*.

High-Frequency Words

when	and
my	because

Targeted Word Family

-ell

OBJECTIVES

ABC Poem and Picture Charts

Phonemic Awareness:
Identify the /y/ sound

Letter Recognition:
Recognize **Y** and **y**

Sound-Symbol Awareness:
Associate the /y/ sound with the letters **Yy**

Early Reading:
Engage in repeated readings of the poem "When I Get Up in the Morning"

Early Writing:
Write a class journal entry about what children did yesterday

Student Edition

Phonemic Awareness:
Identify the /y/ sound

Letter Recognition:
Recognize **Y** and **y**

Sound-Symbol Awareness:
Associate the /y/ sound with the letters **Yy**

Early Reading:
Read picture labels that begin with **y**

Early Writing:
Write **Yy**; use developmental spelling to write about a morning routine

---

Language and Cultural Differences

The letter **y** at the beginning of a word or syllable stands for a consonant glide (also called a "semivowel"). In producing /**y**/, the tongue is pushed forward and up toward the roof (or palate) of the mouth, and the jaw is barely open. As a glide, /**y**/ begins with /ee/ and then glides into the vowel that follows, as in **yellow** /**ee-eh-loh**/.

For children who are acquiring English, point to pictures in this unit. Say the picture names slowly, emphasizing the /**y**/ sound, and have children repeat after you.

Using the ABC Poem and Picture Charts: Yy Poem Chart

Phonemic Awareness and Sound-Symbol Awareness

Read "When I Get Up in the Morning" aloud, pointing to each word. Ask children to stand and act out the waking-up motions as they recite the poem.

Say **yellow**. Explain that **yellow** begins with the **/y/** sound. (**Note:** Be sure to say **/y/**, not **/yuh/**, to isolate the consonant sound.) Have children repeat **/y/**, noticing how the mouth looks and feels. Associate this sound with **Yy** at the top of the chart.

Use **Meeting Individual Needs** below to develop phonemic awareness and sound-symbol awareness.

School/Home
You may wish to duplicate the page that follows *Teacher Edition* page T153 so that children have their own copy of the poem.

Yy

When I Get Up in the Morning

When I get up in the morning
I tumble out of bed,
I yawn*and stretch and
   stretch and yawn
And scratch my sleepy head.

When I get up in the morning
I always rub my tummy,
Because I know
   my breakfast's waiting—
Yummy yummy yummy.

—Clive Webster

★**Note: Basic Words** are starred.

Meeting Individual Needs

Stage 0 Spellers

Read the poem, asking children to clap for words that begin with **/y/**. Read the poem again, pausing to allow children to shout the rhyming words **bed** and **head, tummy** and **yummy**.

Stage 1 Spellers

Use the Stage 0 activity. Then ask questions about letters and sounds in the words. For example, ask, *"What letter spells the /y/ sound in yawn?"* (y) *"What letter spells the /m/ sound in yummy?"* (m)

Stage 2 Spellers

Cover the poem. Ask volunteers to write **yawn** and **yummy** on chart paper, giving one letter for each sound they hear. Accept developmental spellings (e.g., **YON** for **yawn** and **YME** for **yummy**).

Stage 3 Spellers

A few children may be ready for more spelling patterns. Start with **yawn**. Make new words using the **-awn** pattern. (dawn, lawn, fawn)

For more information on the Stages of Spelling Development, see pages Z10–Z15.

High-Frequency Words
when, and, my, because

Point out **when, and, my,** and **because** in the poem. Ask volunteers to name the letters in each word. Clap and chant the spellings. Ask volunteers to find the words in the poem. Add the words to your word wall or to a list of words for writing.

Using Manipulatives

Provide yellow yarn, construction paper, and glue. Ask children to choose a **y** word such as **yellow, yo-yo,** or **yak,** to model with yarn on the paper. Encourage children to trace their tactile yarn words with their fingers and to pass them around the room to share.

Using the ABC Poem and Picture Charts:
Yy Picture Chart

Phonemic Awareness
and
Sound-Symbol Awareness

Invite children to describe the scene on the chart. Children may wish to talk about a time they rode on a school bus.

Point to **Yy** and ask children what sound it makes. (/y/) Use **Meeting Individual Needs** below to develop phonemic awareness and sound-symbol awareness according to the needs of the children in your class.

Yy

Pictured Words. . . . .
★yellow, yo-yo, ★yawn, ★yarn, yard,
★yell, yak, yogurt

Meeting Individual Needs

Stage 0 Spellers

Prompt children to find pictures of items whose names begin with **/y/**. Ask, *"Do you see some yogurt? Yogurt begins with /y/."* Write each word on chart paper. Ask a volunteer to underline **y** in each word.

Stage 1 Spellers

As children find pictures whose names begin with **/y/**, stretch and count the sounds in several words (e.g., **yell = /y/ + /ĕ/ + /l/**). Write the words, asking children to provide letters for prominent sounds.

Stage 2 Spellers

Challenge children to find all eight pictures that begin with **/y/**. Pronounce the words and ask children to write a letter (or choose a magnetic letter) for each sound. Accept developmental spellings (e.g., **YELO** for **yellow**).

Stage 3 Spellers

A few children may be ready for more spelling patterns. Write **/y/** words children identify. Point out the double consonants in **yell** and **yellow**. Remind children to include **ar** in **yarn**.

For more information on the Stages of Spelling Development, see pages Z10–Z15.

ABC Poem and Picture Charts

Use dry erase markers on the laminated pages to highlight and emphasize words, pictures, and targeted sounds.

- Highlight letters on the **Poem Chart**.
- Underline high-frequency words on the **Poem Chart**.
- Circle pictures on the **Picture Chart**.
- Label objects on the **Picture Chart**.

Spelling and Writing

See page Z17 for more information.

On chart paper, write a class journal entry about what the children did yesterday. Ask each child to contribute a word or sentence. As you write, ask children to provide letters for prominent sounds they hear.

Using the Student Edition: Page 53

Phonemic Awareness and Sound-Symbol Awareness

Help children follow the directions on *Student Edition* page 53.

Use **Meeting Individual Needs** below to extend the practice activities according to the needs of the children in your class.

One-Minute Handwriting Hint

Y and **y** include several slant strokes. To practice slant strokes, have children use triangle shapes to draw pictures of tents, sailboats, cat ears, etc.

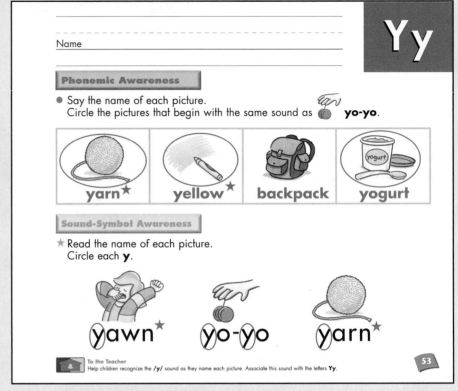

★**Note: Basic Words** are starred.

Meeting Individual Needs

Stage 0 Spellers

Practice the **/y/** sound. Tell children you will say the last part of a word and you would like them to say the whole word by adding **/y/** to the beginning. Use these word parts: **am** (yam), **awn** (yawn), **ard** (yard), **ear** (year), **ell** (yell), **es** (yes), **ou** (you), **oung** (young), **ellow** (yellow), **esterday** (yesterday). You may wish to give a yellow smiley face sticker for each correct response.

For more information on the Stages of Spelling Development, see pages Z10–Z15.

Stage 1 Spellers

Use the Stage 0 activity. After children say each **y** word, ask questions about its sounds and letters. For example, ask, *"What letter spells /y/ in yellow?"* (y) *"What letter spells the /n/ sound in yarn?"* (n)

Stage 2 Spellers

Use the Stage 0 activity. Ask children to count the sounds in several of the words on *Student Edition* page 53 as you say them slowly (e.g., **yo-yo** = /y/ + /ō/ + /y/ + /ō/). Show how to write the words with one letter for each sound.

Stage 3 Spellers

A few children may be ready for more spelling patterns. Use the Stage 0 activity. Start with **yam** and **yell**. Make new words with the **-am** and **-ell** patterns. (jam, ham; bell, sell)

Spelling and Writing

See page Z17 for more information.

Ask children to describe their usual routine for waking up and getting ready for school. Encourage them to number and illustrate each step in the process. Accept developmental spelling.

Using the Student Edition: Page 54

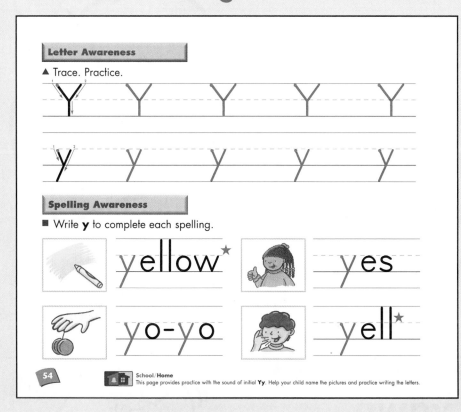

Letter Awareness

and

Spelling Awareness

Share these letter chants. Ask children to write the letters in the air as you chant together.

Y

Slant right. Lift. Slant left.
Then pull straight down.
Write to Yasmin, Yetta, and Yoko
To invite them to town.

y

Slant right. Lift.
You're not done yet.
To finish small **y,**
You've got to slant left.

Point out the red directional arrows and the green dots that show where to begin each letter.

Guide children in tracing and writing **Y** and **y** to complete the activities on *Student Edition* page 54.

Use **Meeting Individual Needs** below to extend the practice activities according to the needs of the children in your class.

Meeting Individual Needs

Stage 0 Spellers

Have children sculpt **Y** and **y** from clay. Encourage them to trace the clay letters with their fingers, using the correct starting point.

Stage 1 Spellers

Use the Stage 0 activity. Slowly say words from the **Spelling Awareness** activity on *Student Edition* page 54. Ask children to sculpt letters from clay to match prominent sounds they hear.

Stage 2 Spellers

Write the words from the **Spelling Awareness** activity on large cards and laminate them. Allow children to use them as a base for building the words with clay.

Stage 3 Spellers

A few children may be ready to produce conventional (correct) spellings. Call out words from the **Spelling Awareness** activity and ask children to write them or sculpt them with clay. Have children use their books to check spelling.

Building Words With Word Families

bell, fell, sell, tell, well, yell, shell, spell

Point out the word part **-ell** in the **Spelling Awareness** activity on *Student Edition* page 54. Give a clue for each **-ell** word you want children to make. For example, say, *"This is what happened to Jack when he went up the hill."* (fell) Ask children to supply the beginning sound and corresponding letter for each word. Add the **-ell** words to your word wall or to a list of words for writing.

Unit Assessment

See page Z16 for more information.

You may wish to check progress by having children write **Y, y,** and one or more **Basic Words** (**yawn, yarn, yell, yellow**). Note spellings to determine each child's stage of spelling development.

Have children record one **y** word in their **My Words** book (following *Student Edition* page 56).

Yy

When I Get Up in the Morning

When I get up in the morning
I tumble out of bed,
I yawn and stretch and
    stretch and yawn
And scratch my sleepy head.

When I get up in the morning
I always rub my tummy,
Because I know
    my breakfast's waiting—
Yummy yummy yummy.

—Clive Webster

Copyright © 1996 by Clive Webster. Reprinted by permission of Clive Webster.

School/Home
Read the poem several times with your child. Read the poem again as you act out the waking-up motions. Then look for words in the poem that begin with **Y** or **y**. Read and write the **y** words together, emphasizing the **/y/** sound heard at the beginning of **yellow**.

MATERIALS

ABC Poem and Picture Charts

Zz Poem Chart: "In Winter When
It's Zero"

Zz Picture Chart

Student Edition

Pages 55–56

Teacher Edition

Pages T155–T160

Basic Words

zero	zebra
zoo	zip

★Note: **Basic Words** are starred where they appear in this *Teacher Edition*.

High-Frequency Words

when	home
play	all

Targeted Word Family

-ip

OBJECTIVES

ABC Poem and Picture Charts

Phonemic Awareness:
Identify the /z/ sound

Letter Recognition:
Recognize Z and z

Sound-Symbol Awareness:
Associate the /z/ sound with the letters Zz

Early Reading:
Engage in repeated readings of the poem "In Winter When It's Zero"

Early Writing:
Write sentences with z words and arrange them in a Z shape

Student Edition

Phonemic Awareness:
Identify the /z/ sound

Letter Recognition:
Recognize Z and z

Sound-Symbol Awareness:
Associate the /z/ sound with the letters Zz

Early Reading:
Read a sentence related to the poem "In Winter When It's Zero"

Early Writing:
Write Zz; use developmental spelling to write facts about an animal for a zoo sign

---

Language and Cultural Differences

For /z/, the tongue is curled slightly and raised while air is forced through the rounded space. Young children who have lisps due to missing front teeth may pronounce /z/ as /th/. Realize that children may not be able to pronounce /z/ until their front teeth appear.

If you whisper **zebra,** you will hear a voiceless /s/ instead of /z/. Some languages, like Spanish, have only the voiceless /s/ and lack /z/ (as pronounced in English words) altogether. A few languages, including Hawaiian, have neither /s/ nor /z/.

Using the ABC Poem and Picture Charts: Zz Poem Chart

Read "In Winter When It's Zero" aloud, pointing to each word. Read the poem again. Invite children to jump up and down in place as they chant the poem together.

Say **zoo**. Explain that **zoo** begins with the /z/ sound. (**Note:** Be sure to say /z/, not /zuh/, to isolate the consonant sound.) Have children repeat /z/, noticing how the mouth looks and feels. Associate this sound with **Zz** at the top of the chart.

Use **Meeting Individual Needs** below to develop phonemic awareness and sound-symbol awareness according to the needs of the children in your class.

School/Home
You may wish to duplicate the page that follows *Teacher Edition* page T159 so that children have their own copy of the poem.

Zz

In Winter When It's Zero

In winter when it's zero★
I zoom straight home
   from play,
But when the springtime
   sun is bright
I zigzag
   All
The
   Way!

—Margaret and
John Travers Moore

★**Note: Basic Words** are starred.

Meeting Individual Needs

Stage 0 Spellers

Invite children to chant the poem while clapping. Read the poem again, asking children to clap only for words that begin with /z/. Point to the z words and ask children to finger-trace a **Z** shape in the air.

Stage 1 Spellers

Say and stretch the sounds in each **z** word from the poem (e.g., **zero** = /z/ + /ē/ + /r/ + /ō/). Ask children to blend the sounds to say the word. Then ask questions such as *"What letter spells the /ō/ sound in zero?"* (o)

Stage 2 Spellers

Tape a blank card over **zero, zoom,** and **zigzag**. Say the words slowly and then write them on the cards, asking children to provide a letter for each sound. Accept developmental spellings (e.g., **ZRO** for **zero**).

Stage 3 Spellers

A few children may be ready for more spelling patterns. Start with **zig** and **zag**. Ask children to write new words with the **-ig** and **-ag** patterns. (dig, big; bag, wag)

For more information on the Stages of Spelling Development, see pages Z10–Z15.

High-Frequency Words
when, home, play, all

Point out **when, home, play,** and **all** in the poem. Ask volunteers to name the letters in each word. Clap and chant the spellings. Ask volunteers to find the words in the poem. Add the words to your word wall or to a list of words for writing.

ABC Using Manipulatives

Ask children to cut a **Z** shape from drawing paper and decorate it with zebra stripes. Invite children to use their decorated letters in a learning center along with magnetic letters or plain letter cards to spell words such as **zoo, zebra,** and **zip**.

Using the **ABC** Poem and Picture Charts:
Zz Picture Chart

Invite children to describe the scene on the chart. Children may wish to make up a story that tells why the zebra has left the zoo.

Point to **Zz** and ask children what sound it makes. (/z/) Use **Meeting Individual Needs** below to develop phonemic awareness and sound-symbol awareness according to the needs of the children in your class.

Pictured Words....................
★zebra, zipper, zigzag, ★zero, ★zoo, ZIP code, zoom

Meeting Individual Needs

Stage 0 Spellers

Prompt children to find pictures of items whose names begin with /z/. Ask, *"Do you see a zipper? Zipper begins with /z/."* Write each word on chart paper. Ask a volunteer to underline **z** in each word.

Stage 1 Spellers

Ask children to find pictures whose names begin with /z/. Stretch and count the sounds in each word (e.g., **zoo** = /z/ + /o͞o/). Write the words, asking children to provide letters for prominent sounds.

Stage 2 Spellers

Challenge children to find all seven pictures that begin with /z/. Pronounce the words and ask children to write a letter (or choose a magnetic letter) for each sound. Accept developmental spellings (e.g., **ZEBRU** for **zebra**).

Stage 3 Spellers

A few children may be ready for more spelling patterns. Write /z/ words children identify. Explain that the sound at the end of **zebra** (i.e., the schwa sound) is difficult to spell because the letter is difficult to hear. In **zebra,** it is spelled **a**.

For more information on the Stages of Spelling Development, see pages Z10–Z15.

ABC Poem and Picture Charts

Use dry erase markers on the laminated pages to highlight and emphasize words, pictures, and targeted sounds.

• Highlight letters on the **Poem Chart**.
• Underline high-frequency words on the **Poem Chart**.
• Circle pictures on the **Picture Chart**.
• Label objects on the **Picture Chart**.

Spelling and Writing

See page Z17 for more information.

Provide a strip of paper for each child. Ask children to write a sentence on the strip that contains at least two **z** words. (You may wish to supply a list of **z** words.) Staple the sentences to a bulletin board in a **Z** shape.

Phonemic Awareness
and
Sound-Symbol Awareness

Help children follow the directions on *Student Edition* page 55.

Use **Meeting Individual Needs** below to extend the practice activities according to the needs of the children in your class.

One-Minute Handwriting Hint

Show children how to pause (without lifting the pencil) before and after the slant stroke in **Z** and **z**. Emphasize that each horizontal line is written from left to right.

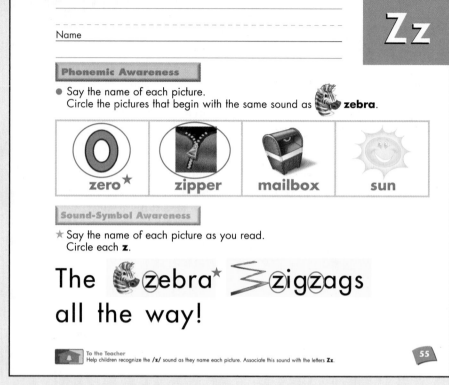

★**Note: Basic Words** are starred.

Meeting Individual Needs

Stage 0 Spellers

Distribute self-sticking notes and ask children to draw a zoo animal on each note. Draw a large circle on the chalkboard and label it **ZOO**. Tell children they can return their animals to the zoo by listening to words you say and changing the beginning sound to **/z/**. Use these words: **hero** (zero), **tip** (zip), **rap** (zap), **boom** (zoom), **dipper** (zipper), **bone** (zone), **moo** (zoo), **best** (zest). For each response, have a child place his or her animal in the zoo.

For more information on the Stages of Spelling Development, see pages Z10–Z15.

Stage 1 Spellers

Use the Stage 0 activity. After each child places an animal in the zoo, repeat the **/z/** word. Ask the volunteer questions such as *"What letter spells the /z/ sound in zoo?"* (z) *"What letter spells the /p/ sound in zipper?"* (p)

Stage 2 Spellers

Use the Stage 0 activity. After each child places an animal in the zoo, ask him or her to write the **z** word on the chalkboard, giving one letter for each sound. Accept developmental spellings (e.g., **ZEPR** for **zipper**).

Stage 3 Spellers

A few children may be ready for more spelling patterns. Use the Stage 0 activity. Write **zip** and **zap**. Ask children to write new words with the **-ip** and **-ap** patterns. (lip, rip; map, nap)

Spelling and Writing

See page Z17 for more information.

Invite children to draw an animal and its habitat at the zoo. Ask them to write a sign for the exhibit that gives two common facts about the animal. Encourage the use of developmental spelling.

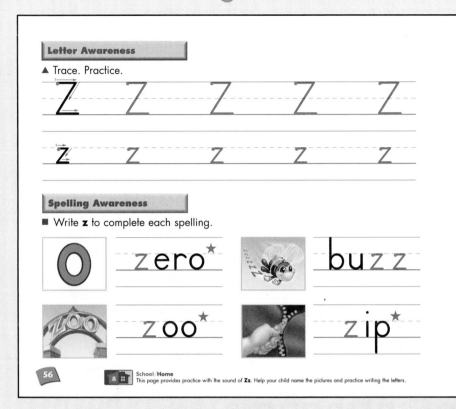

Share these letter chants. Ask children to write the letters in the air as you chant together.

Z

Begin **Z** with a slide—
Make sure you slide right!
Slant left to the baseline;
Then end with one more slide right.

z

Slide right.
Slant down left and then slide right.
Both **z**'s are the same—
Except for the height.

Point out the red directional arrows and the green dots that show where to begin each letter.

Guide children in tracing and writing **Z** and **z** to complete the activities on *Student Edition* page 56.

Use **Meeting Individual Needs** below to extend the practice activities according to the needs of the children in your class.

Meeting Individual Needs

Stage 0 Spellers

Provide a zip-top bag for each child. Spread a small amount of washable paint in each bag and seal it. Ask children to lay the bags flat and use them as "magic slates" for finger-tracing **Z** and **z**. Check to make sure they are following the correct stroke sequence.

Stage 1 Spellers

Use the Stage 0 activity. Slowly say words from the **Spelling Awareness** activity on *Student Edition* page 56. Ask children to trace letters for prominent sounds they hear in the words.

Stage 2 Spellers

Use the Stage 0 activity. Slowly say words from the **Spelling Awareness** activity. Ask children to write a letter for each sound they hear. Accept developmental spellings (e.g., **ZIRO** for **zero**).

Stage 3 Spellers

A few children may be ready to produce conventional (correct) spellings. Call out words from the **Spelling Awareness** activity. Ask children to trace them on the "magic slates" and then check their spelling.

Building Words With Word Families

dip, lip, rip, sip, tip, zip

Point out the word part **-ip** in the **Spelling Awareness** activity on *Student Edition* page 56. Ask two volunteers to stand and hold a short length of rope between them. Use a clothespin to attach a card with **ip**. Invite volunteers to pin cards with **d, l, r, s, t,** and **z** beside **ip**. Read the new words together. Add the **-ip** words to your word wall or to a list of words for writing.

Unit Assessment

See page Z16 for more information.

You may wish to check progress by having children write **Z, z,** and one or more **Basic Words** (**zero, zebra, zoo, zip**). Note spellings to determine each child's stage of spelling development.

Have children record one **z** word in their **My Words** book (following *Student Edition* page 56).

Zz

In Winter When It's Zero

In winter when it's zero
I zoom straight home
    from play,
But when the springtime
    sun is bright
I zigzag
    All
The
    Way!

—Margaret and
John Travers Moore

School/Home
Read the poem several times with your child. Encourage him or her to zoom a toy car or animal around a tabletop while reciting the poem. Then look for words in the poem that begin with **Z** or **z**. Read and write the **z** words together, emphasizing the **/z/** sound heard at the beginning of **zoo**.

Using the Student Edition: Pages 57–64

Children can show their spelling progress by writing and illustrating one word for each letter of the alphabet on the **My Words** pages. Words may include **Basic Words** or other words from each unit, words you choose, or words that children self-select based on their interests. A complete list of words included in *Spelling Connections for Kindergarten* begins below. **More Words for Writing** are also suggested for each letter.

As children write their words, encourage the use of developmental spelling. You may wish to use the completed pages during parent conferences as the year progresses to explain the value of developmental spelling and showcase children's growing knowledge of sounds and letters. A child's writing on the pages will provide a means to assess his or her stage of spelling development. (See pages Z10–Z15.) At the end of the year, help children tear out the **My Words** pages and attach a construction paper cover to make a book to take home.

S	= **Student Edition**
Po	= **Poem Chart**
Pi	= **Picture Chart**
★	= **Basic Word**
HF	= **High-Frequency Word**

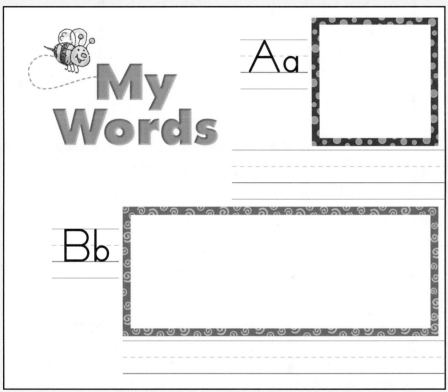

Aa

a (HF), about (Po), acorn (Pi), acrobat (Pi), all (HF), ★alligator (S, Pi), alphabet (Pi), am (Po), anchor (S, Pi), ★and (S, Po, HF), anthill (Pi), ★ants (S, Po, Pi), ape (Pi), ★apple (S, Pi), apron (Pi), are (HF), arrow (Pi), as (HF), astronaut (Pi), at (Po, HF), away (Po), fan (S)

More Words for Writing: act, add, address, after, ask, ax

Bb

baa (Po), ★bag (S, Pi), bags (Po), balloon (Pi), barn (Pi), baseball (Pi), ★bat (S, Pi), be (HF), because (HF), bee (S, Pi), bicycle (Pi), big (S, HF), bingo (Pi), bird (S, Pi), black (Po), blue (HF), bow (Pi), ★boy (S, Po, Pi), ★bus (S, Pi), but (HF)

More Words for Writing: baby, banana, bear, bed, birthday, book

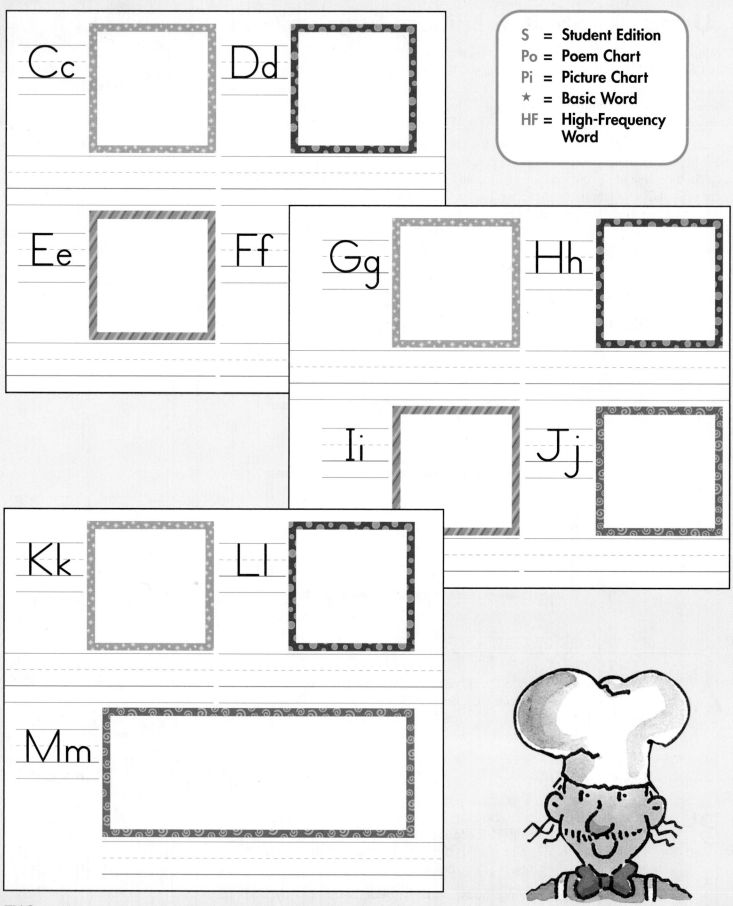

Cc Dd Ee Ff Gg Hh Ii Jj Kk Ll Mm

S = Student Edition
Po = Poem Chart
Pi = Picture Chart
★ = Basic Word
HF = High-Frequency Word

TI62

Cc

came (HF), camera (Pi), ★can (S, Po, Pi, HF), candy (Pi), cap (S, Pi), ★cat (S, Pi), catch (Po), caterpillar (Pi), cloud (Pi), computer (S, Pi), corn (Pi), cow (Pi), ★cows (S, Po), ★cup (S, Pi)

More Words for Writing: calendar, camel, camp, carrot, coat, color

Dd

day (S), deer (S, Pi), dinosaur (Pi), ★dish (S, Po, Pi), do (HF), ★dog (S, Po, Pi), doll (Pi), dolphin (Pi), doughnuts (Pi), ★down (S, HF), dress (Pi), drum (Pi), ★duck (S, Pi)

More Words for Writing: dad, did, dig, dollar, drink, dust

Ee

eagle (Pi), ear (Pi), ★egg (S, Po, Pi), eggplant (Pi), elbow (S, Pi), elephant (S, Pi), eleven (Pi), ★elf (S, Pi), engine (Pi), envelope (Pi), eraser (Pi), ★Meg (S, Po, Pi), ★net (S, Pi), regular (S, Po)

More Words for Writing: echo, edge, elevator, elk, end, every

Ff

fan (Pi), farmer (Pi), fee (S, Po), ★fence (S, Pi), ★finger (S, Po, Pi), fire engine (Pi), firefighter (Pi), ★fish (S, Pi), flag (Pi), flamingo (Pi), flashlight (Pi), fly (S), fog (S), for (HF), forest (Pi), ★fox (S, Pi), frog (Pi)

More Words for Writing: face, fall, fast, feet, fork, four

Gg

★game (S, Pi), garbage (S, Po), garden (Pi), ★gate (S, Pi), geese (S, Po, Pi), gift (Pi), ★girls (S, Po, Pi), go (S, HF), goat (Pi), ★goats (S, Po), good (Po, HF), got (S), grapes (Pi), grass (Pi), great (Po), guitar (S, Pi)

More Words for Writing: get, giggle, give, gold, gorilla, green

Hh

hammock (Pi), hand (S), happy (S), happy face (Pi), ★hat (S, Pi), have (HF), hay (Pi), heart (S, Pi), hedgehog (Pi), ★hill (S, Po, Pi), hippo (Pi), hive (Po, Pi), ★hole (S, Po, Pi), home (HF), hook (Pi), horn (Pi), hose (Pi), hot dog (Pi), ★house (S, Po, Pi, HF)

More Words for Writing: hair, hamster, hatch, helicopter, hero, horse

Ii

I (HF), ice skates (Pi), icicle (Pi), if (HF), igloo (S, Pi), iguana (Pi), ill (S, Po), ★in (S, Po, HF), ★inch (S, Pi), inchworm (Pi), ★ink (S, Pi), insects (Pi), invitation (Pi), iron (Pi), is (HF), itty-bitty (Po), ivy (Pi), pig (S, Pi), ★pin (S, Pi)

More Words for Writing: idea, inside, invention, island, itch

Jj

Jack (S, Po, Pi), ★jam (S, Pi), ★jar (S, Pi), jeep (S, Pi), jelly beans (S, Pi), ★jet (S, Pi), jewels (Pi), jokes (Pi), juice (Pi), ★jump (S, Po)

More Words for Writing: jack-in-the-box, jeans, job, juggle, jungle

Kk

kangaroo (Pi), ★keep (S), keeping (Po), ketchup (Pi), kettle (S, Pi), kettle's (Po), ★key (S, Po, Pi), king (S, Pi), kiss (Pi), kitchen (Po, Pi), ★kite (S, Pi), ★kitten (S, Po, Pi), koala (Pi)

More Words for Writing: kayak, keyboard, kick, kind, kiwi

Ll

★ladder (S, Pi), lady (Pi), ladybug (Pi), lamb (Pi), lamp (S, Pi), ★lap (S, Po, Pi), lazy (S, Po), lemon (S, Pi), lemonade (Pi), leopard (Pi), let (Po), lid (S), lies (S), like (HF), likes (HF), lion (Pi), lips (S), ★little (S, Po, HF), lizard (Pi), lobster (Pi), ★lock (S, Pi), log (Pi), lollipop (Pi), love (HF), lying (Po)

More Words for Writing: lake, last, leaf, leg, letter

Mm

macaroni (Pi), make (HF), ★man (S, Po, Pi), map (S), marshmallow (Pi), me (HF), meatball (Pi), ★milk (S, Pi), mirror (Pi), ★mop (S, Pi), mountain (Pi), ★mud (S, Pi), muffin (S, Po, Pi), mushroom (Pi), my (HF)

More Words for Writing: mask, math, men, mile, moon, music

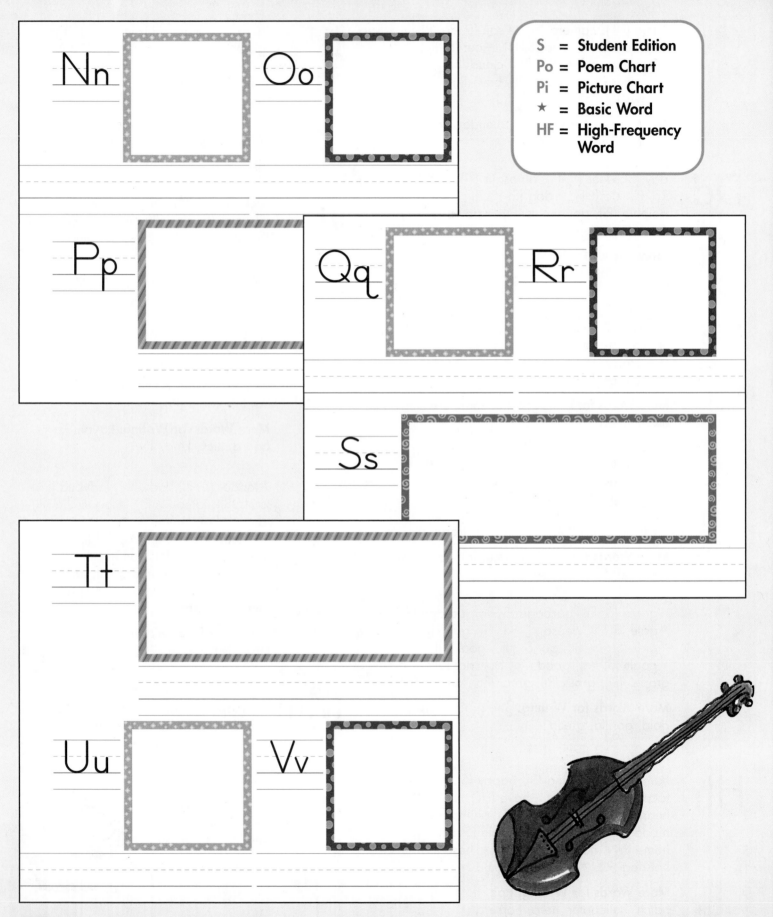

Nn Oo

Pp

Qq Rr

Ss

Tt

Uu Vv

S = Student Edition
Po = Poem Chart
Pi = Picture Chart
★ = Basic Word
HF = High-Frequency Word

Nn

nail (S, Pi), napkin (Pi), necklace (Pi), ★nest (S, Pi), ★net (S, Pi), newspaper (Pi), nickel (Pi), ★nine (S, Pi), no (S), noodles (S, Po), nose (Pi), not (HF), nurse (Pi), ★nuts (S, Pi)

More Words for Writing: name, nap, neck, new, nice, number

Oo

boat (S, Pi), ★dock (S, Pi), oatmeal (Pi), ocean (Pi), octopus (S, Pi), ★off (S, Pi), oiled (Po), olives (Pi), ★on (S, Pi, HF), one (HF), only (Po, HF), or (HF), orange (Po), Oscar (Pi), Oscar's (Po), ostrich (S, Po, Pi), otter (Pi), over (HF), overalls (Pi), owl (S, Po), ★ox (S, Pi)

More Words for Writing: October, OK, onion, open, other

Pp

paint (S, Pi), pajamas (Pi), ★pan (S, Po, Pi), pancake (S, Po, Pi), pancakes (S), parachute (Pi), parrot (Pi), peanut butter (Pi), peas (S, Pi), ★pen (S, Pi), pencil (S, Pi), ★pig (S, Pi), pillow (Pi), pink (Pi), plate (Pi), play (S, HF), ★pop (S, Po), porcupine (Pi), purple (Pi)

More Words for Writing: pack, panda, prize, puppet, puppy, puzzle

Qq

★quack (S, Pi), quacking (Po), quail (Pi), quarter (S, Pi), ★queen (S, Po, Pi), question mark (S, Pi), quick (Po), ★quiet (S, Pi), quills (Pi), ★quilt (S, Pi), Quincy (Po)

More Words for Writing: quart, question, quit, quiz

Rr

rabbit (Pi), ★rain (S, Pi), rainbow (S, Pi), raincoat (Pi), raindrop (Po), rake (S, Pi), ★red (S, Pi, HF), ribbon (Po), ★ring (S, Po, Pi), river (Pi), robin (Po, Pi), rocket (Pi), rocks (S, Pi), roller skates (Pi), ★rose (S, Po, Pi), rowboat (Pi), ruby (Po, Pi)

More Words for Writing: read, rest, robot, rope, run

Ss

sail (Pi), ★sand (S, Po, Pi), say (HF), sea (Pi), seal (S, Pi), seaweed (Po), see (S, HF), seven (Pi), shell (S, Pi), shoes (Pi), shovel (Pi), ★six (S, Pi), sleep (Po), slowly (Po), snail (S, Pi), snails (Po), so (HF), ★sock (S, Pi), starfish (Po, Pi), stones (Po), ★sun (S, Pi)

More Words for Writing: seed, side, sit, skate, spell, stop

Tt

tail (Pi), tape (Pi), teacher (Pi), teddy bear (S, Po, Pi), ★ten (S, Pi), ★tent (S, Pi), that (Po), the (S, HF), tie (Po), tiger (S, Pi), time (S), to (HF), tools (S, Pi), ★top (S, Pi), touch (Po), tulips (Pi), ★turn (S, Po), turtle (S, Pi), two (Pi)

More Words for Writing: table, take, team, ticket, toad

Uu

★bug (S, Pi), umbrella (Pi), ★umbrellas (S, Po), umpire (S, Pi), ★under (S, Po, Pi), unicorn (Pi), unicycle (Pi), ★up (S, Pi, HF), upside down (S, Po), us (S)

More Words for Writing: uncle, undo, uniform, until, upstairs

Vv

vacuum cleaner (Pi), valentine (S, Po, Pi), Valentine's Day (Pi), ★van (S, Pi), ★vase (S, Pi), vegetables (Pi), very (S, HF), ★vest (S, Pi), ★vine (S, Pi), violets (Po, Pi), violin (S, Pi)

More Words for Writing: vacation, vanilla, volcano, vulture

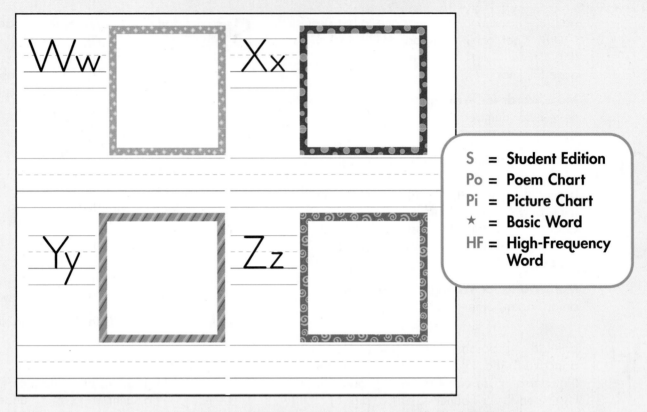

S = **Student Edition**
Po = **Poem Chart**
Pi = **Picture Chart**
★ = **Basic Word**
HF = **High-Frequency Word**

Ww waggle (Po), wagon (S, Pi), watch (S, Pi), ★water (S, Pi), waterfall (Pi), watermelon (Pi), way (HF), ★web (S, Pi), what (S, HF), when (HF), white (Pi), why (HF), wiggle (Po), will (HF), window (S, Pi), ★wing (S, Pi), with (HF), woodpecker (Pi), woods (S, Pi), ★worm (S, Pi)

More Words for Writing: wait, wall, week, wet, win, wish

Xx ax (S, Pi), ★box (S, Po, Pi), exit (S, Pi), ★fox (S, Po, Pi), mix (S, Pi), ★ox (S, Po, Pi), ★six (S, Pi), wax (Pi)

More Words for Writing: fix, X-ray, xylophone

Yy yak (Pi), yard (Pi), ★yarn (S, Pi), ★yawn (S, Po, Pi), ★yell (S, Pi), ★yellow (S, Pi), yes (S), yogurt (S, Pi), you (HF), your (HF), yo-yo (S, Pi), yummy (Po)

More Words for Writing: yam, year, yet, yolk

Zz buzz (S), ★zebra (S, Pi), ★zero (S, Po, Pi), zigzag (Po, Pi), zigzags (S), ★zip (S), ZIP code (Pi), zipper (S, Pi), ★zoo (S, Pi), zoom (Po, Pi)

More Words for Writing: fuzz, zap, zone

Elkonin Boxes Practice Page _____

To the Teacher: See page Tl68 for directions.

**Start
with
markers
here.**

2 sounds

3 sounds

4 sounds

How to Use the Elkonin Boxes Practice Page

Phonemic awareness, i.e., the ability to break words into individual sounds and to manipulate those sounds, is an important step in becoming a good reader, writer, and speller. **Elkonin Boxes,** also known as **Say It, Move It Boxes,** can help children build phonemic awareness and help teachers assess growth in this important area. A reproducible **Elkonin Boxes Practice Page** appears on page T167 in this *Teacher Edition.* Use these steps to show children how to use the practice page.

Elkonin Boxes Practice Page
To the Teacher: See page T174 for directions.

Start with markers here.

2 sounds

3 sounds

4 sounds

Copyright © Zaner-Bloser, Inc.

This page may be reproduced for classroom use.

1. Begin by modeling the use of the boxes. On the board, draw two boxes like the boxes labeled "2 sounds" on the practice page. Write "2 sounds" below the boxes. Tell the children that each box represents one sound in a word.

2. Say the word **at** aloud. Ask the children how many sounds they hear in this word. Guide them to realize that **at** has two sounds, /ă/ and /t/. It is not important that the children identify the sounds (e.g., **short a**), only that they realize the word is composed of two different sounds.

3. Say **at** again. As you say /ă/, tape a paper circle (or use magnetic markers, if possible) in the first box. As you say /t/, place a marker in the second box.

4. Now say the word **as** aloud. Ask the children which sound changed, the first sound or the second sound. Move the marker in the second box to demonstrate that the second sound has changed from /t/ to /s/.

5. Repeat the procedure with a variety of words with two sounds (e.g., **am, all, add, an**).

Duplicate and distribute copies of the **Elkonin Boxes Practice Page** to the children. Make sure the children have at least four markers (buttons, etc.). They should always begin with their markers in the large circle and then place one marker in each box as they identify the number of sounds in each word you say. As the children become more adept, you may wish to isolate a single sound and ask the children to move the marker that represents the single sound. For example, say, "Move the marker that stands for /t/ in **at**."

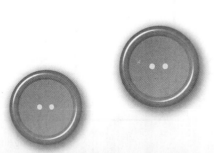